A MANDARIN
AND THE MAKING OF
PUBLIC POLICY

A MANDARIN
AND THE MAKING OF
PUBLIC POLICY

REFLECTIONS BY NGIAM TONG DOW

Introduced and edited by Simon S. C. Tay

NUS PRESS
SINGAPORE

© NUS Press
National University of Singapore
AS3-01-02, 3 Arts Link
Singapore 117569

Fax: (65) 6774-0652
E-mail: nusbooks@nus.edu.sg
Website: http://nuspress.nus.edu.sg

First Edition 2006
Reprint 2006
Reprint 2007
Reprint 2008
Reprint 2016

ISBN 978-9971-69-350-3 (Paper)

National Library Board Singapore Cataloguing in Publication Data

Ngiam, Tong Dow.
    A mandarin and the making of public policy: reflections by Ngiam Tong Dow /
introduced and edited by Simon S.C. Tay. – Singapore: NUS Press, c2006.
    p. cm.
    Includes index.
    ISBN: 978-9971-69-350-3 (pbk.)

1. Ngiam, Tong Dow – Political and social views.   2. Singapore – Officials and
employees, Retired – Anecdotes.   3. Singapore – Politics and government – 1965–90.
4. Singapore – Politics and government – 1990-   5. Singapore – Economic policy.
6. Singapore – History.
I. Tay, Simon.   II. Title.

DS610.7
959.5705 – dc22   SLS2006017463

Typeset by: International Typesetters Pte Ltd
Printed by: Markono Print Media Pte Ltd

To

My wife Jeanette Gan,
and our family
Ngiam Siew Ching and Lee Cheng Dee,
Ngiam Shih Kwang and Ong Yean Sze.
My grandchildren Shaun, Clarissa and Daniel.
My brothers and sister.

CONTENTS

LIST OF ILLUSTRATIONS

INTRODUCTION: A MANDARIN AND THE MAKING OF PUBLIC POLICY

Reflections by Ngiam Tong Dow

Simon S.C. Tay

Telling the Singapore Story

The success story of Singapore has increasingly been recognised. From the early and uncertain years after independence in 1965, after separation from Malaysia, and into the early decades of economic boom in the 1970s and 1980s, Singapore has climbed from "third world to first".[1] The small island state has achieved a level of economic development, combined with social and political stability that has eluded many other developing countries in Asia and Africa that emerged as independent states after World War II.[2]

Much of this has been closely associated with the extraordinary leadership of Mr Lee Kuan Yew.[3] It is beyond debate that Mr Lee Kuan Yew was the undisputed leader of the founding generation of Singapore. Others however also contributed towards laying the foundations of modern Singapore. The contributions, characters and views of this founding generation have not however been fully captured to date. Only some works have sought to review the role of the politicians of the founding generation, who stood alongside

---

1   Mr Lee Kuan Yew's memoirs, *From Third World to First* (Singapore: Singapore Press Holdings, 2000).

2   Bill Easterly, *The Elusive Quest for Growth* (Cambridge: MIT Press, 2002); World Bank, *The East Asian Miracle* (New York: Oxford University Press, 1993).

3   Mr Lee Kuan Yew's memoirs come in two volumes: *The Singapore Story* (Times Publishing, 1998); and *From Third World to First* (Singapore Press Holdings, 2000). There are in addition many studies of his life and work, including some controversial and critical volumes, such as, *No Man Is An Island: A Portrait of Singapore's Lee Kuan Yew*, by James Minchin (Sydney, NSW: Allen & Unwin, 1990). For a more general account of Mr Lee and Singapore during the years of independence and separation, see Dennis Bloodworth, *The Tiger and the Trojan Horse* (Singapore: Times Books International, 1986).

Lee Kuan Yew, or brought together their key speeches and views.[4] Even less attention has been given to the roles played by the founding and early civil servants who worked under and alongside these political pioneers.[5] This is notwithstanding that the study of Singaporean politics and public policy has underlined the close working relationship between Singaporean political servants and their bureaucrats. Thus, while most might acknowledge the relative success story of Singapore, there have been relatively few stories and story tellers of that success.

It is in this context that this book brings together the reflections of Mr Ngiam Tong Dow. The book seeks to make a contribution to the history and study of Singaporean politics and policy-making, and fill some of the gaps in the telling of the Singapore story. And, beyond scholarly interest, it is hoped that this book will assist those who have participated and indeed those who are still participating actively in policy-making processes.

This book may attract some controversy. Mr Ngiam has, since his retirement in 1999, been willing to revisit and review some of the public policy strategies and directions from Singapore's past. This is not only for historical purposes. Mr Ngiam has also reviewed policies and decisions in the context of present and emerging trends and policies. In doing so, he has recorded his views not only on the successes, but also on what he sees to be some potential or existing shortcomings of the Singapore system and policies. A number of the speeches and interviews given by Mr Ngiam and collected and edited in this book have, as such, stimulated considerable interest and discussion.

This book is not however a denunciation of the Singapore system and its achievements. To the contrary, reading Mr Ngiam more closely, the reader will find that he embraces very many elements of the Singapore success story. This is to be expected. As a senior civil servant serving this founding generation of political leadership, he has been very much a part of the system. But he does voice points of difference and concern about both some past decisions and some emerging trends for Singapore. These differences have attracted controversy.

---

4   The speeches by Dr Goh Keng Swee, a former Deputy Prime Minister and regarded by many as Singapore's economic architect have been collected in several books, including *The Practice of Economic Growth* (Singapore: Federal Publications, 1977); *The Economics of Modernization* (Singapore. Federal Publications, 1995); and *The Wealth of East Asian Nations: Speeches and Writings* (Singapore: Federal Publications, 1995). Speeches by S. Rajaratnam, another colleague of Mr Lee and the first Foreign Minister, were collected in *The Prophetic & the Political: Selected Speeches & Writings of S. Rajaratnam*, ed. Chan Heng Chee and Obaid ul Haq (Singapore: Graham Brash, 1987). *Lee's Lieutenants: Singapore's Old Guard*, ed. Lam Peng Er and Kevin Y.L. Tan (St. Leonards, NSW: Allen & Unwin, 1999) is a collection of essays on Lee's political contemporaries and colleagues. *Leaders of Singapore* is a well researched and handsome book of essays and photographs, written by Dr Melanie Chew, then a Senior Fellow of the Singapore Institute of International Affairs.

5   Even among the private sector, there have been few memoirs from the pioneering generation of business leaders that go beyond their business and touch on their relationship to broader development of Singapore. For an exception, see Ho Rih Hwa, *Eating Salt* (Singapore: Times International, 1990).

In considerable part, this seems to arise from the very idea of a former senior civil servant airing his views and differences in public. It is not common in Singapore to do so, especially where such views may differ with government. It would seem to be no accident that there have been few such writings from those who have been within the public administration system.

As Mr Ngiam himself acknowledges, the elite in the administrative service have been likened to "a priesthood" by some of the early senior civil servants and Dr Goh Keng Swee, the founder member of the cabinet, who is widely acknowledged as Singapore's economic architect and served as Defence Minister, Finance Minister and eventually Deputy Prime Minister.[6] This analogy of a priesthood suggests vows of confidentiality and silence.

Looking at prevailing practices in the Singapore civil service, it is not at all common for a civil servant to attribute or seek attribution of any achievement or policy initiative to a particular individual, or even to state an individual view publicly. Instead, there seems to be an idea of a broader collective responsibility within the civil service, and deference to their political masters in citing achievements and initiatives.

These may be reasonable and indeed positive characteristics. They are certainly part of the separation and differentiation between the roles of the senior civil servants and their political leaders.

However, even good characteristics can be taken to extremes. A culture of silence is neither warranted nor beneficial to Singapore (unless of course there are matters of state secrecy and confidentiality involved). Ministers have, after all, called for a "remaking of Singapore". Prime Minister Lee Hsien Loong has since entering office spoken of leaving no "sacred cow" unquestioned.[7] There have indeed been calls for more discussion within government and the civil service, as much as between the government and the wider civil society and citizenry.[8] The system of governance in Singapore has deliberately evolved to emphasise consultation and increasingly the active participation and ownership of citizens.

Mr Ngiam has, since retirement, been energetic in giving speeches and interviews on a broad range of issues, from looking at economic issues to considering land and transport policies. He has also spoken to diverse audiences, from government civil servants to private sector businesses and, in one set of seminars, to government officials from China anxious to know

---

6   Page 201.

7   The current Prime Minister, Mr Lee Hsien Loong, when he served as Deputy Prime Minister and Minister for Finance, promised to leave not even "sacred cows" unquestioned in considering recommendations from the Ministerial committee on "Remaking Singapore" and from the Economic Review Committee, in which many private sector leaders were involved. He made these points at the Tenth Parliament on 4 April 2002, and the Remaking Singapore Committee (February 2002). Information available at: <www.parliament.gov.sg/Publication/Htdocs/H0404.htm, http://app.mti.gov.sg/default.asp?id=505> and <http://www.remakingsingapore.gov.sg/> [10 Jan. 2006].

8   Simon S.C. Tay, "Towards a Singaporean Civil Society", *Southeast Asian Affairs* (1998).

something about the Singapore story. Mr Ngiam has also had time for some reflections on the political leaders of the founding generation that he served with, as well as recollect a little of his days in school and ties to church.

As the editor, I have tried to make a selection of Mr Ngiam's speeches and writings that would be of interest to those interested in his perspectives on the Singapore story, whether as student, researcher or participant.

In bringing these disparate speeches and writings together, I have tried to make the texts represented in this book at once both cohesive and yet fairly representative. I have edited Mr Ngiam's words sparingly. Editorial comments and footnotes have been added with a particular eye to smoothing transitions from one point to another, and to supplying background information for those who may not know Singapore, its history and public policy making in Singapore as well as Mr Ngiam's original audiences did. Additionally, where some books and views would add to the background that readers can glean from Mr Ngiam's writings, I have sought to make reference to them, including to some books and writings that may differ in their views. I have also added interviews that Mr Ngiam has given as well as excerpts of some speeches that he has addressed to his schools and church, which touched on more personal things. But primarily my task as editor has been to allow Mr Ngiam to speak for himself.

In this introduction, my aims are three-fold. First, I briefly review Mr Ngiam's long career in public administration and key appointments he has held. I hope this will give some context to Mr Ngiam's viewpoints. Second, I outline the book and the three sections into which Mr Ngiam's various thoughts and writings have been organised. Third, I provide an overview of Mr Ngiam's recurring themes, and examine where his views agree with or differ from some of the existing policies and prevailing wisdoms in Singapore.

As editor, I also offer a concluding epilogue, after the text of selected speeches and talks given by Mr Ngiam. There, I give a brief overview of the academic literature about the public service in Singapore, especially as it relates to the policy-making processes and interplays with the political leadership. I hope this will provide a broader context for the reflections offered in the book.

A Mandarin in Modern Singapore

Mr Ngiam Tong Dow entered the elite administrative service of the civil service in 1959, the year he graduated from the University of Malaya (precursor of the National University of Singapore) with a rare First Class Honours in Economics. In 1964, he became one of the first civil servants from Singapore to be sent to Harvard University, where he obtained his Master in Public Administration.

In 1972, at age 35, he became the youngest ever Permanent Secretary and remained at the apex of the civil service as a Permanent Secretary in economic and infrastructure ministries until his retirement. He served in the Ministries of Finance (1972–9 and 1986–99), Trade and Industry (1979–86), Communications (1970–2) and National Development (1987–9), and concurrently as Permanent Secretary (Prime Minister's Office) (1979–94).

He has been the Chairman of a number of key statutory boards, including the Economic Development Board (EDB, 1975–81), Central Provident Fund Board (CPFB, 1998–2001) and Housing & Development Board (HDB, 1998–2003), and was involved in several major government-linked companies, serving as Chairman of the DBS Bank (1990–98) and of Sheng-Li Holding Company Pte Ltd, 1981 to 1991. In 2003, he was made Chairman of the HDB Corporation Pte Ltd, the privatised arm of the HDB. It has since been renamed Surbana Corporation. Mr Ngiam served a total of 40 years before retiring in 1999.

Early in his career, as he recounts in this book, Mr Ngiam has worked closely with two of the founding political and administrative leaders of Singapore. First was, Dr Goh Keng Swee, former Deputy Prime Minister and an intellectual heavyweight and economic architect of Singapore, who established the Ministry of Finance and EDB, and later headed the key Defence and Education Ministries. Second was, the late Mr Hon Sui Sen, former Permanent Secretary and later Finance Minister, whom Mr Ngiam describes as an economic "administrator and builder". As Permanent Secretary (Prime Minister's Office), Mr Ngiam served both the founding Prime Minister of Singapore, Mr Lee Kuan Yew, and the second Prime Minister, Mr Goh Chok Tong.

His contributions have been recognised with four National Day Awards. The first, the Public Administration Medal (Gold) was awarded to him in 1971. Second, he received the Meritorious Service Medal in 1978. In 1995, he received the Long Service Award, and in 1999, shortly before his retirement, he was conferred the Distinguished Service Order.

The citation of his National Day award, in 1971, recognised his character and attributes: "Mr Ngiam has brought to the service a rare combination of ability, versatility, and a practical bent gained with experience.... These qualities enabled him to help formulate and implement a re-organisation of the system of public transportation, and thereby contributed towards making the traffic problem in Singapore manageable."

In 1978, when Mr Ngiam received the Meritorious Service Medal, the citation especially recognised his efforts in the mid-1970s to deal with the economic challenges in the aftermath of the oil crisis. It acknowledges how Mr Ngiam, as Chairman of the Economic Development Board (EDB), was able to "turn around the pessimism about Singapore as an export manufacturing base" and generate sufficient investments so that full employment could be sustained. He was also credited with undertaking the task of restructuring Singapore's economy to meet "the current complex of problems brought about by the unfavourable global economic climate and growing protectionism".

In 1999, when he was awarded the Distinguished Service Order for a lifetime of service, the citation recognised that, "Mr Ngiam's astute advice in economic and fiscal policy, mixed with a good dose of wisdom and pragmatism, have contributed in no small measure to the success story of Singapore."

It is clear that in his distinguished career in public service, Mr Ngiam has been a major contributor to government policy and work in many sectors, especially in economics and development planning.

Yet in his speeches and interviews Mr Ngiam does not dwell on the milestones achieved by Singapore and these agencies during his tenure. This is, to my mind, partly a result of personal modesty. Equally, however, it is a function of a mindset among the civil service in Singapore: they may help achieve many things but far less often are they allowed to talk about it or, even more, claim those achievements as part of their personal contribution.

The role of the elite in the Singaporean civil service, known for efficiency and quality, has often been analogised to the system of mandarins that served in the Chinese empire. They are selected after the most demanding examinations. They are inducted into a life-long service. They are entrusted by the leaders with considerable powers and discretion.

He does not of course apply the term, "mandarin" to himself. Indeed, Mr Ngiam may find the term, "mandarin" somewhat out of place as he often emphasises his Hainanese roots, with their more humble South China origins, and that he is more comfortable in English. Yet the term is appropriate. Mr Ngiam has clearly been a "mandarin" in the Singapore civil service and, under the guidance of the political leadership, has contributed greatly to the success of Singapore.

Reflections and Criticisms: Past, Present and Future

Although Mr Ngiam has achieved many things in his career, this book is not a memoir about those past contributions. It is, rather, more about his reflections, present and future of Singapore in the context of his experience. What does Mr Ngiam talk about? His writings and reflections, given after his retirement from the civil service, are presented in this book in three sections.

The first section of this book introduces Mr Ngiam and some of his reflections on the pioneering years and generation of Singapore. While this book is not a biography, section one gives some personal insights and reflections of the man and his time, to allow the reader to situate Mr Ngiam in the broader history of Singapore. The section features three interviews that he has given since retirement. The first, with Ms Susan Long of The Straits Times, attracted considerable attention, not only because it was one of the earliest public interviews that Mr Ngiam gave but also because Mr Ngiam voiced some questions and differences over government policies, both past and present.

The second interview was conducted by Dr Melanie Chew, author of the well-known book *Leaders of Singapore*,[9] as part of her research into the Fullerton Hotel, previously a government office building where Mr Ngiam worked when he served the EDB. The third interview, with Mr Sonny Yap, was conducted as part of a larger project to review the political leadership and history of the PAP. While Mr Ngiam is not a PAP member, he worked very closely with senior figures in the party and drew on this experience to share quite personal and close up perspectives on these PAP leaders and also on his cohort of civil servants.

In addition to these interviews, the first section of the book also includes brief excerpts from speeches that Mr Ngiam delivered at his former schools, Serangoon English School and St. Andrew's, and to the Christian fellowship of the Economic Development Board. His brief recollection of these pioneering years in Singapore offer a snapshot of life in the Singapore of that period, and his naming of so many school mates and contemporaries demonstrates the smaller and more familial circle of Singapore in the past.

Section two of this book moves away from recollections of personalities and the personal to Mr Ngiam's insights and analyses of policies in Singapore's development. This is drawn from seminars he has given to visiting officials from China under a programme organised by the Nanyang Technological University. While Mr Ngiam is not an academic, his experiences enrich his expositions on the lessons to be drawn from the Singapore story. Mr Ngiam recognises that Singapore's experience may not be of direct relevance to larger countries:

> In comparing China and Singapore, we need to recognise the differing circumstances of each country. China is a continental size country with a long unbroken civilisation. Singapore, on the other hand, is a tiny city state. We became an independent country only on 9 August 1965.[10]

But he argues that Singapore's experience in "baking the cake first" may be of relevance:

> Some developing countries that have elected governments struggle with other factors and institutions. One of these is the role of the army and other armed forces. The army must remain above party politics. Its role is to protect and defend the nation, and not to prop up any particular party or group. In reality, however, the army has often intervened in many developing countries, taking over power from behind the barrel of the gun. No economic development is possible in a country prone to coups and countercoups.
>
> After spending forty years engaged in the economic development of Singapore, I am convinced that the most important condition for success is

9   Melanie Chew, *Leaders of Singapore* (Singapore: Resource Press Pte Ltd, 1996).
10 Page 87.

good Government. A good Government is one led by able, honest, selfless men and women.[11]

He analyses the experiences of Singapore in providing the basics of housing and jobs for the people, and developing its infrastructure and industry. He also considers the role of education in driving the economy, and outlines the Singaporean approach in finding and seizing opportunities for growth.

It is well known that Singapore's early economic and industrial policy defied the conventional wisdom of the time by inviting in multinationals and exporting to the world. Mr Ngiam does more than recount this story. He deflates the idea that the Singapore government had a grand theory or plan. He instead emphasises the simple necessity of this thinking, and the expedience to respond to immediate needs and concerns for Singapore:

> Like other developing countries in the 1960s, Singapore tried to kick-start industrialisation through a policy of import substitution, advocated religiously by academic UN economists. Import tariffs were imposed on the full range of consumer products to give fledgling domestic industries time to grow.
>
> As Singapore's domestic market was minuscule, we sought a common market with Malaysia through political merger. The creation of a Malaysian common market was aborted when Singapore separated from Malaysia because of irreconcilable differences.
>
> On gaining independence on 9 August 1965, Singapore dismantled all its import tariffs. Through force of circumstances, we had to learn very quickly to face frontally the head winds of global competition. Singapore is probably the original global economy even before the concept was conceived by the WTO.
>
> Fortunately for Singapore, we were the exception in a world of infant industry protection. Multinational companies invested in Singapore because we practised a free and open economy, without exchange controls or protected industries.[12] [....]
>
> When Singapore, by force of circumstances, plunged into export-led industrialisation, we offered multinational companies (MNCs), and our own people, a large measure of these attributes. And, we welcomed all manufacturing investment — foreign and indigenous, low tech, high tech, or no tech. In the early years, Singapore stood out as a rare exception welcoming MNCs, and Asian companies. The truth is that we made a virtue out of necessity. But I would add, we did so also because of the hard knocks of our adverse experience in searching for a Malaysian common market.[13]

---

11 Page 88.
12 Page 92.
13 Page 106.

Even outside the classroom, there is much to interest the more general reader, especially as Mr Ngiam reflects not only about the past and present of Singapore, but also considers its economic prospects for the uncertain future in the knowledge-based economy and increasing global competition. He suggests that there are some constants from Singapore's past that should help shape the country's future: "If you were to ask me to sum up Singapore's industrial strategy in a few words, I would say it has been a process of 'finding niches, and seizing opportunities'."[14]

This theme of looking back to Singapore's foundational experiences and trying to navigate ways forward is further explored by Mr Ngiam in the third and final section of this book. The writing in this section are drawn from speeches that Mr Ngiam gave to a variety of audiences; some were hosted by private sector companies and others given to audiences consisting primarily of present and former government employees. The section does not however republish Mr Ngiam's speeches completely, or in chronological order. Instead, excerpts have been selected and ordered around the themes of economic achievement and challenges, and of leadership and the lessons to be learnt from others.

It is notable in this section that Mr Ngiam is willing not only to share his thoughts on the successful policies but also to consider the mistakes he feels have been made.

There are points throughout this book, where Mr Ngiam voices doubt and disagreement with government policies in the past, and what he sees to be negative tendencies and trends in the present. Some of these relate to the political and executive institutions in Singapore.

For example, some in Singapore argue that the political dominance of the PAP government, so long as legitimately won and renewed by free and fair elections, is good for Singapore as it offers continuity. He offers the view that:

> It is the law of nature that all things must atrophy. The steady state does not exist in nature. And unless SM [Lee Kuan Yew] allows serious political challenges to emerge from the alternative elite out there, the incumbent elite will just coast along. At the first sign of a grassroots revolt, they will probably collapse just like the Incumbent Progressive Party to the left-wing PAP onslaught in the late '50s. [...] I think our leaders have to accept that Singapore is larger than the PAP.[15]

Another point Mr Ngiam made that caused some stir was in relation to the civil service. While he has been in that service for all his working life, he offers a critique that:

---

14 Page 129.
15 Page 22.

We have been flying on auto-pilot for too long. [...] There is also a particular brand of Singapore elite arrogance creeping in. Some civil servants behave like they have a mandate from the emperor. We think we are little Lee Kuan Yews.[16]

In contrast, Mr Ngiam, at various points, recalls a civil service that was more open and that encouraged exchange and debate, even if the administrative service was itself an elite group. For instance, Mr Ngiam recalls how the economic development department comprised just four people when it started, and how Mr Hon Sui Sen, his Permanent Secretary at the time, advised him to treat the office attendant, Mr Sani, as an equal member of the team.[17] More than this, the relative openness in the service seems to have derived, in my view, from the sense of urgency and innovative hard work that marked, for Mr Ngiam, the necessary character of the founding generation of key civil servants and their political masters.

Mr Ngiam also raises questions and criticisms that relate to specific and past policy debates. For example, he touches on the different views and proponents in the debate over land transport, and the decision over whether to build an underground system. His comments reveal that Dr Goh Keng Swee preferred the proposal for an all-bus system instead of the proposal for the Mass Rapid Transit (MRT) we see today. Even as he surveys the reasons that Dr Goh and others expressed their doubts — because of cost, ideas of prudence and the priorities for infrastructure — Mr Ngiam also reveals how some, including himself, were pro-MRT and continued to lobby for the project.[18]

Another example of differences over past policy, threaded in different parts of the book, is the Central Provident Fund (CPF) and wages. Mr Ngiam shares some of the thinking over the setting up of what has become a central policy in Singapore, touching on social services, demand for housing and wage costs. He recollects the decision, taken in the brief recession that Singapore experienced in the mid-1980s, to sharply cut the CPF, thereby bringing down wage costs in Singapore. Mr Ngiam argues that this cut was a correct policy to help address Singapore's lack of competitiveness at the time. However, he argues against the smaller cut made in the late 1990s because he feels that it was not a substantial measure to address competitiveness and could breed uncertainty among employers and corporations.

Mr Ngiam defends the policy of the 1980s to let wages rise in what has been derided as a "high wage policy". He was closely associated with this policy, which was eventually reversed during the recession period. He argues that the policy was right in economics to force industries to upgrade or else relocate.

---

16 Pages 22 and 23.
17 Page 174.
18 Pages 150–2.

However, Mr Ngiam insists, this was let down by implementation and the giving of exceptions in terms of foreign workers and other concessions.[19]

There are other policy debates and decisions of the past that Mr Ngiam recollects in this book, in some detail.

Some may wonder why he may wish to recount old differences when policies were agreed and implemented by all in the government, whatever their personal preferences and arguments. Certainly, governments cannot function effectively if civil servants and politicians would insist on their views, even after a collective decision has been made.

However, in my view, this has not been Mr Ngiam's intention, whether when he was in the civil service or now, in penning these recollections after retirement. What I hope readers will gain from these recollections is not the reigniting of old quarrels and differences, but a close observation of the robust debate of the policy-making process within government. Some may also draw insight from the fact that those who argued for the MRT prevailed despite the concerns of a "heavyweight" minister such as Dr Goh. These are insights for those studying the Singaporean processes of policy making and politics, more generally. This is especially given the prevailing view that politics in Singapore is less about a competition between political parties, but a species of bureaucratic politics, given the one-party dominance of the PAP.

Seen in this light, Mr Ngiam's recollection of policy debates assures us that it is a robust and rational process; a system in which ideas and sound arguments win out, and in which power does not command meek obedience from "yes" men. It helps explain, to both Singaporeans but also especially to the foreign observers, why and how the Singapore has continued to survive and even excel, without the sound and fury of checks and balances in a liberal democratic system.

Mr Ngiam's writings also describe the role of individuals within the Singaporean system of policy making. His observations of the founding generation of politicians offers not just rich praise but also an understanding of the differences of their roles in the "team" that shaped Singapore. Anecdotes he offers of Dr Goh Keng Swee, whom Mr Ngiam describes as "the economic architect" and the "best minister" in the founding cabinet, are both light and insightful.

> Dr Goh was a very analytical man. He has a brilliant mind. You know, he used to write his own budget speeches within the space of three hours. He would come to the office on a Sunday morning, and tell his secretary, Miss Chia, "I'm going to dictate my budget speech." Within three hours, he had dictated the whole budget speech! [....]
> He would draft his speech and say to me, "OK, now you go and find the figures for me. And if the figures click, then I use your figures, otherwise,

---

I'll change my text to suit your figures." But of course, he knew the figures. They were in his mind. He has a brilliant mind. Dr Goh has a great intellect.

And yet he is a practical man. I'll give you an example: in 1968 I followed him to the World Bank meeting. And there of course, with me being the only officer around, we began to talk. And he said, "Ngiam, when we get back, please write a short project paper on starting a Bird Park in Singapore." I was a young officer, and he was in a good mood, so I said, "Sir, why do we want a bird park? Why can't we have a zoo?" We had no zoo, then. So he turned around and said, "Ngiam, bird seed costs less than meat!" [...] He's remarkable — a brilliant economist, yet down-to-earth.[20]

Mr Ngiam similarly shares stories about Mr Hon Sui Sen, with whom he worked very closely and regarded as a mentor.

> I recall with great delight a lesson in managing people that Mr Hon taught Mr Lee (Kuan Yew) and Dr Goh (Keng Swee). One day, when both of them were bemoaning that a particular officer with great potential had yet to deliver on his promise, Mr Hon spoke up. He told them that they were like impatient gardeners. Having just planted a seedling both of them could not wait for the tree to grow and bear fruit. Impatient, they pulled out the young sapling to see whether it had deep roots. As Mr Hon was a quiet man who spoke little, both the Prime Minister and Deputy Prime Minister nearly fell out of their chair![21]

Such first-hand recollections allow us to see the founding generation of politicians and policy makers as human beings, both in their brilliance and in their personal traits. These insights are important for the succeeding generations of Singaporeans who will not have the privilege of knowing these founding politicians, let alone to work closely with them as have Mr Ngiam and other civil servants of that generation.[22]

Prime Minister Lee Hsien Loong has noted with concern that younger Singaporeans do not know the pioneer political leaders. He said: "It has only been since 2000 that we began teaching our students about the Singapore story post independence — the people we are, the challenges we faced, the problems we solved, and the nation we built. As a result, we now have a lacuna in the generation of Singaporeans who were too young to know our pioneering leaders first-hand, and at the same time did not learn in school about their roles in building modern Singapore."

---

20 Pages 34 and 35.

21 Page 62.

22 See Prime Minister Lee Hsien Loong's speech on 8 April 2006 at Raffles Junior College. See *The Straits Times*, 9 April 2006, "PM to Rafflesians: Step up to serve nation". Also archived in Singapore Press Releases on the Internet (SPRINTER), <http://app.sprinter.gov.sg/data/pr/20060408995.htm> [9 April 2006].

Yet Mr Ngiam's writings may generate interest not only for such recollections of the past, but even more for his observations of the present and suggestions for the future of Singapore, or indeed for other countries that seek to develop their economies. Mr Ngiam suggests that Singapore's future is not in hard technology and should not over emphasise basic research. His analysis is that:

> We do not have the resources to make and sell hard technology. But we do have the soft knowledge to persuade others to do business with us. [....]
>
> Developing our soft knowledge — in education, medicine, and wealth management — is the way to go. We can do hard science, but the rewards will be long in coming. Why not be true to ourselves and use the soft skills we have now?[23]

This analysis differs in emphasis from Singapore government's plans for developing basic research and innovation in different fields, including biotechnology and creative services.

Another difference in emphasis that may be noted between Mr Ngiam and some of the present government's policies relates to the role of multinational companies (MNCs). He acknowledges that these MNCs have played a necessary and important role in Singapore's early decades, and indeed he himself actively courted and worked with such companies. Looking ahead, however, Mr Ngiam argues that Singapore must "grow its own timber", to develop Singaporean companies.[24] To that end, Mr Ngiam advocates both the need to encourage more private sector enterprises and small to medium enterprises, and the need for government-linked companies to demonstrate a renewed sense of state entrepreneurship to grow new businesses, and not just to acquire assets overseas.[25]

His differences with existing government policies are not only economic, but also concern social issues. In education, Mr Ngiam argues that the early emphasis in Singapore on "hard skills" needs to be supplemented by other knowledge, as a foundation for creativity.

> Out of sheer necessity, we concentrated on the economic imperative in education. Efficiency, rather than effectiveness, was the name of the game. Along the way, we also lost some of our cultural roots and ethnic instincts. [...]
>
> Today, we cannot go back to the *status quo ante*, to what was before. It will be pointless to restore dialect programmes back to our airwaves. The generation of grandparents today do not speak any dialects at all, having grown up under the non-dialect regime. What can be done?

---

23 Page 137.
24 Page 23.
25 Pages 160–3.

A back of the envelope solution might be to encourage our English-speaking to read Chinese history, literature, and even poetry, in English to enthuse their grandchildren about their Chinese heritage. [...]

It is not only Chinese culture that has been affected. ... [E]ven in English-speaking schools, technical education was preferred over subjects such as literature and history.

With the neglect of English literature in school, young Singaporeans do not have enough command of English to absorb the essence of western culture. Instead, Hollywood is their western cultural diet.

At the same time, unable to speak to their grandparents, they cannot relate what little culture they are taught in their Mandarin lessons to their daily lives. [...]

In education, as in any field of human endeavour, we have to face reality. Our single-minded pursuit of economic prosperity has brought us to a crossroads. In a knowledge-based global economy, inputs of land, labour, and capital are necessary, but not sufficient for growth and prosperity. We have to learn to apply knowledge creatively.[26]

In looking at current social policies to help citizens deal with economic uncertainties, Mr Ngiam questions whether the Singapore government is doing too much for too many. He suggests that:

We should just concentrate on helping the poorest 5 to 10 per cent of the population, instead of handing out a general largesse. Forget about asset enhancement, Singapore shares and utility rebates.[27]

The root of his criticism was that the lessons from the founding years should be reinforced, to emphasise the means for ordinary people to make good. His prescription is that the social compact of Singapore should return to its original promise, "That you shall be given the best education, whether it be academic or vocational, according to your maximum potential."[28]

How do we see these and other differences of opinion? In what context should we set these instances of criticism that Mr Ngiam voices? What are the recurring themes of the concerns that Mr Ngiam raises?

Context and Themes

In considering Mr Ngiam's reflections in context, we would do well first to recognise the many areas in which he agrees with government policies. His concurrence with and support for many decisions made and directions set are

---

26 Pages 118–9.

27 Page 26.

28 Page 26.

apparent in his writings and speeches, and perhaps clearest in those collected in the second section of this book.

He agrees that "the most important condition for success is good government", which he defines as "one led by able, honest, selfless men and women". He makes it clear that he regards Singapore as an exemplary case. Mr Ngiam agrees that Singapore was right to emphasise the need for jobs and housing to meet basic needs of the people. He also concurs with the decision to invite in multinational companies (MNCs) in the face of the failure of the merger and common market with Malaysia, "by switching from an inward-looking import substitution strategy to an international export-oriented policy", even if this was, in his view, making a virtue out of necessity. He emphasises the difficulty in this strategy and credits the leaders and others who made this work.

His recollections of state entrepreneurship, in which he played a considerable part, are positive. He emphasises how the government civil servants helped build many and indeed most of the companies that are associated with today's economy, often from scratch. The decisiveness of the leaders of the time, and the trust they had in the administrators they selected, are also emphasised.

In finance, Mr Ngiam emphasises that Singapore has been correct to practise "fiscal rectitude" in which "we do not spend more than we earn". For similar reasons, Mr Ngiam supports the Singapore government's policy to acquire land for public purpose, while paying compensation only on the price of the undeveloped land. He emphasises the open, fair and transparent system of compensation behind this land acquisition and the overarching goal to free the land for development. As Singapore ventured into capital-intensive industries, such as petro-chemicals, Mr Ngiam again states his belief that "good and stable government (is) a *sine qua non* of investment".

Looking at education, he recognises the appropriateness of matching investment to the skills that Singaporean workers could offer and the need to increase training in order to offer higher skilled production to MNCs. This approach culminated, as Mr Ngiam relates, in the decision to increase the number of universities and especially the number of places offered for engineering, seen as essential for the high tech jobs that the EDB sought to bring to Singapore.

In this context, some themes that cut across Mr Ngiam's writings and speeches may be noted.

First, he emphasises the urgency of the early days of Singapore's independence and the personalities that gave life to the young state. Mr Ngiam rightly and respectfully gives the spotlight to the political leaders — especially Mr Lee Kuan Yew, Dr Goh Keng Swee and Mr Hon Sui Sen. But he also recognises his fellow civil servants who supported them ably, private sector leaders, and the suggestions given by foreigners who invested and were interested in Singapore, including of course Dr Albert Winsemius, the government's economic adviser in Singapore's early years.

Second, Mr Ngiam gives insights into the qualities of flexibility, inventiveness and instinct that were applied to making many key decisions and undertakings. He talks of Dr Goh's "back of envelope" calculations and common sense approach to projects.

Third, he emphasises the need to recognise the imperatives of meeting basic economic needs in society and the stages of development that Singapore met and passed through in sequence.

From this, Mr Ngiam's writings can be read as his version of the "Singapore story". He draws on his personal recollections to lend particular insights and emphasis, but his telling is similar to those by government agencies and indeed Minister Mentor Lee Kuan Yew in emphasising the hard work and tough minded and often unconventional decisions that lie behind the success story.

Given this, how do we understand the areas and points on which Mr Ngiam differs from government policies?

Largely, I believe, these differences emerge from two concerns. The first is a mix of both personal and patriotic sentiment. As Mr Ngiam says poignantly in an interview: "I'm taking a long term view because I've got three grandchildren. So I want to be sure that in 50 years' time, that there will be a Singapore that they will be proud of. That's very important."[29]

The second reason relates more to his views on economic policy and competitiveness. His concerns are that what he regards as fundamental concerns and lessons from the past are being eroded on one hand or, on the other, being preserved and over-extended without thinking as the civil service and government continue on "auto pilot".

This drives him to suggest new directions and clusters of ideas that would, together, help keep Singapore ahead in an increasingly open and competitive world economy. These suggestions include: reforming education to broaden its range and make it more creative; growing networks for Singapore beyond our physical territory to include Singaporeans abroad and friends of Singapore; growing an external economy; fostering a new generation of Singaporean companies and businesses, whether from government-linked entrepreneurship or private sector small and medium-sized enterprises; and emphasising the "soft" skills of Singapore in key areas.

These ideas differ from the policies that Mr Ngiam and those in the same founding generation implemented. But, Mr Ngiam and others would argue, while those policies were right for their time, the world has changed, and Singapore too must change. The ideas may also differ from those in place at the time that Mr Ngiam penned these thoughts. They are not however beyond the range of suggestions contemplated by various blue ribbon consultation committees that were led by younger government ministers in the 1990s and

---

29 Page 53.

since the year 2000, such as the committees on "Remaking Singapore" and "Singapore 21".

Mr Ngiam's ideas are, in this regard, by no means singular to himself. Some or indeed more thinkers about policy may share similar ideas, in part or whole. His writings and reflections, as such, represent a broader strand of thinking about Singapore's future.

They are offered to be read and studied not as personal musings but as reflections in context of a mandarin who has participated closely in the founding decades of Singapore, who has sought to distill vital lessons from those experiences, and thought to apply them in thinking of the future of his country.

In parallel with this has been a growing recognition that, now beyond its 40th year, Singapore needs to give more space and emphasis to its history. More funding has been put into the study and public education of Singapore's history. The country's compulsory education system has introduced "social studies", a subject that gives a prominent place to the modern history of Singapore. Such an emphasis on history should see not just a single master narrative of the Singapore story. Rather, it would seem desirable that there be a growing number and range of memoirs and reflections from a cross section of those who have contributed to various aspects of the Singapore story.[30]

As Prime Minister Lee Hsien Loong has noted: "Dr Goh Keng Swee once observed that 'one of the most notable character traits of the Singaporean is his unconcern for the history of his country.'... Things have improved since then. But we still need to do better. We are updating the Social Studies and History syllabi for primary and secondary schools, so that the new generation growing up will learn about our founding fathers, and understand how we got here, why it could easily have turned out very differently, and why Singapore can be defended, and is worth defending. More importantly, interest in history cannot be driven solely by the government or the education system. It must be a process animated by many voices that keep alive the story of Singapore and its heroes in our collective memory."

This book, I hope, will find its place among such tellings of the Singapore story.

---

30 See *The Straits Times*, 9 April 2006, "PM to Rafflesians: Step up to serve nation". Also archived in Singapore Press Releases on the Internet (SPRINTER), <http://app.sprinter.gov.sg/data/pr/20060408995. htm> [9 April 2006].

Part 1
A Person and the Policies

"MEETING A MANDARIN": INTERVIEW WITH THE STRAITS TIMES

Since Mr Ngiam Tong Dow retired from the civil service in 1999, affairs of the state have been weighing heavily on his mind. The Chairman of HDB Corp worries over Singapore's long-term survival and what kind of society will be passed on to the next generation. Mr Ngiam, who was born on 7 June 1937, insists he is "no radical", just a concerned Singaporean with three grandchildren, who asks the vexed question "whether there will be a Singapore for them in fifty years' time".

The small-built, straight-talking economist was recruited to the elite Administrative Service in 1959, just after the People's Action Party came to power. He saw Singapore through its fledging years, when unemployment was over 10 per cent and the political situation was "tinder dry".

He counts among his mentors, former Finance Ministers Hon Sui Sen and Dr Goh Keng Swee, as well as Senior Minister Lee Kuan Yew. From 1970 to 2000, he served variously as Permanent Secretary to the Ministry of Communications, Trade and Industry, Prime Minister's Office, National Development and Finance and as Chairman of the EDB and the HDB.

Today, he belongs to a deeply respected circle of grey eminence whose views are sought on a myriad of policy and strategic matters.

In this rare interview, he gives a candid appraisal of the sameness of the civil service today, the creeping arrogance that is afflicting some among the Singapore elite, and the lack of an alternative leadership to People's Action Party and its repercussions for the country.

Edited from original interviews by Susan Long, "S'pore 'bigger than PAP'", The Sunday Times' Tea with Think section, *The Straits Times*, 28 Sept. 2003, p. 39; "Stop dancing to the tune of the gorilla", The Sunday Times' Tea with Think section, *The Straits Times*, 5 Oct. 2003, p. 33.

Q With all this pessimism surrounding Singapore's prospects today, what's your personal prognosis?[1] Will Singapore survive Senior Minister Lee Kuan Yew?[2]

A Unequivocally yes, Singapore will survive SM Lee, provided he leaves the right legacy.

What sort of legacy he wants to leave is for him to say, but I, a blooming upstart, dare to suggest to him that we should open up politically and allow talent to be spread throughout our society, so that an alternative leadership can emerge.

So far, the People's Action Party's tactic is to put all the scholars into the civil service because it believes the way to retain political power forever is to have a monopoly on talent. But in my view, that's a very short term view.

It is the law of nature that all things must atrophy. The steady state does not exist in nature. And unless SM allows serious political challenges to emerge from the alternative elite out there, the incumbent elite will just coast along. At the first sign of a grassroots revolt, they will probably collapse, just like the incumbent Progressive Party faced with the left-wing PAP onslaught in the late '50s.

I think our leaders have to accept that Singapore is larger than the PAP.

Q For starters, what would be a useful first step in opening up?

A For Singapore to survive, we should release half our talent, our President and Overseas Merit scholars, to the private sector. When ten scholars come home, five should turn to the right and join the public sector or the civil service; the other five should turn to the left and join the private sector.

Of course, we'll always be short of talent but you need to spread it out throughout your society and economy and not just siphon it away to public service. These scholars should serve their bond to Singapore — not to the government — by working in or for Singapore overseas. As matters stand, those who wish to strike out have to break their bonds, pay a financial penalty and worse, be condemned as quitters.

But it takes a certain temperament and mindset to be a civil servant. The former head of the civil service, Sim Kee Boon, once said that joining the administrative service is like entering a royal priesthood. Not all of us have

---

1 At the time of the interview, the Singapore's economy was experiencing sluggish growth and the rate of joblessness was relatively high.

2 Senior Minister Lee Kuan Yew was appointed Minister Mentor by Prime Minister Lee Hsien Loong in Aug. 2004.

the temperament to be priests. However upright a person is, the mandarin will in time begin to live a gilded life in a gilded cage.

For example, as a Permanent Secretary, I never had to worry whether I could pay my staff their wages. It was all provided for in the Budget. As Chairman of DBS Bank and executive director of government-linked trading firm Intraco, I worried about wages only 20 per cent of the time.

I now face my greatest business challenge as Chairman of HDB Corp, a new start-up spun off from HDB.[3] I spend 90 per cent of my time worrying whether I have enough to pay my staff at the end of the month. It's a mental switch.

Q Personally, what's your biggest worry about the civil service today?

A The greatest danger is we are flying on auto-pilot. What was once a great policy, we just carry on with more of the same, until reality intervenes. Take our industrial policy, for instance. At the beginning, it was the right thing for us to attract multinationals to Singapore. But we didn't realise that World Trade Organisation (WTO) would be coming into the picture.

If you think about it, WTO ushered in the knowledge-based global economy. Knowledge resides in people and institutions. So if the institutions belong to other people, do you think Singapore will have the knowledge?

For some years now, I've been trying to tell everybody: "Look, for God's sake, grow our own timber." If we really want knowledge to be rooted in Singaporeans and based in Singapore, we have to support our Small and Medium-sized Enterprises (SMEs). I'm not a supporter of SMEs just for the sake of more SMEs but we must grow our own roots. Creative Technology's Sim Wong Hoo is one and Hyflux's Olivia Lum is another but that's too few.[4]

We have been flying on auto-pilot for too long. The MNCs have contributed a lot to Singapore but they are totally unsentimental people. The moment you're uncompetitive, they just relocate.

---

3 HDB Corp, the corporatised arm of Singapore's Housing & Development Board has changed its name to Surbana Corp. from 1 July 2005.

4 Mr Sim Wong Hoo is the CEO of Creative Technology, which is well known for sound cards such as the famous Sound Blaster for the PC, portable media player and MP3 players. Sim is a business all-star in Singapore, in the classic poor-local-boy-makes-good mold. More information on Mr Sim can be found at <http://64.233.179.104/search?q=cache:61ciuTAGuJsJ:www.pathfinder.com/asiaweek/technology/2000/0929/acom.cover.html+about+Sim+Wong+Hoo&hl=en&gl=sg&ct=clnk&cd=1> [28 Feb. 2006]. Ms Olivia Lum is Group CEO & President and founder of the Hyflux Group. She started corporate life as a chemist with Glaxo Pharmaceutical and left in 1989 to start up Hydrochem (S) Pte Ltd, the precursor to Hyflux Ltd. Hyflux became the first water treatment company to be listed on the Singapore Stock Exchange in 2001 and became an index stock on the Straits Times Index since March 2005. Today, it is one of Asia's leading water and fluid treatment companies specialising in membrane and related technologies for liquid/solid separation. The core businesses for Hyflux are water; industrial processes; structured projects; consumer and material sciences. Its main markets are in China, Middle East and Singapore.

Why has this come about?

I suspect we have started to believe our own propaganda. There is also a particular brand of Singapore elite arrogance creeping in. Some civil servants behave like they have a mandate from the emperor. We think we are little Lee Kuan Yews.

SM Lee has earned his spurs, with his fine intellect and international standing. But even Lee Kuan Yew sometimes doesn't behave like Lee Kuan Yew. There is also a trend of intellectualisation for its own sake, which loses a sense of the pragmatic concerns of the larger world. The Chinese, for example, keep good archives of the Imperial examinations which used to be held at the Temple of Heaven and presided by the Emperor himself. In the beginning, the scholars were tested on very practical subjects, such as how to control floods in their province. But over time, they were examined on the Confucian Analects and Chinese poetry composition. Hence, the intellectuals of China became emasculated by the system, a worrying fate which could befall Singapore.

But aren't you an exception to the norm of the gilded mandarin with zero bottomline consciousness?

That's because I started out with Economic Development Board in 1961. Those days, we had to sell the idea of Singapore, chasing after any kind of manufacturing industries for jobs. Investment promotion then was all about hard foot slogging and personal persuasion, which teaches you to be very humble and patient.

Out of 100 cold calls, you were lucky if 10 CEOs replied to you or if 10 who picked up the phone agreed to talk to you. You were lucky if two people agreed to visit, and you were damn lucky if you could get one to locate here. I learnt to be a supplicant and a professional beggar, instead of a dispenser of favours.

These days, most civil servants start out administering the law. If I had my way, every administrative officer would start his or her career in the EDB.

The idea of creating an alternative elite is not new. What do you think of the oft-mooted suggestion of achieving that by splitting ranks within the PAP?

Quite honestly, if you ask me, this idea of a Team A and a Team B within the PAP is a synthetic and infantile idea. If you want to challenge the government, it must be spontaneous. There must be a risk involved. You have to be prepared. The PAP is right in saying that if you challenge us, then you had better be prepared for hardball.

You have to allow some of your best and brightest to remain outside your reach and let them grow spontaneously. How do you know their leadership will not be as good as yours? But if you monopolise all the talent, there will never be an alternative leadership. And alternatives are good for Singapore.

Q In your calculation, what are the odds of this alternative replacing the incumbent?

A Of course there's a political risk. Some of these chaps may turn out to be your real opposition but that is the risk the PAP has to take if it really wants Singapore to endure.

In Singapore today, politics is all or nothing, which is not a good thing. A model we should work towards is the French model of the elite administration. The very brightest of France all go to university or college. Some emerge as Socialists and others as Conservatives; some work in industries and some work in government. Yet, at the end of the day, when the chips are down, they are all Frenchmen. No member of the French elite will ever think of betraying his country, never.

That is the sort of Singapore elite we want, political but not totally partisan; and at the end of the day, when the crunch comes, will stand side by side and fight for Singapore.

But it doesn't mean that all of us must belong to the PAP. That is very important.

Q What do bad times have in store for the PAP, which has based its legitimacy on providing the economic goods and asset enhancement? Is its social compact with the people in need of an update?

A Oh yes. And my advice is: Go back to SM Lee's old credo, where nobody owes us a living. After I had just taken over as HDB's Chairman in 2000, an astute academic and Singapore observer asked me: "Tong Dow, what's your greatest problem at HDB?" Then he diagnosed it himself: "Initially you gave peanuts to monkeys so they would dance to your tune. Now you've given them so much peanuts that the monkey has become a gorilla and you have to dance to its tune. That's your greatest problem."

Our people have become over-fed and today's economic realities mean we have to put them on a crash diet. We cannot starve them because there will be a political explosion. So the art of government today is to put everyone on a diet, beginning with the dispensable items.

We should just concentrate on helping the poorest 5 to 10 per cent of the population, instead of handing out a general largesse. Forget about asset enhancement, Singapore shares and utility rebates. You're dancing to the tune of the gorilla.

I don't understand the urgency of raising the GST[5] which effectively increases the tax on the lower income people. Why tax the lower income, and then return it to them in an aid package? It demeans human dignity and creates a growing supplicant class who habitually hold out their palms. That is not the way to treat people. Despite the fact that we say we are not a welfare state, we act like one of the most welfarish states in the world. You should instead appeal to their sense of pride and self-reliance.

I think political courage is needed here. And my instinct is that the Singaporean will respect you for that. Even if the PAP's percentage wins drops from 75 per cent to 55 per cent, it is still worth it for the sake of Singapore's survival.

So what should this new compact consist of?

It should go back to what was originally promised: "That you shall be given the best education, whether it is academic or vocational, according to your maximum potential."

And there should be no judgment whether an engineer is better than a doctor or a chef.

My late mother was a great woman. Although illiterate, she single-handedly brought up four boys and a girl. She used to say in Hainanese: "If you have one talent which you excel in, you will never starve."

I think the best legacy to leave is education and equal opportunities for all. When the Hainanese community came to Singapore, they were the latest arrivals and the smallest in number. All the commanding heights of the economy had been taken up by Teochews, Hakkas and the Cantonese.

The Hainanese had no patron saint. So they had no choice but to become humble houseboys, waiters and cooks. But they always wanted their sons to have a better life than themselves. The great thing about Singapore was that we could get an education, which gave us mobility, despite coming from the poorest families. Today, the Hainanese as a

---

5 Goods and Services Tax (GST) is a tax on domestic consumption. The tax is paid when money is spent on goods and services, including imports. It is a multi-stage tax which is collected at every stage of the production and distribution chain. GST was introduced in Singapore on 1 April 1994. The GST rate was increased from 3% to 4% in 2003 and from 4% to 5% in 2004. More information on GST can be found at <http://www.mof.gov.sg/taxation_businesses/gst.html> [28 Feb. 2006].

dialect group form proportionately the largest number of professionals in Singapore.

You advocate focusing on education. What is at the top of your wish list for remaking Singapore's education system?

Each year, the PSLE creams off all the top boys and girls and despatches them to only two schools, Raffles Institution and Raffles Girls' School. However good these schools are and however brilliant their teachers are, the problem is that you are educating your elite in only two institutions, with only two sets of mentors.

These boys and girls may turn out brilliant but they are all more or less cast in the same mould. Now I don't believe in diversity for the sake of diversity but we must be prepared to face unknown and unexpected challenges. It worries me that Singapore is only about "one brand" because you never know what challenges lie ahead and where they will come from.

I think we should spread out our best and brightest to at least a dozen schools. Otherwise, with a single track, you risk being irrelevant.

Otherwise, you're optimistic that Singapore can get out of this economic funk?

Oh yes. I think in Singapore, we always tend to be too extreme, black and white. We should have some shades of grey. Well, Dr Albert Winsemius, a Dutch economist who used to be Singapore's economic adviser, used to tell me, you Singaporeans are remarkably unbalanced people because you stand in a very small pond. When the water is just below your nose and the sun is shining, you think everything is well and good, and you're filled with euphoria. But the moment the water rises by an inch and suffocates you, you think that's the end of the world.

So we have to ask ourselves: Why are we unbalanced? I think it's because we are too black and white. We need to have diversity even in nature and particularly in human affairs, since all of us are born with different qualities, different characters and different temperaments.

So you're advocating a more inclusive mindset all around?

Yes, intellectually, everyone has to accept that the country of Singapore is larger than the PAP. But even larger than the country of Singapore, limited by size and population, is the nation of Singapore, which includes a diaspora.

My view is that we should have a more inclusive approach to nation building. So we have started the Majulah Connection,[6] an international network where every Singaporean, whether he is a citizen or not, so long as he feels for Singapore or was born in Singapore or his parents still live here, is included as part of our diaspora.

I don't agree with the "quitters" and "stayers" labels because most Singaporeans who have worked abroad and remain abroad still have feelings for Singapore in some corner of their hearts.[7] We have to include them as Singaporeans in the larger sense. Similarly, we should include the foreigners who have worked and thrived here as friends of Singapore. That's the only way to survive. Otherwise, its just four million people living on a little red dot of 600 square kilometres. If you exclude people, you become smaller and smaller, isolate yourself, and in the end, you'll disappear.

What is the kind of Singapore you hope your grandchildren will inherit?

I'm not a great historian but look at Sparta and Athens, two city states in Greek history. Singapore is like Sparta, where the top students are taken away from their parents as children and educated. Then, cohort by cohort, they each select their own leadership, ultimately electing their own Philosopher King. When I first read Plato's Republic, I was totally dazzled by the great logic of this organisational model where the best selects the best.

But when I reached the end of the book, it dawned on me that though the starting point was meritocracy, the end result was dictatorship and elitism. Once selected, only God can remove the Philosopher King. If he is a good dictator, then all is fine and good. But if he's bad, the whole state collapses. In the end, Sparta, a martial state known for being disciplined and strong, crumbled.

On the other hand, there was Athens, a city of philosophers known for its diversity and different schools of thought. Most people consider philosophers bloody useless fellows but at least they dare to argue and think. At the end

---

6   Majulah Connection was launched in November 2002 to connect the overseas Singaporeans and friends of Singapore (collectively called the Singapore Alumni) with Singapore, and provide platforms that offer business and personal opportunities to this community. Majulah Connection website can be found at <http://www.majulah.net/> [28 Feb. 2006].

7   Mr Ngiam refers to a debate provoked by then PM Goh Chok Tong which seeks to distinguish between those who quit on Singapore and those who stay on in the country. "Fair-weather Singaporeans will run away whenever the country runs into stormy weather. I call them 'quitters'. Fortunately, 'quitters' are in the minority. The majority of Singaporeans are 'stayers'. 'Stayers' are committed to Singapore. Rain or shine, they will be with Singapore." National Day Rally Address by PM Goh Chok Tong, University Cultural Centre, 18 Aug. 2002. Speech can be found at <http://www.gov.sg/nd/ND02.htm> [10 Jan. 2006].

of the day, Athens survived. Sparta is long forgotten. What does this tell us about OB markers?[8]

So SM Lee has to think very hard what legacy he wants to leave for Singapore and the type of society he wants to leave behind. Is it to be a Sparta, a martial, well-organised, efficient society but in the end, very brittle; or an Athens, untidy, chaotic and argumentative, but which survived because of its diversity of thinking?

Personally, I believe that Singaporeans are not so "kuai" (Hokkien for docile) to become a Sparta: This is our saving grace. As a young senior citizen, I very much hope that Singapore will survive for a long time, but as an Athens. It is more interesting and worth living and dying for.

---

8   Mr Ngiam refers to the bounds of public discussion in Singapore which are often referred to as "OB markers"; an analogy to the "Out of Bound" markers used on golf-courses.

A Personal History of Men, Institutions and Policies

Mr Ngiam, you are Hainanese.

Yes, my father came to Singapore as a young boy from Hainan. He was really remarkable. He came with just one year of secondary school. Yet, within three years, he picked up enough English to pass the Senior Cambridge Certificate — in the old days that was the "O" level. Remarkable! My Dad was a linguist. He worked as an interpreter. So he would interpret from English to Chinese, in most dialects. During the Japanese occupation, he learned Japanese very quickly and became an interpreter for the Japanese.

My mother was also a remarkable woman. She was widowed very early in life, and with five children to raise — four sons and one daughter. She worked as a servant, and managed to put all of us through school. She was a woman of true grit. It was remarkable, the way she raised her family. All four sons went to University on either bursary or scholarship.

Did your brothers and sister do as well as you?

In fact they did better! I'm the eldest. I only had a bursary, an Open Bursary. My younger brother, Tong Yuen was a Colombo Plan scholar. He did engineering. Now he's a chemical engineer, just about to retire from Exxon Chemicals. And the third brother is Associate Professor in Pharmacy, Dr Ngiam Tong Lan. My youngest brother is Dr Ngiam Tong Tau, head

Interview with Mr Ngiam Tong Dow on 12 Aug. 2000 with Dr Melanie Chew.

of the Agri-food & Veterinary Authority (AVA). My sister did not go to university but all of her three children are engineers. My brother-in-law read physics in University.

So do you believe in genes? I think that my father, although he died very young, left us with a rich genetic inheritance. I'm not a believer in genes totally, I believe in both nurture and nature.

We are blessed. We came from a little village in Hainan, to Singapore. Singaporeans don't realise how blessed they are! The more I visit countries and study their economics, the more I realise how blessed we are. Are you a Christian? I think the Lord is with Singapore.

In 1959, you graduated from the University of Malaya: Who were your classmates?

At that time, the Honours Class was quite small, 14 or 15 in all. The Singaporean classmates were Mr Haider Sithawalla, Mr Ernest Wong, not of UOB but another Ernest Wong.[1] The rest of my class were Malaysians.

In fact I still keep in touch with them, for instance, the Chief Secretary of Malaysia, Tan Sri Sallehuddin. Ramon Navaratnam, he was in Treasury. Wong Kum Choon, he was in Primary Production. All quite interesting fellows!

The smartest in my class was a lady, Lulu Teh. Being a woman in those days, they would not give her a proper job. So she became a librarian in Bank Negara. And from there, she picked up enough investment knowledge and made, well, a fortune! Remarkable!

When you joined the civil service in 1959, which figures were amongst your cohort?

I joined the Administrative Service in 1959. There were three of us. Herman Hochstadt was one year ahead of me in University, but he did two Honours degrees.[2] So he entered the Admin Service in my batch. Sarjit Singh, but he's Malaysian, so after the break up he went back to head the Rubber Research

---

1 He was Mr Ernest Wong Thian Yow.

2 Herman Hochstadt is the former Chairman of NOL, ECICS Holdings (Temasek Holdings unit) and Vice Chairman of Thakral Corporation. He also served various positions on the boards of several government, quasi government and private organisations. He was a former Permanent Secretary in the civil service.

Institute. There was a Eurasian boy, Reutens, but he decided to join the private sector.

I would say that I was the first PAP civil servant. I joined on 1 August 1959. The PAP won the elections on 30 May 1959.[3] I was posted first to the Ministry of Commerce and Industry. Mr Abu Bakar Pawanchee was the Permanent Secretary. When the PAP took over, James Puthucheary was made Director of the Industrial Promotion Board.[4]

I was there for about two or three months. After that, Dr Goh who was the Finance Minister formed the Economic Development Division of the Ministry of Finance, with Mr Hon Sui Sen as the Permanent Secretary. I was posted to the Economic Development Division.

When I arrived, I discovered that I was the only young cadet around! The Economic Development Division was composed of four persons: the Minister, Dr Goh Keng Swee.[5] Mr Hon Sui Sen was the Perm Sec.[6] I was the young cadet Administrative Assistant and the office boy.

There were only four of us in the Economic Development Division — the Minister, the Perm Sec, the Admin Assistant and the Office Boy. That was the beginning of the Economic Development Division!

My predecessor, Mr Henry Oh, was the Principle Assistant Secretary. But he had left to join IBM. So I took over his place. And then, within a year, I was joined by Joe Pillay,[7] from Kuala Lumpur. I think he was working in Shell. But he knew Dr Goh when they were in London, when they were members of the Malayan Forum. I remember writing the letter of appointment for him. He joined as an Engineer, Special Duties.

---

3 The elections resulted in a landslide victory for the PAP. The Party won 43 out of the 51 seats contested.

4 James Puthucheary was an anti-colonial soldier and leader, economist, trade unionist, lawyer and pioneer of the Central Provident Fund and Industrial Promotion Board (now Economic Development Board). A collection of his writings can be found in his book: Puthucheary, Dominic and Jomo K.S., *No Cowardly Past: James J. Puthucheary —Writings, Poems, Commentaries* (KL: INSAN, 1998).

5 Dr Goh is affectionately known as the architect, engineer and hand-craftsman of modern Singapore. He created and played key roles in the schemes and plans of the EDB, PSA, JTC, HDB, MOE and CPF Board in "A Tribute to Dr Goh Keng Swee" by the Defense Science Organization, information available at: <http://www.dso.org.sg/home/publications/comm/2-Tribute.pdf> [10 Jan. 2006].

6 Mr Hon Sui Sen was Singapore's former Minister of Finance from 1970–83. He had devoted 44 years of his life serving the nation, first as a top civil servant, then as a senior cabinet minister. During that time, he played a major role in Singapore's industrial development and banking activities. He helped to consolidate Singapore as an international financial market and was a significant force behind Singapore's economic growth, in *A Tribute to Hon Sui Sen* by the Havelock Citizen's Consultative Committee & Havelock Community Centre Management Committee (1984).

7 Mr J.Y. Pillay is the Chairman of the Singapore Exchange Ltd Board since Nov. 1999. He has held a variety of positions in the government of Singapore (1961–95), rising to Permanent Secretary in 1972. He served in the ministries of finance, defence and national development. Between 1985 and 1989, Mr Pillay was the Managing Director of the Monetary Authority of Singapore and of the Government of Singapore Investment Corporation. For his full biography, please refer to <http://www.sgx.com/ir/board/index.html> [28 Feb. 2006].

So there was Joe Pillay, myself, Mr Dhanabalan,[8] and a lady, a very intelligent woman, Miss Heng Hong Ngoh. She was my senior in University, one of the few girls to get First Class Honours in Economics. She was the same batch as James Puthucheary. So that was it — four of us.

Were you involved in the Five Year Plan?

I remember Dr Goh took Joe Pillay, Miss Heng and Mr Hon to the Changi Chalet and wrote the plan over the weekend. It was required by the World Bank because we were looking for a loan! I stayed back in the office, getting the figures. The rest went to Changi Chalet and wrote the Five Year Development Plan. Dr Goh is a remarkable man. I was, really, very lucky to work under him and for Mr Hon Sui Sen also.

In what way?

Dr Goh was a very analytical man. He has a brilliant mind. You know, he used to write his own budget speeches within the space of three hours. He would come to the office on a Sunday morning, and tell his secretary, Miss Chia, "I'm going to dictate my budget speech." Within three hours, he had dictated the whole budget speech!

Dr Goh wrote all his own speeches in those days. Of course, he did his own homework, he would call for all the files and he'll read through. So in his own mind, he knows exactly what he wants to say. Even a major Budget Speech is done within a few hours. Today it is done by many officers over weeks and months! He is a really fantastic man.

He would draft his speech and say to me, "OK, now you go and find the figures for me. And if the figures click, then I use your figures, otherwise, I'll change my text to suit your figures." But of course, he knew the figures. They were in his mind. He has a brilliant mind. Dr Goh has a great intellect.

And yet he is a practical man. I'll give you an example: in 1968 I followed him to the World Bank meeting. And there of course, with me being the only officer around, we began to talk. And he said, "Ngiam, when we get back, please write a short project paper on starting a Bird Park in Singapore." I was

---

8 Mr Dhanabalan is the Chairman of Temasek Holdings Pte Ltd. He was also previously the Chairman of DBS Group Holdings Ltd and Singapore Airlines Ltd. He started his career in the Singapore Civil Service in 1960 and later served in the Economic Development Board from 1961 to 1968. He entered politics in 1976 and while a Member of Parliament, he held a number of cabinet positions — Minister of Foreign Affairs (1980–8), Minister for Culture (1981–4), Minister for Community Development (1984–6), Minister for National Development (1987–92), and Minister for Trade and Industry (1992–3). More information can be found at <http://www.temasekholdings.com.sg/2005review/tr2005_10.pdf> [28 Feb. 2006].

a young officer, and he was in a good mood, so I said, "Sir, why do we want a bird park? Why can't we have a zoo?" We had no zoo, then. So he turned around and said, "Ngiam, bird seed costs less than meat!"

He's remarkable — a brilliant economist, yet down-to-earth. How does he do his analysis? Nowadays we need all these blooming economists to gather statistics, and write analysis. I went with him to Bangkok to attend the ECAFE meeting.[9] And after dinner, he said, "Let's take a walk down the street." I protested, "Sir, why should we walk? It's so hot and dusty!" And he said, "No, no, let's walk." And after walking a while, I asked, "Sir, what are you doing?" He replied, "I'm looking at the prices of all the things in the shops." He was checking on the shops, to form an opinion on the state of the Thai economy. This was back in the 1960s. He was a real practical person.

Was he a believer in the merger with Malaysia?

No. I don't think Dr Goh ever believed in Malaysia. Because he knew that it was going to be very difficult. I'll give you an example. In those days we had this immigration deposit scheme, where people could come into Singapore if they had a million dollars. I was in the EDB then, so I used to write supporting papers for him, to accept Mr So-And-So.

In 1963, just two weeks before we went to Malaysia, he called me up and said, "Ngiam, just give me a list of all the applicants. You don't have to write any analysis. Just put down the name, the amount of money they are bringing in, and send it up." So I sent it up to him, he approved them all. I said, "Hey how can you approve them all, just like that?"

He said, "The moment we enter Malaysia, this is going to go up to KL. They will make sure that we don't get anybody. They will not approve anyone!" So he was very shrewd. He said, "We had better take all the decisions we want now, because they are going to control us."

He was involved in the currency talks with Malaysia. At that time, Mr Lim Kim San was the Minister of Finance.[10] So I remember going up with

---

9 Established in March 1947, at Shanghai, as ECAFE — The Economic Commission for Asia and the Far East was founded to assist in post-war economic reconstruction. The Commission moved its Headquarters to Bangkok in January 1949. The name was changed, in 1974, to better reflect both the economic and social aspects of development and the geographic location of its members. Available at Department of Public Information United Nations (UN) "UN Regional Commissions" in the Department of Public Information UN website <http://www.un.org/issues/reg-comm.asp> [12 Jan. 2006].

10 Lim Kim San served as the first Chairman of the Housing & Development Board, and was credited for leading the successful public housing programme in Singapore in the early 1960s. After Singapore's independence in 1965, Lim served as Minister for Finance and as Minister for the Interior and Defence. Lim retired from politics in 1981, and held appointments in the Public Utilities Board, Monetary Authority of Singapore and the Port of Singapore Authority as Chairman. He also served as Executive Chairman of Singapore Press Holdings from 1988 to 2002, and remained in the company as Senior Advisor until the end of 2005 at the age of 89.

him, with Sim Kee Boon[11] and Elizabeth Sam.[12] There were many rounds of meetings and talks. So Dr Goh, he was in Defence at that time, and he told us, "I don't think there will ever be a common currency agreement. There will come a breaking point. You know what the breaking point will be? Control over the reserves."

You see, at first, the Malaysians allowed us to issue currency against our own reserves. The Malaysians issued currency against their own reserves; the "S" series and the "M" series. It was the Currency Board system, so you could only issue currency up to the amount of reserves that you held.[13]

At first we thought that the Malaysians were agreeable to the common currency. Then Tan Siew Sin, the Malaysian Minister of Finance, at the last moment, decided: "Yes, you can issue against your reserves. But your reserves must be managed by me." That was the breaking point: the control over the reserves. Dr Goh predicted it *very* accurately.

Q This was in 1973 when the two currencies split.

A Yes. But before that, we had many rounds of negotiation. And Dr Goh, he's a very shrewd man. He predicted the breaking point.

Senior Minister Lee was at that time Prime Minister. He is also very shrewd. I remember him telling us, "Whatever correspondence you have with the Malaysians, you write it, knowing very well that one day, it is going to be made public."

---

11 Mr Sim Kee Boon joined the Civil Service in 1953 and became Head of Civil Service in 1979 until he retired in 1984. Soon after, he was appointed Executive Chairman of Civil Aviation Authority of Singapore (CAAS) until he stepped down 15 years later in 1999. He was also the Executive Chairman to Keppel Corporation Ltd and group of companies before retiring in 2003. Mr Sim is currently a member of the Temasek Advisory Panel, and Advisor to the CAAS and Lum Chang Group; President Commissioner of Bank Danamon; and Board Director of Asia Financial Holdings Pte Ltd. More information about him can be found at <http://www.temasekholdings.com.sg/2005review/tr2005_10.pdf> [28 Feb. 2006].

12 Mrs Elizabeth Sam is the Independent Director of Boardroom Ltd. She chairs the Nominating Committee and is a member of the Audit and Remuneration Committees. Mrs Sam is a Director of SC Global Developments Ltd and AV Jennings Homes Ltd, Australia. Mrs Sam has over 40 years of experience in the financial sector having held senior appointments in the Ministry of Finance, the Monetary Authority of Singapore, Mercantile House Holdings Ltd, and OCBC Bank where she retired in the position of Deputy President. More information about her can be found at <http://www. boardroomlimited.com/coinfo_bddtrs.asp> [28 Feb. 2006].

13 The Currency Board system was managed then by the Board of Commissioners of Currency (BCCS) which was set up in 1967. It has merged with the Monetary Authority of Singapore (MAS) since 2002. The features of the Currency Board system (then) were: the exchange rate was fixed between the domestic currency and a specified foreign currency; domestic notes and coins were fully convertible at the fixed exchange rate; and the domestic currency was fully backed by foreign assets or gold. Today, the only feature of the Currency Board system that Singapore has retained is the full backing of currency-in-circulation by external assets. More information can be found at <http://app.mof.gov. sg/news_speeches/speechdetails.asp?speechid=62> [28 Feb. 2006].

So Mr Lee Kuan Yew, and Dr Goh, they were both prepared for a breakdown. So every letter had to be written, ready to be made public one day. He really taught us how to write letters. We always appeared very, very reasonable. The facts had to be on our side. Because he warned us, "It will be published one day." So Senior Minister told us, "Whatever you write, you write it knowing very well it will be published one day."

I think all Foreign Affairs officers should also know that. When you write to another government, always remember that one day, when it comes to a fight, your letter will be exposed. So within weeks of the breakdown in the currency talks, we came up with a Green Paper, telling our side of the story.

Q When did SM start to lose faith in Malaysia?

A Senior Minister believed in Malaysia. But Dr Goh believed the contrary.

Q Can I take you back to 1960. Do you remember Dr Winsemius?

A Yes, I worked very closely with him. He came to Singapore in 1961. As I said, I was the only young officer in the Economic Development Division! So I went to the airport to receive them. I remember, I was asking Dr Winsemius[14] for his passport and he said, "You can ask young Mr Tang for the passports." Mr I.F. Tang was Secretary to the UNDP Mission.[15] Dr Winsemius and I.F. Tang, I would say, they are true friends of Singapore. They really put their hearts and souls into Singapore.

Q When did the IPB become the EDB?

A In 1961. I helped Mr Hon establish the EDB. Then I went over with him to EDB. He brought along Joe Pillay, Dhanabalan and I.

---

14 Dr Albert Winsemius, a Dutch Economist was Singapore's long-time economic advisor. He worked closely with first generation leaders like MM Lee (the PM) and former Finance Minister Goh Keng Swee. Later he was consulted by SM Goh (then PM) and his second-generation team. During his term as Singapore Economic Advisor from 1961 to 1984, he visited Singapore two or three times a year without fail to review economic performances indicators and to discuss macro-economic strategy with government planners. More information on Dr Winsemius can be found at <http://www.ntu.edu. sg/DO/Home/Professorships/Albert+Winsemius.htm> [28 Feb. 2006].

15 Mr Tang I-Fang who is Chairman & Executive Director of WBL Corporation Ltd and Chairman of United Engineers Ltd, also has had a distinguished career in the private and public sectors. Mr Tang was a China-born mechanical engineer by training and he came to Singapore in 1960 as a member of the United Nations Industrial Team led by the late Dr Winsemius. He has served as Chairman of the Economic Development Board and the Jurong Town Corporation. More information about Mr Tang can be found at <http://www.wbl.com.sg/bod_tif.shtml> [28 Feb. 2006].

Q *Who was left in the Ministry of Finance?*

A Sim Kee Boon and Howe Yoon Chong.[16] They were left upstairs.

Q *So you moved to the second floor.*

A Yes, that's another anecdote which I must tell you. Hon Sui Sen reminded me of this incident. When the EDB was being formed, Hon Sui Sen told me to go down to the Town Club on the second floor of the Fullerton Building, and tell them to vacate from their premises. Mr Hon remembers that my face went white; absolutely white. Mind you, I was a very young officer. And I had to go down to the Town Club, to serve them notice. To evict them from their premises!

Q *You served notice on the Town Club?*

A Yes! I was a young officer. The Town Club in those days was *the* club. It was the best club in those days, the bastion of British capitalism. All the Chairmen of the big companies, Shell and the trading houses, were all members. I was the one to give the orders for them to leave. Hon Sui Sen told me to go and chase them out. He reminded me years later, "Your face went white." I think the Secretary was Captain Pavitt, the Director of Marine. I served the notice on him.

Q *Did they resist? They had some legal title.*

A No, they had no legal title. They were just a tenant. I went to see Captain Pavitt, and said to him; well you are only a tenant. So please vacate by such and such a date. So then the EDB moved down to the premises of the Singapore Town Club. That is why the EDB had such nice premises with high ceilings. That was the best club of those days. That was in the 1960s. The Town Club was still a very powerful club.

I joined Mr Hon as his only Admin Officer. I had to do everything, from square one, from the ground up. If I had joined another place, say, the Treasury side of the Finance Ministry, there would be any number of

---

16 Mr Howe Yoon Chong is the Chairman of The Straits Trading Company Ltd since 1992. He was also the CEO of the Group until he stepped down in 2000. Prior to joining the Group, the former top civil servant, politician and banker held many senior appointments including Head of Civil Service, Permanent Secretary to major ministries, as well as Chairman and Chief Executive of major statutory boards like HDB, PSA and others. He was the Chairman CEO of DBS Bank Ltd (1985–90), the Minister of Defence (1979 to 1982) and Health (1982 to 1984). Information obtained from <http://www.stc.com.sg/bod.php> [28 Feb. 2006].

HEOs[17] doing the work for you. So you never learn. The best way to learn is to do things yourself. I always believe in that. Don't ever be served by people. You will never learn.

Q Who was on the Treasury side?

A They were the terror of the civil service. The Establishment people: Tan Chok Kian and George Bogaars,[18] they were the traditional Treasury; the Controllers. It was called Budget and Establishment in those days. But the Economic Development Division was different. It was the "new economy" organisation. So we were very different. We were a very small organisation. But we had very good leadership: Dr Goh and Mr Hon.

Dr Goh was really a brilliant man. OK, you can call me a civil servant of the old school. But I've said in public, Singapore was very lucky to have a winning team. Lee Kuan Yew, the political visionary. Goh Keng Swee, the economic architect. And you have Hon Sui Sen as the builder. It was a winning combination.

But don't ask me if there is such a thing in today's Cabinet. I will not commit myself! But they should have such a team: the political leader, the economic architect and the builder. This is very important for Singapore. But today only MM is left, the other two are gone.

Q Can you have another team like them? All of them were products of their circumstances.

A That is true. But there must be a team. In any team, I would say, the paramount leader is the political man. That is Lee Kuan Yew. You must have a political leader. You must also have an economic architect. A man who can design and plan economic policies. And then you must have somebody who can deliver. You must have three such men. That's a winning team.

Q You were in EDB from 1961.

A 1961 to 1963, and then from there I went to Harvard, and then I came back, then went back to EDB for one or two more years. I was Estate Officer for Jurong. And that's where I disagreed with Dr Goh.

---

17 Higher Executive Officer.

18 The late George Edwin Bogaars was the Head of the Civil Service as well as Permanent Secretary at the ministries of Finance (Budget), Interior and Defence and Home Affairs. He was also instrumental in setting up the Armed Forces and Temasek Holdings and in re-organising the Special Branch.

You know, we built all the flats there. And the industrialists refused to move the workers into the flats. So Dr Goh had this idea of collecting tolls. Every time a bus or lorry of workers goes through his gantry, he wanted to collect a toll on those going in. This was to encourage the workers to live in Jurong, within the gantry areas. But luckily for me, I didn't have to enforce his idea. Mr Woon Wah Siang, Mayor of Jurong, he built the gantries. But I think the economic tide turned and people just moved into the residential quarters because then they needed housing. Keng Swee is a brilliant man, but this was one of his ideas that I didn't agree with.

What happened after the Separation on 9 August 1965?

Mr I.F. Tang played a great role in our economic development. Before that, we were pursuing import substitution. So the aim was to get local industry going, and that is why we had duties and tariffs. The Malayan Common market was the flavour of the day.

But the moment we left Malaysia, there was no more Common Market. There was no more domestic market. So I.F. Tang told Dr Goh, "OK, from now on, we must be export-oriented." And in one stroke, we removed all the duties and tariffs.

You had over 300 tariffs or tariff categories at the time.

Yes, we just took them all off. I felt sorry for the Small and Medium-sized Enterprises (SMEs) because they believed in us. We sold them the idea of Malaysia: The Malaysian Common Market. And then we put duties to protect the Common Market, so they built factories and started their businesses.

So when we left Malaysia they were left holding the can. Quite a number of them suffered as a result. I remember one man who lost his entire business. I felt very sorry for him. He had a factory making Swan socks. He was a textile trader who believed that we had to go into the Malaysian Common Market. They believed in us, the SMEs. And when there was no Common Market, they were just left there. And then we invited the MNCs in. So sometimes it is difficult. We have to adjust. When we were wrong, the businessmen carried the burden. I felt very sorry for the SMEs.

But now, I'm glad to see that the SMEs have become independent. They are the ones who are producing the components, the contract manufacturers. I would say that the EDB had a role in this because in the EDB we set up training centres; the Industrial Training Centres. And the people who joined the EDB training were those with barely an education. Through these centres, they learned a skill. So they could go and join the workforce of the MNCs, for Rollei and other factories. And these are the ones who are doing well now. The SMEs have really become independent.

So the present day entrepreneurs came up from the EDB programmes?

Yes! And when we were training them, we never believed that they were our stars of the future. This is another irony. The late Ong Wee Hock was in charge of industrial training. So as the Chairman I used to tease Ong Wee Hock, "Wee Hock, you want to throw pearls before swine." He was very angry with me!

What I'm saying is that the least promising material, the boys from the Industrial Training Centres, turned out to be the *real* entrepreneurs. Life is always like that. It is just like a lily that grows in a pond. The pond is so muddy, but suddenly, a beautiful flower comes out of the mud.

So now I can tell you, the local companies, our private sector, they were started by the boys from the Industrial Training Centres. Some came out and started small factories, some engineers joined the MNCs and came out later. They are the backbone of local manufacturing. The SMEs have come a long way.

So when we do life sciences, I begin to wonder. You are now concentrating on the academic stars. Will they be the ones who will create the new businesses? That's one of my worries. Well, I hope they succeed because they are the future. We have put our bets on them.

So I think all my successors in EDB, when they promote industries, they should remember this part of our history. The persons who really struggle and succeed are the ones that have the least resources. In the early days, we didn't have any money. So we couldn't put our bets on anybody. So the entrepreneurs in the SMEs, they had to find their own way.

They had to fight their own way up. Is that the secret of success?

You know, when I was Chairman of EDB, we never believed in giving grants. To give grants to somebody means that he is basically not profitable. You know? So we gave tax incentives, we help train the labour in the Industrial Training Centres, we help to promote exports. But we do not give out grants.

But today more and more are asking for grants. Personally I don't think it is a healthy trend. Other countries have given grants. In the end, the industries don't come from the grants!

I remember distinctly, when I was Chairman EDB there was an Irish American fellow, Chairman of the Hyster company, which manufactured forklifts. He came to Singapore and wanted to establish a plant here. And my boys were *very* anxious to have him. And in those days, a forklift truck was *the* technology. So I called him and said, look, we can give tax incentives, we can find you a site, we can train your people. And he said, "No, this is not enough. You must give me a grant!"

So I thought, if he is asking for a grant, this means that he is not sure of his company. And he said, "Mr Ngiam, if you don't give me a grant, I'm going to go to Ireland and I will build my factory in Ireland. The Irish Government has offered me a grant." So I said, "Yes, well, good luck to you." He went to Ireland. And it gave me no end of satisfaction to read, three years later, in the *Financial Times*, that his company in Ireland went bankrupt, in spite of grants from the Irish government.

If a company is not competitive, then it needs a grant. We should be very wary of this. I would say as a country, we finance education and infrastructure, but not to give a grant to a company. I'll never believe in it.

Then you were in the Ministry of Finance with Sim Kee Boon and Elizabeth Sam from 1965 up to 1970.

Yes. After Harvard, I went back to the EDB for just a while. Then Sim Kee Boon became the Perm Sec of Economic Development, so Joe Pillay and I, we went back to the Finance Ministry. Mr Dhanabalan remained in EDB. Then Mr Hon established the Development Bank of Singapore and Dhanabalan went over to head the bank. So I was back in the Economic Development Division, Sim Kee Boon was the Perm Sec.

That was the time we had to deal with the split from Malaysia: Everything split. Currency, tariffs, everything. No more Common Market. And we also had the British withdrawal to cope with.

Those were very difficult times.

I. F. Tang was really the pioneer of this new economic policy. It was after the Separation. He told Dr Goh, "Forget about domestic markets. There are no more common markets. You'd better look at the rest to the world as your market." Export manufacturing was the only way. And we had to bring in the MNCs. I.F. Tang and Chan Chin Bock;[19] they were the ones who brought in the MNCs into Singapore.

In those days it was quite shocking to turn your back on the development of local industries.

No choice! There was no more Common Market. The day we left Malaysia we had no more Common Market. But I tell you, in retrospect, I realise that

---

19 Mr Chan Chin Bock was the former Chairman of the Economic Development Board and current Chairman of EDB Consulting Group. He is also the lead author of "Heart Work" — a commemorative book on how the Economic Development Board steered the industry development of Singapore from the 1960s into the 21st century. For more information about him, please refer to <http://www.sedb.com/etc/medialib/downloads/media_releases.Par.0004.File.tmp/Heart%20Work%20Press%20Release%20Annexes.doc> [28 Feb. 2006].

protection was definitely the wrong route. I remember the day they removed the duties. There was a steep duty on toothpaste. And Colgate was making toothpaste in Singapore. So we removed the duty. But they didn't drop their price!

So I called up the expatriate manager, and said, "Look Mr So-And-So, we removed the duty. Your price should drop by so-many cents." He said, "No Mr Ngiam, we set at what the market can take. Why should I drop the price just because you removed the duty?" So they never dropped their price. So having domestic industries does not mean that prices will drop at the marketplace. Only competition does that. So later on, you had other brands of toothpaste coming in. Only then did the prices drop.

So I think competition is the key to efficiency, not protection. And if you remove the protection, it doesn't mean the manufacturers will drop their prices. No, only competition does that.

And then you were instrumental in the Ministry of Finance.

At one point, I was in the role, *de facto,* of head of Singapore's central bank. I say this because I used to travel to all the meetings of the various Governors of the Central Banks; with Tun Ismail of Malaysia, Dr Puay Ungpakorn of Thailand, and the Philippines, Mr Castro. You see, at that time, we didn't have the Monetary Authority of Singapore.[20] So I used to represent Singapore at these meetings of Central Bank Governors.

I was always the youngest at those meetings. And that's how I got to know the present Governor of the Thai Central Bank. At that time he was also a young boy, carrying Dr Puay's bag. Now he is Central Bank Governor himself. This was before we started the Monetary Authority of Singapore.

Why didn't we call it Central Bank?

That was to Dr Goh's great credit. He believed in the Currency Board system. I would say there are two very successful policies in Singapore, which we claim to be our own. First, the Central Provident Fund. Second, the Currency Board. Both were actually British colonial policies, which worked so well that we retained them even when we were on our own.

---

20 Prior to 1970, the various monetary functions associated with a central bank were performed by several government departments and agencies. As Singapore progressed, the demands of an increasing complex banking and monetary environment necessitated streamlining the functions. The Monetary Authority of Singapore (MAS) was formed in 1971 and the MAS Act gives MAS the authority to regulate all elements of monetary, banking and financial aspects of Singapore.

You look at the Currency Board. It was started before the war; as early as that. And it all started when the British colonials, the chaps in Whitehall, were thinking, "Look, these chaps in the colonies, we should not trust them with the power to issue currency notes!" So they designed a Currency Board system. And with a Currency Board, before you can issue a dollar, you must have so many pounds banked with them as a reserve. Every dollar is fully backed by reserves. The system maintains its own stability. It is a beautiful system. It can never lead to currency depreciation. Every dollar is fully backed by reserves, which were locked up in Whitehall.

The Currency Board was a very clever idea. Very clever. So even after the Brits left, Dr Goh did not change the Currency Board system. He believed that our currency must be backed; fully backed. Today our currency is still fully backed. It is still a Currency Board system. So that's why our currency will always be stable. The Finance Minister will never be able to issue currency unless he has the reserves to back the currency. Singapore can never print money. So we will never have runaway inflation.

The currency board system was thought up by the British colonial civil servants, because they couldn't trust the colonies to issue currency properly. What the British imposed on us turned out to be a great virtue!

How did the CPF start?

Well, the Singapore civil servants, we all were entitled to pensions. So when we retired, we would all expect a pension from the British Government. I can imagine somebody in the British Treasury thinking, "Why should Britain keep a pension fund for all these chaps? Why should we fund them? We had better make them pay for themselves."

So they started a Singapore Central Provident Fund. So all us civil servants had to save our own money for our pensions. So the British started this Central Provident Fund because they didn't want to have the burden of caring for our old age, funding all our pensions. That was the start of the Central Provident Fund. The British imposed a Central Provident Fund system on the colonies.

By the way, they never imposed these measures on themselves. They imposed a Currency Board for the colonies, but they never imposed it on themselves. So their own sterling pound went haywire, and they could never get it under control. So these are colonial measures that turned out to be good for Singapore. It was very good control, very good discipline.

Dr Goh would say the Englishman is the smartest. For every ounce of effort, he gets the most return. Only trouble with him is that he doesn't put in too many ounces of effort! But for these two measures, we have to credit the British. They really instilled strict discipline on the colonies. This was to our overall benefit; our great benefit.

Q You are credited with starting some of today's financial institutions.

A Because I used to work with Elizabeth Sam and Sim Kee Boon. We were the Admin Officers that created the Monetary Authority of Singapore. At that time Mr Hon was the Finance Minister.

But Dr Goh, again, his thinking — he's such a brilliant man. He said, "Look. We must have two institutions. MAS can manage the short-term volatilities. And the Government Investment Corporation (GIC)[21] to do the long-term investments." So he split the Central Bank into two organisations, the MAS and the GIC. So the MAS doesn't fool around with our reserves. It was another brilliant stroke. Goh Keng Swee is a brilliant man.

Q In 1967 there was a drop in sterling.

A That one — Mr Lim Kim San, he played a great role in that. And Dr Goh, he's really very prescient. Before the drop, he moved our funds out of sterling. And this was despite the Brits writing us any number of letters asking us not to move out. You know in those days, there was the Sterling Bloc, and the British were pressuring us to stay in. So thanks to Dr Goh, we didn't suffer too much from the British depreciation.

Q You didn't follow the devaluation, as the Malaysians did.

A No, we didn't. We had already moved out of sterling.

And even gold — I must tell you the story of gold. Our first 100 tons of gold reserves, Dr Goh must be given the credit. Dr Goh, when he was the Minister, used to carry in his pocket a '555' booklet. You know, in the old days, even the breadman used to carry the '555' booklet to record down how much bread he has given you on credit. But the great man himself, Dr Goh Keng Swee, used to carry a '555' booklet in his pocket.

So every morning when he came into the office, he would call up Kee Boon or myself or Joe Pillay. And he pulls out his '555' booklet and looks for a page, and he says, "Go and do research on this topic." It was all written in the booklet!

So one day he asked me to write him a paper about gold to see whether the gold system could continue. So I wrote him a paper, saying, "I don't

---

21 The Government Investment Corporation (GIC) is a global investment management company established in 1981 to manage Singapore's foreign reserves with the aim of achieving long term returns on state assets while managing its risk. GIC invests internationally in equities, fixed income, money market instruments, real estate and special investments.

think so." So he said, "In that case, we had better go and buy gold from the South Africans."

In 1968, we went to the World Bank meeting. The South Africans were there and we invited the South African Finance Minister to our hotel room. He came and said, "Before we talk, we must switch on the TV very loud." Right in the heart of Washington! So we said, OK, and we switched on the TV, full volume. And Dr Goh said, "We're interested in buying gold." Dr Goh wanted to buy gold at a fixed price, rather than a floating market price. So we agreed to buy 100 tons, a substantial amount, at $40 US dollars. At that time the gold price was only $35. So we paid him a premium, in order to fix the price.

The South African agreed, "OK, you send your man to Switzerland, we'll deliver the gold to you in Switzerland and you pay us in Switzerland." Then he took out this US one dollar note. And sliced it into halves! Just like that. He gave half to me and said, "You keep this. I will keep the other half and my man will meet you in Switzerland."

A few months later, Wee Cho Yaw[22] and I, we went up to Switzerland, to the Swiss Bank Corporation. The first question the Swiss banker asked us was, "Do you have your half?" I said, "Yes." I handed the sliced US dollar note over. He took out the other half. It matched! The serial numbers were the same.

He said, "OK. Your identity has been established." It was so simple, instead of bringing letters of authentication, documents of identity. No need for all of that! So we bought 100 tons. In our reserves, I think we still have a lot of surplus on the gold account. We bought at $40. Today, even if it drops to $250, we still make a lot of money.

That was Singapore's first purchase of gold. We broke the embargo on South Africa! We bought quite cheap, just before Nixon went to demonetise gold. We were very lucky.

Subsequently, more gold was bought, but at a higher price. But the first tonnage of gold was bought by me and Wee Cho Yaw as my advisor.

Q But it was your report which started Dr Goh's thinking to buy gold.

A When you read economic reports, you must have a sense of the market. How the market is moving. It is something you have to develop. In that way, Dr Goh was an excellent teacher. You know, when the MAS was started by

---

22 Mr Wee Cho Yaw is the Chairman and CEO of United Overseas Bank since 1974. He is a well-known banker, entrepreneur and a leader in the commercial domain of Singapore. He is also a member of the Asia-Pacific Advisory Committee, New York Stock Exchange; Honorary President of Singapore Chinese Chamber of Commerce and Industry; and was appointed Pro-Chancellor of Nanyang Technological University in 2004. More information can be found at <http://www.uobgroup.com/assets/pdfs/AR2004.pdf> [1 March 2006].

Dr Goh, and he was the first Chairman, he used to invite me to his Monday meetings. I tell you, this was a real terror to all the MAS officers. Every Monday was an ordeal to these poor fellows. Ng Kok Song[23] was among them. Each week, Kok Song had to produce the US dollar exchange rate, and give last week's rates. And Dr Goh would ask, "What will it be next week?" Kok Song would have to make a guess. The following week, Dr Goh would surely match the actual rate against Kok Song's prediction, I can tell you!

It was a very good training! Within five minutes, these chaps must produce their prediction. And today they are the central bankers or in the private sector banks. Dr Goh Keng Swee was like a professor, and he used to put them all through his test, like a tutorial. You should have seen them squirm. But they really had good training from Dr Goh.

How would you compare Dr Goh and Mr Hon?

If the civil service has a hero, that's Hon Sui Sen. Hon Sui Sen would get all the ideas from Dr Goh. But he will implement them in a very efficient way. You have a team, the triumvirate. You have the political leader, the architect, and then the builder. The builder is Hon Sui Sen. He built up the civil service. That's why Joe Pillay, Dhanabalan and I, we all really hero-worshipped him. He never lost his temper, I can tell you that. Never.

You knew when he was angry, he became even quieter. Then you know he's angry. He was a Perm Sec who really knew his people. He never admonished you. He would correct you, and *very* gently.

And Dr Goh?

Dr Goh — he'll test you the first time. And he'll make up his mind, whether you are worthy of his training or not. Otherwise he'll write you off. Just like that. But his temper is mercurial. It happened to me only once. One day when I was just a junior officer, I went into his office at the Fullerton.[24] When I went in, he was smiling, he looked at my work, said, "Yes, OK." Then he suddenly thought of something else, and within minutes, from sunshine, he was like thunder. And he took his pencil and threw it at me!

---

23 Mr Ng Kok Song is the Managing Director (public markets) of the Government of Singapore Investment Corporation (GIC). Before joining GIC in 1986, Mr Ng served in various management positions at the Monetary Authority of Singapore (1971–86). He was also the founding Chairman of the Singapore International Monetary Exchange (SIMEX) from 1983 to 1987. More information can be found at <http://www.temasekholdings.com.sg/2005review/tr2005_10.pdf > [1 March 2006].

24 The Ministry of Finance and EDB then had offices at the Fullerton; today converted into a five-star hotel. The neo-colonial building was built to be a fort and has also served as the general post office.

So I walked out! I went to tell Miss Chia, his secretary, "Hey, the Minister just threw a pencil at me! So I walked out!" And Miss Chia said, "That's the right thing to do." Well, he never even noticed that I had left the office. That was my only experience of his temper. He changed from sunshine to thunder. So when you want to deal with him, you had to handle him properly.

But I learned a great deal from Goh Keng Swee and Hon Sui Sen. They were great teachers. When you submitted something to Dr Goh, he will take the trouble to polish up your draft. Yes! By changing a word here and there; putting a question mark against your figures. He would send it back to you. And you go and correct it, and resubmit it. And he will then approve. That's the best training. It was just like in school.

Nowadays our children don't write essays. But in those days, a good teacher will be able to mark your essays in such a way that it improves. He'll just change a word here and a word there, and polish. And from a rough draft, comes a polished product. And Goh Keng Swee and Hon Sui Sen, they used to do that.

These two men really taught me. They took the time to teach me, to correct me. These days you talk about a learning organisation. We were already a learning organisation, years ago! We learned from our bosses. They taught us, one on one.

Of course, we were a smaller civil service. But I think, today, the size of your staff is no excuse for not teaching your young officers. I tried to practise this when I became a Perm Sec. I would discuss the job with the officer concerned. And let him work. And then, I would correct his work. That was something I learned from these two men. One on one.

Q It must have been a privilege to work for them. It was a good education.

A Even Senior Minister. He's a lawyer, he's a fantastic teacher. If you are secretary to the Senior Minister, you should never second-guess what he wants. Wong Chooi Sen, he was secretary to Lee Kuan Yew when he was Prime Minister. And SM, he has quite neat handwriting. He makes his comments on the side. And Wong Chooi Sen would do the corrections, exactly. And he would say, you can never interpret Lee Kuan Yew. You see for yourself, what he has written. Nowadays the Private Secretaries try to paraphrase the great guy, which is wrong. Don't try to interpret your boss. Especially these three great men.

Q After 1965 the economic growth shot up!

A The moment we left Malaysia, we decided that import substitution was the wrong policy, the Common Market was gone, and the whole underpinning had changed. We changed to exports. We went to the world market. The best thing that happened to us, in retrospect, was for Malaysia to have kicked us out. Then we had the freedom to roam the whole world.

And I still believe that Singapore is a small economy, and we are a small population. As long as we are competitive, we can survive, we can make a living. That is my fundamental belief.

But we should never, never overprice ourselves. That is the great danger. Other than that, it's quite easy to be the Finance Minister of Singapore. The problems of Singapore are very finite. You can solve them within a matter of five or ten years. If you are the Finance Minister of China or India, you will need three or four lifetimes to solve the problems.

The high growth continued to the oil crisis in 1973, and then you came back to the Ministry of Finance.

Yes. I spent two years in Communication. Then I came back to Finance. The oil crisis hit us hard in 1974. But I think we survived this crisis through our good leadership. Again, I talk about the team of leaders — Lee Kuan Yew, Dr Goh, and Mr Hon, who was by then the Finance Minister.

The oil crisis came. Many countries tried to control the oil prices. But Mr Hon decided very early that he was not going to give any subsidies for oil. He said, "Let the oil price go up." Mr Hon Sui Sen made one remark which I will never forget. He said, "You'd better swallow your medicine in one gulp." A very wise man. That was how we weathered the oil crisis. We swallowed our medicine in one gulp. It was like the Japanese. They also allowed the oil price to go up. The first oil crisis, in 1974, they got hold of all the steel plants and electrical companies and literally closed down the inefficient ones. So they restructured (Now, of course, well, they seem to have lost their way). Other countries tried to slow down the oil prices by subsidies or other measures, which was wrong. We never did that.

Then there was a massive US dollar drop in 1973.

That was when the US dollar devalued. But by then, from 1972 onwards, we had already solved our problem of unemployment. We had full employment by 1972. Up to then, we had kept our wage levels way down, below the global wage level. So factories, MNCs, were coming in. We no longer had unemployment. The first phase of our industrialisation for "labour-intensive" industries — which were to create jobs, any job — was over.

That was why we started the second phase. It was the so-called "high-wage high-skills policy". At that point, we were underpricing ourselves. As much as we should not overprice ourselves, we also should not underprice ourselves. So we started pushing up the wage levels. That was when we brought in the National Wages Council (NWC), and they really jacked up the wages. And, instead of the wage-earners getting the money, and spending it on consumer goods, we decided we put the money into the Central Provident Fund (CPF).

So from 1972, we raised the wages. This started the "skills-intensive" phase of industrialisation. We pushed the labour force to become a high wage, high skills force. That was our second phase of industrialisation.

The first phase — to bring in low-cost, "labour-intensive" industry. To get the people into jobs. The second phase was to force the employers to train the workers and give them skills, pay them more. The extra money, we channelled to CPF, which allowed the workers to buy their homes from the HDB.

And the third phase, from about the 1990s, we progressed into the "knowledge-based" industrialisation.

The knowledge-based economy, I think, brings the greatest opportunity for Singapore. It also poses the greatest challenge. For the first two phases, we could solve the problems on our own. The third phase, "knowledge-based", is a matter of the global economy.

As an economist, I try to simplify things. Classical economic says that the factors of production are land, labour and capital and Singapore has very little of each. Therefore our potential GNP or GDP cannot grow beyond a certain size.

But in the knowledge-based economy, you can use knowledge to leverage on all three factors of production. So you can grow *beyond* your land, labour and capital. Your potential is far, far greater. That's the economic theory I believe in. So I would say, the knowledge-based economy liberates Singapore.

However, the other side of the coin is this: it's a global economy. Knowledge is available to everyone, all over the world. It is very mobile. And therefore we must be globally competitive. Our doctors can only be paid as much as the next-best doctor in the world. The engineer also has to price himself very carefully. And so on. The price is a global one.

So all these pay increases have to be thought about. In the global economy, information is freely available. It's a perfect market. And Singapore is a price taker, we cannot overprice ourselves, even for one day. Now Singaporeans have to compete with the best in the world.

I have friends who are business people and they are very sharp. They said to me, "You think the barber is protected from international market forces?" I thought, yes, of course, he's a local service. But I was wrong. Anyone can go to Johor Baru and have a haircut. Even without the Internet!

I tell you, this is the real meaning of the "knowledge-based" global economy. On the one hand, the knowledge-based economy liberates Singapore from the constraints of land, labour and capital. But in the new global economy, the Singapore economy has to compete and cannot be priced more than the rest of the world.

Q *And we must give quality.*

A Of course. We must give the best quality. Global quality. Now, the Singaporeans must compete with the best. You want to be the best, the best doctor in Singapore, you want to earn a million dollars? You must be as good as the best doctor from anywhere in the world. You need not be paid one cent less, but neither can you ask for one cent more. You must be amongst the best, and you must compete with the best. That is the law of the global economy. Perfect competition.

That is something; somehow, this message must go through. Singapore cannot overprice itself. That is something that which I have always held.

Q *In your days, you were not paid a very high salary.*

A I remember when I went in, my first pay was $680. Luckily for me I went in *after* Dr Goh cut the allowance,[25] so I never felt the cut. Sim Kee Boon went in before. He took a pay cut! Kee Boon used to drive a Rover. After the cut, he said, "I have to switch to a Volkswagen."

So my pay was $680 per month. My greatest ambition in life was to become a Perm Sec, and to be paid $1,950. By the way, this was Mr Hon Sui Sen's pay when he retired. He said to me, "Ngiam you are very lucky. On my pension, Mrs Hon and I, we cannot even afford two days of rice porridge."

Q *Why were you all willing to work for so little money?*

A In those early days there was a sense of mission. Pay wasn't on our mind. It was getting the job done. We were seeing Singapore through. It was an inspiring kind of situation. There was less calculation. I think the first twenty years were like that.

Q *You didn't have many promotions in those days. No fast track!*

A You know, I had my first promotion only in my fifth year of service. It took me five years! I joined in 1959, I was only promoted in 1964. From Admin

---

25 Salary in the civil service only improved radically after 1990. When self-government started in 1959, Civil Service was recruited by the British with very few locals. Motivation stemmed from the drive to change the nature of the society and the economy rather than salaries (<http://stars.nhb.gov.sg/data/pdfdoc/2000063010.htm>). The current government's policy is to pay people according to their market value and contribution so as to build a first-class public service.

Assistant to Assistant Secretary. But then, this showed another side of Hon Sui Sen's greatness. I remember, Joe Pillay and I, we felt a sense of impatience. For years, we had no promotion. So one day, one of us wrote to him, and he wrote back these simple words: "There is always room at the top."

What he meant was this: there were so many jobs, so much work to do. If you are able, you'll be promoted. In those early days, we were creating so many institutions. And therefore the opportunities were great. If you were able, if you could do the work, sure there will be room for you! There were plenty of jobs to go around. So that is what he meant. I'll never forget his words, "There is always room at the top."

Q *How can we get the same spirit, under modern circumstances? It is a different world.*

A If you ask me to give advice to the Cabinet, I would say they are taking too clinical an approach to the problems. I mean, in life, there must always be some untidiness, some chaos. As a government, you must be prepared to respond to it. You know? So I think I hope that they will not create a sterile kind of environment for the civil service. It should be a vibrant kind of environment.

It takes all kinds to make the civil service. There are some who are very good organisers but very poor at writing policy papers. There are some very good at policy papers, but can't even organise a picnic. So I think we have to look at the spectrum of talent.

Today, I think they have a new system which is bound by rules. Now, you can be a Perm Sec for only ten years and Deputy Secretary for five years. In my view, that is a negative way of moving people up and out. It is too mechanical. Maybe in the army, it's OK. But in other aspects of public service, I would say, it is not an active approach. You should not worry that you have too many talents in the system. You should worry that you have not enough talent!

Again, I go back to Hon Sui Sen. His policy was, he finds a talent, he gives him a role, a job which suits his talent. That's what he meant by, "There's always room at the top." That's Hon Sui Sen.

He once told me, "Look, when you are my subordinate, I try to identify your strong points. And I use your strong points to do the work. You also have weak points, but I'll not stress that too much. I'll try to help you use your strong points. When you are the boss one day, you look at a person, what are his strong points. Use his strong points. It is much more satisfying than harping on a weakness." That is Hon Sui Sen. A great leader.

At one stage there were three Perm Secs in the Finance Ministry. There was George Bogaars, who came back from Defence to Budget. Joe Pillay was Perm Sec of Revenue, and myself, Perm Sec, Economic Development. There were three of us. So one day somebody commented to Mr Hon, "You have too many Perm Secs!" And he said, "No. But I have three *good* Perm Secs." That's the way the system should be.

Today, you are worried about having the people stay too long. I mean, that's not an active approach to management. I would say that, as a boss, for every talented person you have, you should be able to find a role for him. I mean, for *every* talent. The main thing is to grow Singapore, to create new roles for your talented people.

And Hon Sui Sen, again, gave me another of his principles. He used to say, "My only job is to appoint you to a certain job, because I think you can do the work. I have studied your talent, and I think you can do it. Having appointed you, I leave you to do it. You take the ball and run." Of course, he made appointments very carefully. But once he makes the appointment, he leaves you to the work.

But the Singapore civil service has been seen as a near-flawless institution.

I think we have done very well to institutionalise the system. But, for God's sake, they must keep the spark alive. They must believe in a mission. To be mission-oriented.

I asked some of our young Perm Secs, "What is the mission of the Admin Service today? My mission was to create employment for the unemployed. Your mission is to create an economy and society where our very best will raise their families in Singapore. If you cannot, you are finished. You have failed."

I believe this is very important. Our very best must choose to raise their families in Singapore. They can have their businesses all over the world. But where do they raise the family? That is the acid test. I think that is very important. I'm taking a long term view because I've got three grandchildren. So I want to be sure that in 50 years' time, that there will be a Singapore that they will be proud of. That's very important. So I think we have to inculcate that.

The mission of the Admin Service today is far more difficult. Their job is much harder than Sim Kee Boon's or mine was. Ours was sheer quantity. Achievement of quantitative targets. But the Perm Secs today are going after *qualitative* targets, which is much, much harder.

And they will have to respond to great changes — from the old to the new economy. Even when I was the Chairman of the CPF Board, I said that the CPF model is for the old economy. The model is based on long-term, continuous employment. But in the new economy, you are your own employer. You are a consultant. You are employed for three months, then you go on to another piece of work. Quite a different world altogether.

Soon, all the companies will be subcontracting. And I would say, even the government itself, the public service, should subcontract. They should end up with only a core of the present civil service, say, 10 per cent. Just the thinkers, the leaders — to set a direction. The very top, the Ministerial level, they are the core. They should be purchasers of services.

But for the rest of the civil service? You can form companies and work for yourself.

We have to change the way we structure our Ministries. For instance, our Perm Secs. You know, every Minister requires a Finance Perm Sec for two months of the year. But not for more. He may need another Perm Sec, say, an expert in manufacturing, for three months. There should be a pool of Perm Secs who are specialists in a particular field. And a Minister should be able to draw on whatever skills and specialties that he needs, make full use of them, and then afterwards, release them back, into the pool.

What I am saying is this: the Perm Secs should be consultants. And they should have a team of officers whom they can lead to do the work, on a contract basis. Why do you want a Finance Perm Sec for 12 months of the year? He can be more useful to another Ministry.

You're asking for a more loose and flexible system of deploying the Perm Secs...

In the New Economy, you must all be specialists. Every Ministry requires an economist. So you are the economics Perm Sec, you can do the economic policy-making for them. But you do it as a consultant.

So, with your team of chaps, you move in, do the job, move out. It's a hard life. But these types like McKinsey and Arthur D. Little, those guys are really bright. They go into a topic, they find the facts, do all the analysis, they give you the options. And after the job is finished, you give them a cheque, and they go away and do work for somebody else. You don't keep them on your payroll. That is the way of the future. So the institutional type of civil service has to change, and quite rapidly. That is the true sense of the market.

Which part of your career did you enjoy most?

I enjoyed my whole civil service career. But if I had to name the part I really enjoyed most, it must be my years at the EDB. I regard the EDB as the "centre-forward" of the Singapore "football" team. Because without the investments, there would be no economic growth. Without economic growth, you can have all the dreams in the world; they are not going to be fulfilled.

The EDB boys were given a great deal of freedom right from the start. That's why Dr Goh started the EDB outside of the traditional civil service.

I would say that Philip Yeo[26] has done a brilliant job in the EDB. He has brought it to a higher platform. Because he knows, the EDB, they must always have the freedom to range.

Hon Sui Sen thought the same way. One day he told me, "Ngiam, I envy you as Chairman EDB." He was then my Finance Minister. He went on, "As Finance Minister, when you submit a paper to me, all I do is write yes or no. It gives me no satisfaction. In EDB you are creating, moving things along, and making changes. Creating changes; that is the greatest satisfaction."

So I think we should keep the EDB spirit — this type of organisation. But I must tell you that my friend and I, Chin Bock, we chickened out. Mr Hon said to me, "Ngiam, you want to be a consultant? I will pay you a percentage of the investment commitments that you can bring in. And you take this money; you can do what you like. You can hire ten people, hire one hundred people. I give you complete freedom to run the EDB." So I brought it back to Chin Bock. And we thought about it and he finally says, "What if there is a global recession? We can work very hard for no reward!" So we chickened out. We should have accepted it! In retrospect we should have accepted it.

I mean, I know that the EDB now are great professionals. But if they were hired as consultants, they would have been even greater. I believe that this civil service will run better if you were 75 per cent of your establishment. More than 25, maybe 35 per cent are superfluous. You have more fellows, but instead of working, they are fighting each other.

Achieve 120 per cent result on 80 per cent establishment. That's a true test of a Perm Sec. Of course, Howe Yoon Chong goes as far as 50 per cent! He wants a 50 per cent cut in establishment! He's another radical chap.

The history of HDB cannot be written without him. I would say Lim Kim San, Howe Yoon Chong, Teh Cheang Wan:[27] these are the three people of the HDB.

---

26 Mr Philip Yeo is currently the Chairman of the Agency for Science, Technology and Research. He was the Chairman of the EDB from 1986 to 2001 and then its co-Chairman until 2006. Mr Yeo joined the Administrative Service in June 1970 and served in the Ministry of Defence where he held several appointments including the appointment of Permanent Secretary for Defence in 1979, logistics, technological research & development before assuming his chairmanship in EDB. He retired from the Administrative Service in 1999. For more information, please refer to <http://www.edb.gov.sg/edb/sg/en_uk/index/about_us/senior_management/philip_yeo_co-chairman.html> [1 March 2006].

27 The late Mr Teh Cheang Wan was former Minister for National Development and head of HDB. He was investigated in Nov. 1986 for accepting two bribes and later committed suicide in Dec. 1986.

Eye Witness of a Political Journey: A Civil Servant and the PAP

What was it like to be a student in the tumultuous 1950s?

The leftist tidal wave was fronted by the English-educated leadership in the PAP. They swamped and swept out the colonial English-educated in the Progressive Party. Mr C.C. Tan and Mr John Laycock did not know what hit them.[1] At university then, out of curiosity, I became a fringe innocent member of the Socialist Club helping to distribute the Fajar newssheet.[2] As I recall, it never sold a single copy at the newsstand, but was nevertheless published regularly. I often wondered who was paying the printing cost.

As I was staying at the Dunearn Road hostels, a vivid recollection was that of hundreds of Chinese High School students charging down Bukit Timah Road. Lee Kuan Yew once contrasted the goldfish bowl existence of University of Malaya (UM)[3] undergraduates with the piranha instinct of their Nantah counterparts. To me, the NUS undergraduates were more like "longkang"

Interview with Sonny Yap on 23 June 2003.

1   Mr Tan Chye Ching (C.C.Tan) and John Laycock belonged to an elite group of lawyers and merchants which later united with the Straits Chinese British Association to form the Progressive Party (a mainly elite, English-educated, non-communal party).

2   Fajar was published by the University of Malaya Socialist Club. The editors and associates of Fajar were arrested in May 1954 and tried for sedition, but were later acquitted. More information can be found in: Thumboo, E. "Strands In The Labels —Innovation and Continuity in English Studies: A View from Singapore", *Innovation and Continuity in English Studies: A Critical Jubilee*, IAUPE, Germany (2001:187–208).

3   University of Malaya was founded in 1949 from the union of King Edward VII College of Medicine and Raffles College. The University of Singapore was established in 1962 following the decision of the Governments of Singapore and the Federation of Malaya that the Singapore Division and the Kuala Lumpur Division of the University of Malaya should become autonomous national universities in their respective countries. Information obtained from <http://www.nus.edu.sg/corporate/timeline/1949.htm> [1 March 2006].

guppies in contrast to the Siamese fighting fish of Chinese High once found in the fishponds of Ang Sa Lee (Serangoon Gardens) during my boyhood.[4]

I suspect the real reason why the guppies did not become political activists was because our families had to scrape and scrimp to send us to university. And those of us who had to depend on scholarships and bursaries to get through could not afford to fail even a single day.

Were there many fears among you?

Surprisingly, none. We were young and optimistic. We were also ignorant and naive. There is a saying in my Hainanese dialect that the blind man does not fear the tiger. The tiger was very much in our midst. Mr Lim Chin Siong[5] was Political Secretary to Dr Goh, our Minister for Finance. Mr James Puthucheary was Chairman of the Industrial Promotion Board, the precursor of the EDB. Heng Hong Ngoh, S. Dhanabalan, Joe Pillay and myself worked under the inspiring leadership of Mr Hon Sui Sen, our PS (Economic Development), Dr Goh Keng Swee, our Minister of Finance, and our Prime Minister, Mr Lee Kuan Yew.[6]

The Economic Development Division (EDD) grew to become the Economic Development Board, the Jurong Town Corporation, the Development Bank of Singapore, and now the Ministry of Trade and Industry. But not many people know that the EDD started with only four people, namely the Minister, the PS, the Admin Assistant (yours truly), and the office boy, in a dingy corner on the 5th floor of the Fullerton Building, now the magnificent Fullerton Hotel. In the early pioneering days, we do first and talk later. Today some of us talk first and don't do.

The political strategy was not to fight fire with fire. We fought the heat of Communist agitation with the quenching water of employment.

Are you a PAP member? Have you been asked?

Contrary to the suspicion of many of my friends, no. But on my return to the Ministry of Finance from Communications in 1972, Mr Hon, who was by then the Finance Minister, asked me whether I would like to be considered as a PAP candidate. I asked for time to think it over. After consulting my wife, we decided against it, as my daughter and son were still young. My wife also

---

4   The Siamese fighting fish has a more aggressive nature than the "longkang" (drain) guppies.

5   The late Mr Lim Chin Siong was an influential leftwing politician and trade union leader in Singapore in the 1950s and 1960s. Lim joined the People's Action Party (PAP) in 1954 and later left the party to form the Barisan Socialist in 1961. For more information, please refer to: Tan Jing Quee and Jomo K.S., *Comet in Our Sky: Lim Chin Siong in History.* Selangor Darul Ehsan (Malaysia), 2001.

6   Dennis Bloodworth, *The Tiger and the Trojan Horse* (Singapore: Times Books International, 1986). This is a story of how a small group of young nationalists in Singapore took on the formidable communist movement; the duel between the People's Action Party and the Communist United Front.

thought that I was too straightforward to succeed in politics and politicking. She was right, as years later, then SM Lee told me that he could not appoint me as Head of Civil Service because I lacked guile. I also told Mr Hon that some of us should remain behind to mind the shop. Ever so gently, he smiled and we never discussed the matter again. When Mr Hon passed away in 1983, I had lost a father.

I joined the Singapore Administrative Service in August 1959 together with Herman Hochstadt and Sarjit Singh from Malaysia. We were the first three Administrative Officers to join the Service after the PAP came to power. I would say that we were political, but not partisan. We did not have the colonial mental baggage of our predecessors. This was a great advantage. As officers of the new government, we were taught to get things done starting from first principles when necessary. In plain English, starting from scratch. The older civil servants were good at keeping the wheels of administration turning, maintaining the *status quo*. They were IM bound.[7] Those who could not keep up with the pace of the PAP government left.

The PAP leadership had no choice but to be in a hurry. Unemployment was over 10 per cent. There were many street hawkers and odd job labourers. Singaporeans were living in urban slums and mosquito infested kampongs. Not fearing the tiger, my colleagues and I in the EDB and HDB poured out our youthful energy, chasing after any kind of manufacturing industries for jobs, and building flats by the minute. Slowly, painfully but surely we created the jobs and built the high-rise apartments out of the swamps of Toa Payoh.

The political greatness of Mr Lee Kuan Yew, Dr Goh Keng Swee, Mr S. Rajaratnam, Dr Toh Chin Chye, and the other non-Communist PAP leaders is that they never tried to draw the Civil Service into partisan politics. They fought their own titanic battles against their Communist wing, Chinese chauvinists like Mr Ong Eng Guan, and UMNO.[8] They left us alone to get on with the job of building the economy, the physical and social infrastructure. In reality, this protected the English-educated guppies against the Chinese-educated fighting fish. Although it was hard to swallow at that time, we now appreciate what Dr Goh meant when he said that the English-educated should go on their bended knees and thank the PAP.

Who did you work closest with? Who did you feel were your mentors?

Sui Sen, my first Permanent Secretary; Dr Goh Keng Swee, my first Minister for Finance; and Mr Lee Kuan Yew, my first Prime Minister. One day, when

---

7   The Government Instructional Manual (IM) is the "book of rules" that governs how civil servants execute their duties.

8   Ong Eng Guan was a leading member of the PAP and a popular mayor of Singapore who split from the party to contest for another party. UMNO is the party for Malay unity and nationalism and has led the Malaysian government since independence.

I was more cheerful than usual, Dr Goh told me that I had advanced in my career not because I was cleverer than others, but because I was in the right place at the right time. In like vein, he told me that Singapore had achieved economic progress not because we are clever but that others were more stupid. Dr Goh taught me hardheaded economic analysis. [...].

Dr Goh helped and advised me at critical stages of my career. In 1970, he recalled me from Intraco Ltd to be acting Perm Sec (Communications), my first posting at this level.[9] When I became Perm Sec (Budget) in 1986, he called me in and said that MOF would continue to make mistakes. In our spartan early years, we made mistakes on the back of an envelope. Now that we were more comfortable, we have to beware of making mistakes on the backs of huge computers. Dr Goh was our first Finance Minister and the economic architect in the founding cabinet that laid the foundations for the political and economic success of an independent Singapore.

I worked one on one with PM Lee Kuan Yew only in the later stages of my career when I was appointed Perm Sec (Prime Minister's Office). He asked me once whether he had mellowed. I told him I wouldn't know as I did not work to him when he was a young Prime Minister. But I remember him as a ruggedly handsome Cambridge-trained lawyer full of charisma and vitality, espousing the cause of the largely Chinese-educated electorate of Tanjong Pagar. Modern media with their televised TV debates are no match for the flesh and blood political rallies of SM's generation. SM Lee told me that Dr Goh was his best Minister.

When he was PM, Lee Kuan Yew's art of management was to send the best Minister and best PS to deal with the most critical and protracted priority of the time. In 1959, when the PAP won power, unemployment in Singapore was over 10 per cent. For an urban city state with no agriculture to absorb the unemployed and underemployed, the political situation was tinder dry. The Communist left was just waiting to set it alight. Dr Goh was appointed the Minister for Finance, and Mr Hon Sui Sen, the Perm Sec (Economic Development), to spearhead economic development.

The Minister, the Perm Sec and his rookie EDB officers did not fear the Communist tiger. We put our heart and soul into attracting industry and creating jobs. In one ironic instance, the Communist threat helped. Mr I.F. Tang, who succeeded Mr Eric Meyer (a foreign talent from Israel) as Director EDB, told me how we obtained a textile quota from the Americans larger than what our production capacity justified. I.F. told me that rather than producing facts and figures he took the American delegation round the city after dinner casually driving by premises which were on strike. The fierce anti-capitalist slogans shouting from red banners did the trick, for the Americans gave us a

---

9   Ngiam was the youngest person in the history of the Singapore Civil Service to be appointed to the position of Permanent Secretary.

quota more than we deserved. Mr Tang, a foreign talent from China, stayed on in Singapore to become one of our most outstanding citizens.

What did I learn from SM Lee? He taught me statecraft. As Perm Sec (PMO), I had the privilege of lunching with PM Lee one on one, about twice a year. On such occasions, I am proud to say he treated me as his intellectual equal. He told me that the only basis for a civilised conversation between two people was to treat each other with mutual respect. It is pointless otherwise. Arguments were sharp and to the point. I must admit that I lost more arguments than I won. I remember with pride that Dr Winsemius and I successfully persuaded Mr Lee to expand the enrolment in engineering, which he did by establishing the Nanyang Technological Institute. The Vice Chancellor of the National University of Singapore (NUS) then had taken the view that university education was meant only for the few, the intellectual elite. NUS conjured up the spectre of degree "mills" that churned out jobless and unhappy graduates in order to stop the EDB from seeking an expansion in university education. Yet we knew otherwise. A certain Dr Pannenborg of Philips, who was their R&D Head, told us that the first step was to raise our level of competence by having more university-trained engineers. Only when we had the trained manpower can we hope to attract R&D from MNCs.

What were some of the lessons of statecraft you learnt?

SM told me that to win and retain power, we must have talent. That was why he insisted on bonding every President Scholar in the Singapore Administrative Service. I agreed with the first part of his proposition, but not the second half. However, he taught me that to exercise power, we must have a strong treasury (the economy), control of the gun (the army), and influence over the voice (the media).

To me, a strong economy is the equivalent of the tee-off shot in golf. Without a long and straight tee-off, the golfer is not likely to do a par. A strong economy is the *sine qua non* of good government. Our current economic difficulties need not dismay us. After all, we are only a population of 4 million, which is not even a blip on the horizon compared to China's 1.2 billion, and India's 1 billion.

Singapore should not however navigate on policy auto-pilot. We need to stick to the fundamentals. We should never overpay ourselves. Nor should we overprice ourselves. Wage increases have far outstripped productivity increases. The Singapore dollar should float with the US dollar rather than against a theoretical basket of currencies. International trade is denominated in the US dollar. Even in the best of times, it goes against economic commonsense to think that the Singapore dollar can appreciate against the US dollar. Overpaying and overpricing ourselves must surely lead to economic disaster, eroding the under-pining of our state. The wheels of economic laws grind slowly, but they grind inexorably.

*Q*What were the strengths of the pioneering team that led Singapore?

*A*Mr Lee Kuan Yew's charisma and sheer strength of intellect attracted around him a selfless group of men with strong conviction and courage. They believed in Singapore and fought for our creation and survival as an independent nation.

My civil service career was totally in economic development. In this domain four men stood out, namely Lee Kuan Yew, Dr Goh, Mr Hon and Mr Lim Kim San. Mr Lee outflanked the Communist left who were bent on creating chaos to ride to power on the backs of unemployed workers. They were basically spoilers. Their slogans of being the champions of workers sounded very hollow to young EDB officers out on the road trying to attract manufacturing investments to Singapore from MNCs. If SM is the political Moses, then Dr Goh as the economic architect is the martial Joshua, who scouted the Promised Land. He saw opportunities where others saw only difficulties.

But it was left to great administrators like Mr Hon and astute businessmen like Mr Lim to deliver. What I learnt most from Mr Hon was man management. He said whether as Minister or PS, we should identify the strengths of our officers and use them. Of course, we should not be blind to their weaknesses. It is more rewarding to use a person's strength. It is counter-productive to harp on his weakness. Mr Hon also said that as the boss your first decision in selecting the man for the job is also your last. You may take your time in selecting the warrior to fight the battle. Having chosen him, you should leave your choice to get on with the job and not look over your shoulder to second guess him.

I recall with great delight a lesson in managing people that Mr Hon taught Mr Lee and Dr Goh. One day, when both of them were bemoaning that a particular officer with great potential has yet to deliver on his promise, Mr Hon spoke up. He told them that they were like impatient gardeners. Having just planted a seedling both of them could not wait for the tree to grow and bear fruit. Impatient, they pulled out the young sapling to see whether it had deep roots. As Mr Hon was a quiet man who spoke little, both the Prime Minister and Deputy Prime Minister nearly fell out of their chair!

Mr Lim Kim San had the quick mind and disposition of an entrepreneur. He preferred oral submissions to long elegant memoranda from civil servants. He reads body language better than the written text. He was more interested in the end result rather than the argument or "process" in modern management jargon. Mr Lim was therefore the ideal choice to be the first Chairman of the HDB.

With Mr Howe Yoon Chong as his CEO, he got slum clearance and high rise construction off to a flying start. The citation on the award of the Order of Temasek to Mr Lim reads that he broke the back of Singapore's housing problem. Mr Lim and his HDB team worked feverishly to build the low cost flats that house 90 per cent of our people today, tangible manifestation of progress that won the PAP successive elections.

But all this would not have been possible without the inspiring leadership of Mr Hon as Chairman, EDB. We were young once. We put in prodigious effort to establish manufacturing industries to provide the jobs that paid the wages for us to eat and to be housed. By 1972, Singapore with an unemployment rate of 3 per cent achieved full employment. Anyone who wanted a job would get a job. Full employment however is not a permanent state of affairs. In a knowledge-based global economy, Singapore has to run even harder and faster to keep ahead. We must never overpay nor overprice ourselves. The Singapore premium of good governance counts for nothing if the bottom line is negative.

What about the time of merger as part of Malaysia and the Malaysian Common Market?

In the 1950s and 1960s, much of industrial strategy in developing countries, big and small, such as India, was founded on what is known as the policy of import substitution. The seductive logic is for poor countries to keep imports out so that their markets can be consolidated to achieve economies of scale. Add to this disarmingly simple formula, the politically heady wine of self-reliance advocated by the two political giants of Asia, namely Mao Zedong and Jawaharlal Nehru. Until Deng Xiaoping came along some 40 years later, the two biggest and potentially richest countries in Asia were stuck in the policy *cul-de-sac* of import substitution.

Singapore was not spared either. We ignored the minuscule size of our market and tried to expand it by forming a common market with Malaysia. Even then, all that Malaysia wanted was to close our market for themselves, without allowing us equal opportunity to sell to them in their protected market.

Our two years in Malaysia were the most frustrating and miserable for EDB. It is no exaggeration to say that my contemporaries and I were relieved when separation came. We regained our freedom of action, and under the guidance of Dr Winsemius and Mr I.F. Tang, lost no time switching to an export-oriented industrialisation policy. Instead of staring at our own navel, we looked up and saw clear blue skies. The world is our market. Our GDP potential was many times more than what an import substitution policy would ever give us. The hard part of course is that we must be the most competitive; the world's best in the fields we choose to compete in. We have to be in everybody's economic pyramid, in niches where we are useful and add value to our trading partners.

What was the working relationship like between government agencies like the EDB with the labour movement and the NTUC?

Until the decisive split between the non-Communist PAP and the Barisan wing in 1961, there was only industrial chaos. The Barisan wing instigated and fomented strikes all over the island to create the fertile soil of unemployment to wrest power. During this period, Dr Goh taught me as a young officer how to deal with politically inspired strikes. One of a very small number of industries during the early 1960s was a textile mill in Bukit Timah set up by Mr David Lee, a Shanghainese entrepreneur from Hong Kong. He was locked in by his striking workers. To help him out of his dire predicament, Dr Goh asked me to get in touch with his banker, Mr Lever of the Hongkong and Shanghai Bank.

When I told Mr Lever that the Minister has asked me to call him about the textile mill, Mr Lever without any prompting from me said that he knew what to do. He simply withdrew whatever bank facilities that were left. Without cash, the textile mill closed down. A strike became a lockout. Mr Lee later turned his mill to be a manufacturer of steel windows. Industrial peace was gradually restored. Riding on an MNC-based, export-oriented industrialisation policy, we achieved full employment in a relatively short period of time.

Around this period, Motorola, the handphone pioneer, was success-fully wooed by Mr Chan Chin Bock to consider Singapore as one of their offshore manufacturing bases. Joy turned to anguish when Motorola told us that their company had a "no union" policy. When EDB could not persuade the National Trade Unions Congress (NTUC) to accept this even in principle, Motorola left for Petaling Jaya, Kuala Lumpur (KL) in Malaysia. Every time I went to KL for Currency Board meetings, the gleaming Motorola factories on the way to town turned me green with envy.

How did the government manage the policy towards wages?

Dr Winsemius, until the age of 40, was the Director-General of Industrial Development of the Netherlands. He was the Chairman of the EDB of the Dutch Government. The Dutch people after the Second World War were poor and frugal. Dr Winsemius was very persuasive in his job, so that in a very short period of time, he was able to attract enough industries to achieve full employment for his country. As we had achieved full employment by 1972, he told Mr Hon and then PM Lee Kuan Yew not to repeat Holland's mistake of following a pure market approach as wages would just run away in a tight labour market of full employment.

So Dr Winsemius recommended the formation of the tripartite National Wages Council (NWC). The government, represented by the Chairman of the EDB, workers represented by the NTUC, and employers represented by the Singapore Employers' Federation. We huddled in consultation over a period of two weeks once a year under the cheerful, fair and objective chairmanship of Professor Lim Chong Yah of the National University of

Singapore.[10] Professor Lim was my economics tutor at the university. So when Dr Winsemius asked me to suggest a suitable person to chair the NWC, our thoughts naturally turned to Professor Lim, a fellow economist. Mr Devan Nair who went on to become President represented the NTUC in his capacity as its Secretary-General, and Mr Desmond Neill, Hokkien-speaking President of the SEF, represented the major employer groups. I represented the government, providing the economic statistics.

In the initial years, we allowed wages to go up but behind productivity increases. The policy stance was wage restraint. As the labour market tightened, job-hopping became a Singapore phenomenon. In the employer's mind, job-hopping was bad. However, life-long employment, once a virtue, is now a discredited policy. We thought that by accelerating the pace of wage increases, employers would compete vigorously for scarce labour to the point where marginal productivity of labour equals the marginal wage. And presto, there would be optimum allocation of labour.

To their credit, Devan Nair and his NTUC colleagues had to be persuaded by Dr Winsemius to accept the "high wage" policy which we advocated to speed up the restructuring of the Singapore economy. They feared that if wages rose too fast, there would be unemployment. They knew better than the two of us. It was human nature to accept the reward first and promise to deliver later. As it was NWC mandated, both employers and trade union leaders were just happy to follow the NWC guidelines. There was no hassle and industrial peace reigned.

Although Singapore was short of labour, the government imposed quotas and levies on foreign workers so that they would cost as much as the Singapore worker to provide a level playing field for the Singaporean to compete! I must confess that Dr Winsemius and I as economists could not foresee this perverse and twisted political logic. No wonder Devan Nair hesitated to embrace our high wage policy recommendation. The public service, which faced no competitive pressure, also received NWC wage increases like everybody else.

Today, we find ourselves in the bind of a high cost economy. MNCs tell me that for every Singapore worker they hire they can employ four in Penang, and eight in China, with comparable skills. The Singapore premium of good governance, efficient infrastructure and social stability is not sufficient to close this wage gap. In a global knowledge-based economy, Singapore and Singaporeans can no longer have it all our way. The world does not owe us a living. As Dr Goh would surely say others are no longer more stupid than

10 Professor Lim Chong Yah is the founding chairman of the National Wage Council (NWC) from 1972–2001. He joined the University of Singapore in 1969 and was appointed Dean of the Faculty of Arts and Science in 1971. He later founded the Federation of ASEAN Economic Association (FAEA). In 1992, he retired from NUS and became Emeritus Professor. He is a professor of Economics in NTU. Prof Lim has published several books; his latest book is *Southeast Asia: The Long Road Ahead* (2004), a concise study of various important economic aspects of Southeast Asia.

us. We should snap out of our state of self-denial. I believe that if we face up to reality, we will survive and triumph once again.

Q What role did foreigners like Dr Albert Winsemius and Mr I.F. Tang play in the pioneering years?

A Dr Winsemius of the Netherlands and Mr I.F. Tang of China were two foreign friends of Singapore who made extraordinary contributions to the economic development of Singapore. They came to Singapore as the leader and secretary of the first UN Industrialisation Survey Team in 1961. A young admin assistant then, I was sent by Mr Hon to receive them on arrival at the Paya Lebar Airport. The main objective was to create as much employment as fast as possible. We were to produce goods and services as cheaply as possible to be able to sell them in any market, free or protected. Whether an industry is high tech or low tech never crossed our mind.

Our early industries ranged from garments, toys, and hair-wigs to ship breaking, re-rolling steel plates into steel bars, and to our pleasant surprise oil refining (Maruzen Toyo of Japan was the catalyst for Shell and the other oil majors, to do likewise), ship repairing and rig building. Later, Sumitomo Chemicals of Japan was again the catalyst for our petrochemical industry which followed on from oil refining.

Dr Winsemius and I.F. Tang in their heart of hearts never believed in a Malaysian Common Market. In any case, it turned out to be a pipe dream. Dr Goh in the late 60s also told me not to be overly dependent for markets or even supplies on our neighbours, some of whom can be very prickly. Nor, for that matter, on giant countries like China, which can put the political screws on us when it suits their national interest.

After Mr Hon was appointed Minister, he selected me as the civil service counterpart to Dr Winsemius. Dr Winsemius would spend about two to three weeks once or twice a year advising us on economic development. On each visit, he would have himself invited to dinner by Mr Devan Nair in his capacity as Secretary-General of NTUC and with two Dutch compatriots, Mr Gerzon of Shell, and Mr Van Oonen of the Bank of America. I went along to dinner with Mr Nair, but not with Mr Gerzon and Mr Van Oonen. Dr Winsemius told me that both of them who were his Dutch compatriots would not, could not, speak freely with him if I a Singaporean was present.

Dr Winsemius told me that as a foreigner he can only advise, and not steer the ship for us. He can teach me how to drive or even repair the car, but I as a Singaporean have no choice but to steer the ship, drive the car, or pilot the plane myself. In corporate terms, a Singaporean must be the CEO of a Singapore corporation. Even if we were to crash the vehicle, we should have the satisfaction of doing it ourselves. Others should not have to do it for us. We should be in control of our own destiny.

Personal Reflections: God and School

Trusting God[1]

My journey with God began many years ago except at the time, I did not know that He was with me. My mother was widowed at a very young age left with five children, myself being the eldest at nine years, and my sister the youngest at six months. She had to go out to work as a maidservant with an RAF[2] family. But she sent us to school, a government English language school, where the school fees were modest.

We were a Hainanese dialect-speaking family. Fortunately, we were staying next door to an Indian Christian family. Their eldest daughter gave me a start, teaching the alphabet and spelling for about a year before she married and settled down in India. I was also allowed to read their copy of *The Straits Times* each day after school. That was how I learn to read and write English.

When I completed my 'O' level examination, my only thought was to get a job, any job, to help my mother support the family. So I applied to the GPO[3] for a postal clerk's job. I was delighted when they sent me the

---

In this section, excerpts from three speeches by Mr Ngiam are presented. The excerpts discuss his school days and his participation in church. These personal reflections give insight into the formative influences on Mr Ngiam. The recollections of his school days in early Singapore also touch on contemporaries and other students and give a flavour of growing up in Singapore in the early years.

1   Excerpts of talk on "Trusting God" shared with the EDB Christian Fellowship, held on 19 April 2000.

2   Royal Air Force.

3   General Post Office.

appointment offer, together with a form for the medical examination. Off I went to the X-ray centre at Tan Tock Seng Hospital. I failed the X-ray, so I could not be appointed a postal clerk.

My Christian neighbour then suggested that I should continue with my education into the post school certificate class to prepare for university entrance. Mrs Paul found me a Christian benefactor who gave me $60 monthly to see me through PSC.[4]

At the end of the year, I sat for the partial HSC[5] and then the university entrance. I was successful and was given an open bursary to do an arts course at the University of Malaya.

Though we lost our father at a very young age, the Lord blessed me and my siblings with good intellect. All four boys went on to university on bursary or scholarship. My sister who did not go to university is blessed with three children, two of whom are engineers, with the youngest at NUS also doing engineering.

My wife Jeanette was born into a Christian family. One of her maternal granduncles was the Reverend Chew Hock Hin of the Methodist Church. We married in church and I attended Sunday service diligently with my wife and two children.

However, I procrastinated in accepting God for about 20 years. At a Maundy Thursday evening service, I saw my son's face glowing with faith. As I watched Kelvin, the thought came to my mind that God was telling me, Tong Dow, believe and you shall see. Until that moment I was thinking, Lord let me see and I shall believe.

All at once, everything in my life fell into place. The Lord without my realising it has been walking with me all this while. I then accepted Christ, becoming a member of the Barker Road Methodist Church.

As the eldest son in a Chinese family, it was my duty to attend to the family ancestral altar. I was very diligent burning three joss sticks to my parents' memory in the morning every day. But when I believed, I realised that such an act was just a human practice. I must trust the Lord that though my parents did not know Him in their earthly lives, through God's grace, they are now with Him in his kingdom. Our human earthly relationship of parents and children, husband and wife, will take a form that I do not yet comprehend.

I was also asked to speak on being a Christian in our work place. I must tell you that wherever I am posted in my service career, I have always regarded each posting as God's will for me. I will do my best in each job and through my work shine for Him.

I must confess that I had hoped to be given certain appointments, doing my will. And each time I set my heart on something, my will, I have been

---

4   Post School Certificate.

5   Higher School Certificate.

disappointed. At every fork on the road the Lord, on looking back, has always provided a better alternative for me, doing His will, not mine.

Remember to do our work well, and shine for the Lord wherever we are. Let the Lord lead us, doing His will, not ours. We should be as gently as a dove but be as wise as a serpent.

Serangoon Secondary School[6]

In 1945 to 1946, we all walked to school along country lanes past attap villages and occasionally brick and mortar bungalows. Other than the term examinations (which were minor events) school days, on looking back, were fun, trapping spiders, catching fighting fish, kicking *chatek*,[7] scouting and camping. Sports Day was the big event of the year. It was a treat to take a swim at the beach, or the Mount Emily swimming pool.

School days were happy and carefree. We enjoyed simple pleasures like five cents iceball. Never mind hygiene. We were seldom down with flu, though most of us were undernourished. Eggs and chicken were a luxury. *Ikan bilis*[8] was the staple protein.

You can say that I am nostalgic, looking through rose tinted glasses, but school was not one long holiday either! Grades counted. A Grade 1 in the Senior Cambridge School Certificate examination will gain you admission into the Post School Certificate class to prepare for the university entrance examinations. A Grade 2 will gain you entry into the Teachers' Training College to train as teachers. A Grade 3 provided entry into other jobs such as clerks, the Police Force and nursing. In those days you consider yourself lucky if you can get a job, any job, on leaving school.

Our school, Serangoon English School (SES), in today's context, would be considered a neighbourhood school. We were the Oukang (Hougang) boys. Our friends from Raffles Institution would consider us "ulu" country bumpkins. Our Maths teacher, Mr Campos, only offered Elementary Mathematics. Up to Standard 8, we have not even heard of the 10-year series Elementary Examination Maths papers. Our Science teacher, Mr Lee, was transferred because there was no science laboratory for him to teach us General Science. The new Serangoon Secondary School is indeed fortunate to be one of the first few schools with modern IT-enables classrooms and state of the arts facilities.

What we lacked in learning opportunities, we made up with grit and determination. Two of my classmates took science at the private Singapore

---

6   Excerpts of speech given at Serangoon Secondary School, Millennium Move on 25 June 2000.

7   A toy made of feathers attached by their quills to weights such as round pieces of rubber, which is kicked using the inner side of the foot. The object of the game is to keep a *chatek* in the air by kicking it continuously without allowing it to fall to the ground.

8   *Ikan bilis* are very small fishes, also known as anchovies. They are caught in large numbers, salted and dried for use as a foodstuff.

Institute of Science, and went on to become doctors. Dr Paran joined the school later and taught biology to a whole generation of students, several of whom became surgeons and other medical specialists.

Most of my classmates came from poor or, at most, middle-class families. Our parents were mostly clerks, shopkeepers, farmers, mechanics, delivery boys, washerwomen and maidservants. Only one boy in my class went to school by car.

Though our teachers were themselves men of modest means with families to raise, they were kind to us in very personal ways. One of my primary school teachers, Mr Cher Poh Chia, arranged with his provision shop to supply me with Scott's emulsion cod liver oil to help strengthen the lungs of my brothers and myself. My English teacher, Mr Shepherdson, paid for a correspondence course in English for me from the Regent Institute in London. I am truly grateful to these teachers because they helped when it mattered.

When you look back, some of life's tough lessons were learnt in school. I will recount three vivid recollections of school days, and the lessons I learnt. My first recollection began in Primary 1 at the school in Aroozoo Avenue. I was the youngest boy in class, and the smallest. I went to school wearing a sun helmet made of cork, like the one the white hunter wore in Tarzan films.

One of my older and bigger classmates took great delight in knocking the helmet off my head into the drain. As he was bigger, I did not fight back, discretion being the better part of valour. I fought him on the battleground of examinations instead. As I beat him in exam after exam, his respect for his skinny little classmate grew, and after a while he stopped bullying me.

My second recollection was writing lines. In those early days, if the class was noisy or boisterous, teachers were fond of imposing collective punishment. One memorable day, the literature teacher asked us to write out the whole literature book line by line. So I went home and spent the whole afternoon and half the night copying the literature book. I cannot remember the title of the book but recall that the hero was a character called Bulldog Drummond.

The next morning, with aching fingers, we passed up the whole exercise books to the teacher. I then asked one of my classmates how long he took. I was amazed when he told me less than an hour. Remember that was before the age of the photocopier! He then told me quietly that he wrote out only the first and the last few pages of the book and inserted other material in between. He was confident that the teacher would never check page by page, less line by line.

I felt very foolish then. Yet on looking back, I did not regret writing out every word in the literature book. I did not cheat and my integrity remains intact. Honesty and integrity are the hallmark of SES boys.

During our school days, the most relaxed and for some creative periods were our art lessons. We had a great art teacher in Mr Kadir. He was passionate about art and spent English periods teaching us how to draw.

My classmate drew effortlessly, and in few brush strokes created beautiful watercolour roses and gladioli.

However much I tried, I just could not visualise objects in three dimensions. I just could not draw. One day, Mr Kadir, a very patient man, told me that I could not even draw a straight line with a ruler! He gave up on me and I gave up art.

Art is definitely not one of my talents. But that does not stop me from exercising my imagination. I find that I am more comfortable with words, rather than brush strokes. I write better than I draw. I note with pleasure that SES has produced a poet in Mr Robert Yeo. My classmate, the artist, is now an architect in London.

I had already left school when Mr N.I. Low became the Principal of SES for the second time in 1952. My younger brother, Tong Tau, who was still in the school then told me that one day, without saying a word, the Principal went round the school grounds picking up litter. Soon groups of boys followed him picking up litter as well. Mr Low started the first anti-littering campaign in Singapore without uttering a word. He taught a valuable lesson of life, leading by example. Action speaks louder than words.

While SES boys come from humble families without all the opportunities, I believe that all of us can shine if we use and develop the one singular talent that God has given us. While the Serangoon boy is not cleverer than boys in other schools, neither are we more stupid. With honesty and integrity, through sheer grit and determination, we measure up and hold our heads high.

But I know that out there in the heartlands of Singapore, the HDB estates, there are generations of Serangoon boys and girls who are honest, hardworking, solid citizens, good fathers and mothers raising families.

My Saint Andrew Days[9]

I must acknowledge that I am not a full-fledged Saint. Unlike my classmates who started in Primary 1, I spent only two years in St. Andrew's. I joined the school in the School Certificate year in 1953, on transfer from Serangoon English School (SES), as SES did not teach General Science to my cohort.

In the event, it was too late for me to do General Science. But in the one school certificate year, I was given the opportunity to learn Latin and Additional Mathematics. I went on to prepare for the entrance examination to the University of Malaya. St. Andrew's opened the door to higher education for me. For this I am forever grateful.

Though I spent only two years in St. Andrew's, I was able to absorb its values. As Saints, our overriding value is love and compassion. Instinctively,

---

9 Excerpts of an address as Guest-Of-Honour, "St. Andrew's School 142nd Founder's Day", held on 28 Aug. 2004, St. Andrew's Junior College.

we are for the underdog. We care for the poor and the homeless. We are always willing to give those who have failed another chance.

Why do I say that? Because we put into practice what we believe in. Though most of my classmates were from poor or lower middle class families, a group of us volunteered to spend one Saturday afternoon a month teaching children from even poorer homes at the incipient St. Matthew's Church in Prince Charles Crescent in the Lower Delta neighbourhood. We provided companionship, and even dressed their sores. It was Christian love in action.

Our Principal was the Reverend Canon Adams, known to us schoolboys as the Fighting Padre. An Australian churchman with a craggy face, he was passionate about boxing and wanted every boy to box to build up our character and fighting spirit for the battles of life. Boxing, of course, was not for everyone. Our geography master, Mr Fam Choo Beng, vigorously promoted rugby again as a sport for real men. Our Scout troop, with the distinctive St. Andrew's blue-and-white scarf, was led by Mr Dong Chui Seng.

Academic studies were stressed, but not to the exclusion of everything else. St. Andrew's set out to produce all rounders: men of action and of thought.

Among my contemporaries, we can be very proud of men such as Mr Tan Teck Khim, rugby captain, who became Singapore's first Singaporean Commissioner of Police, Mr Michael Fam, again a rugby captain, who was the first Chairman of the Mass Rapid Transit System (later the MRT Corporation or MRTC). At one stage of the mass rapid transit development, there were four Saints involved, namely Mr Michael Fam, Mr Lim Leong Geok, MRTC's first Executive Director, Mr Herman Hochstadt, Perm Sec (Communications), and myself, Perm Sec (Finance). We were all members of the Board. The word went around that Singapore's mass rapid transit system was being built by four underground Saints!

I am proud to say that St. Andrew's produced some very outstanding civil servants. Dr Andrew Chew, former Head of Civil Service, is now Chairman of the Public Service Commission. Younger men who became Perm Secs are Mr Eddie Teo, Perm Sec (PMO), and Mr Kishore Mahbubani, Perm Sec (Foreign Affairs). What are the qualities that St. Andrew's imparted to us that made us good public servants? In my view, it is simply our honesty and integrity. And above all, being true to ourselves and to God.

St. Andrew's has also produced outstanding business entrepreneurs and leaders such as Mr Koh Boon Hwee. We have in Mr Frank Benjamin, an entrepreneur in high fashion, and earlier, the late Mr Jacob Ballas, the most astute broker of his time. Mr Ballas was also a very generous benefactor of St. Andrew's.

There are many other old Saints who were leaders in the professions and civic society. Saints are proudest of Mr David Marshall, the first Chief Minister of Singapore. Saints are men and women of many and diverse talents.

The principals and teachers of St. Andrew's have brought out the best in us, in the classroom and on the playing fields of Woodsville.[10] [...]

We all know that as Christians that God has created us equal. In his eyes, we are all his children. As in the parable, he has given to all of us at least one talent. To me, there is no such being as a totally stupid person. If we as parents, siblings, friends and neighbours, look hard enough we can always find one skill, one aptitude, one attitude, unique to a child.

We cannot be good in all things. Some of us are more physical, have better motor skills. Some of us are more cerebral, good at abstract thinking. Some have both, like great violinists. Some are artistic, creating paradise with a paint brush. Some cannot even draw a straight line with a ruler, like myself. Yet, we can weave magic with words.

---

10 In his address, Mr Ngiam recounts the familiar "Parable of the Talent" in Matthew 25:14 where each of the three servants was given different amount of talents. *Holy Bible* (New York: Liturgical Press, 2001), p. 28.

Ngiam Tong Dow with Robert Kuok, one of the richest men in Asia and founder of the Shangri-La group of hotels. Mr Ngiam recounts the story of how Kuok founded the hotel, and shares his views that Singaporeans must maintain their ethnic identities. See Part 2, chapter on "Education, Growth and Our Future". (photo courtesy of Singapore Press Holdings)

Mr Ngiam (right) upon graduating in 1959 from the then University of Malaya (predecessor of the National University of Singapore), with first class honours in Economics. Pictured with room mate Mr Lee Wai Mun, who scored a first class honours in Mathematics. (photo courtesy of Singapore Press Holdings)

Mr Ngiam (far left) accompanying Prime Minister Lee Kuan Yew (second from right) on his first visit to China in 1976. The Singapore delegation and members of the Lee family are: (left to right) Mr S.R. Nathan (later the President of the Republic of Singapore), Minister Ahmad Mattar, Ms Lee Wei Ling, Mrs Lee Kuan Yew and Finance Minister Hon Sui Sen. They pose at Lake Taihu in Wuxi. (photo courtesy of Singapore Press Holdings)

As former chairman of the CPF Board (1998–2001), Mr Ngiam (fourth from right) attends the Board's 50th anniversary, at which Prime Minister Lee Hsien Loong is guest of honour. Mr Ngiam regards CPF as one of the key economic policies in Singapore's development. (photo courtesy of Singapore Press Holdings)

As Chairman of the DBS Bank (1990–98), Mr Ngiam (far left) poses with senior representatives of Singapore's leading banks, including Mr Sim Kee Boon, then of Keppel Bank. Mr Ngiam recounts the early days of the DBS Bank. (photo courtesy of Singapore Press Holdings)

Mr Ngiam (left) in 1971, meeting with Mr Goh Chok Tong, who was then CEO of the Neptune Orient Lines. Mr Goh went on to serve as the country's second Prime Minister and is now Senior Minister. (photo courtesy of Singapore Press Holdings)

Mr Ngiam (right) with Finance Minister Hon Sui Sen at an ASEAN meeting. Mr Ngiam was tasked with representing Singapore on regional economic cooperation but was frustrated by the slow progress in early decades. See Part 2, chapter on "ASEAN Economic Cooperation". (photo courtesy of Singapore Press Holdings)

Mr Ngiam (front left) in China in 1980, signing agreement to establish reciprocal commercial representative offices in Beijing and Singapore. (photo courtesy of the Ministry of Foreign Affairs)

Mr Ngiam (front, second from right) in Japan in 1986, accompanying then Minister of Trade and Industry, Lee Hsien Loong. Others in the Singapore delegation include Mr Philip Yeo (front, far right) who chaired the Economic Development Board and now is Chairman of A*STAR, two economic agencies that Mr Ngiam believes essential to Singapore's progress. (photo in personal collection of Mr Ngiam Tong Dow)

PART 2

LESSONS FROM THE SINGAPORE EXPERIENCE

Edited from papers delivered as part of a seminar series held in 2005 at the School of Humanities and Social Sciences, Nanyang Technological University, Singapore, for policy makers from China.

BIG COUNTRY, SMALL COUNTRY: STRENGTHS AND LIMITATIONS

The Asian Giants: Contrasting India and China

When Minister Mentor Lee Kuan Yew launched the Lee Kuan Yew School of Public Policy on 4 April 2005, he spoke of "Lessons from China and India". Mr Lee considered the strengths and limitations of these two giant Asian nations and concluded: China and India will shake the world. Together they are home to 40 per cent of the world's population. Both are among the world's fastest growing economies. China, 8–10 per cent; India, 6–7 per cent. China is the factory of the world. India the outsourcing service centre.[1]

China and India are vast countries with huge populations. Yet their immense potential was unleashed only in the last two to three decades. In China, the redoubtable Deng Xiaoping opened China to the world in 1978. In doing so, Mr Deng was aware that when windows were opened wide, some flies would get in.

India, on the other hand, had been the world's largest democracy all along. Knowing English has produced outstanding Indian jurists and novelists. Yet until very recently, India lagged behind less well-endowed countries. I would venture to suggest that India was held back by its brilliant sons and daughters educated at the London School of Economics after the Second World War.

Seminar given on 18 June 2005.

1   Keynote Speech entitled "Managing Globalization: Lessons from China and India" by Minister Mentor Lee Kuan Yew at the official opening of the Lee Kuan Yew School of Public Policy, 4 April 2005. Full speech can be found at <http://app.mfa.gov.sg/pr/read_script.asp?View,4204,>.

They were steeped in the theories of Fabian socialism stressing social justice more than production and productivity.

In contrast, although the Chinese were ideologically Communist, the Chinese state concentrated on education in science and technology.

Their respective education systems may explain the differences in the levels of economic performance of China and India in recent times. In 1976, I was privileged to be a member of Singapore's delegation, led by our Prime Minister, Mr Lee Kuan Yew, on Singapore's first official visit to China. Mr Hua Guofeng was then China's Prime Minister. Besides meetings in the Great Hall of the People, we also visited the Imperial Palace and the Temple to Heaven. We were told that the Temple to Heaven was the venue for the imperial examinations, presided over by the Emperor himself.

The Chinese kept very good archives. They showed us some of the earliest examination scripts. The best brains of China were asked to write essays on practical subjects, such as flood alleviation. The testing and stimulation of the practical bent of mind led to the building of the Grand north-south Canal, probably the longest man-made inland waterway of all time. The same minds also built the Great Wall, probably history's greatest civil engineering feat. Unfortunately, political science failed the Chinese. The Great Wall did not stop the barbarians from invading China.

The Mongols and the Manchurians were more advanced in the art and science of war. The best Han brains were numbed by rote learning of the Confucian analects. They became unquestioning eunuchs owing absolute loyalty to the Emperor. From being great civil engineers, they became poets and artists. The establishment became effete. Dispossessed peasants rose in revolt and swept away the incumbent dynasties. They established their own, which in turn decayed, and were overthrown.

During the Cultural Revolution, the thoughts of Mao Zedong were studied religiously across the country. Polemics and propaganda became the order of the day. A whole generation of students was lost. Fortunately for China, the literary tradition of Chinese education was replaced by the Stalinist Soviet model of boiler suits and engineering. It is no accident that both President Hu Jintao and Prime Minister Wen Jiabao, and most of the current Chinese leadership are engineers by training. When the shackles of the command economy were dismantled, the engineers who are more practical minded took charge of the state-owned enterprises and transformed them.

In contrast, the Indian Civil Service was staffed by men and women who received what can be broadly described as a classical education in philosophy and politics. They were trained to govern, not to administer. An exception to this is the Indian Institute of Technology, which were established to balance the faculties of law and economics. Still, this was not done on the same scale as in Chinese education. It is therefore not surprising that China, like Japan, excels in manufacturing hardware, while India specialises in services outsourcing.

The Relevance of Singapore?

When I think of the Asian giants of China and India, I wonder what relevance the experiences and perspectives from Singapore might have, especially in the economic field. Would you prefer to be the economic planner of Singapore, or of China? Which is more difficult?

In comparing China and Singapore, we need to recognise the differing circumstances of each country. China is a continental size country with a long unbroken civilisation. Singapore, on the other hand, is a tiny city state. We became an independent country only on 9 August 1965.

In May 1959, the People's Action Party (PAP) swept to power in Singapore's first General Elections, winning 43 out of 51 Parliamentary seats, with 53.4 per cent of the popular vote. The government, led by Prime Minister Lee Kuan Yew, was confronted with a stagnating economy, urban slums, high unemployment and municipal corruption. Bribes, otherwise known as "coffee money", had to be paid for taxi and hawker licenses, planning and building approvals, and a myriad of dispensations from the civil servant. Singapore was like any other third world country.

In 1959, a young Lee Kuan Yew stirred Singaporeans to strive by his slogan that nobody owes Singapore a living. Ten years earlier in 1949, the Chinese Communist Party (CCP) had swept the effete and corrupt Kuomintang out of China, and sent them fleeing to Taiwan, a thorny legacy. China was a large densely populated country dependent on subsistence agriculture. The Chinese government, being socialist in ideology, resorted to Stalinist central planning.

The Chinese government told the world that there was no unemployment in China. Yet a job in a bank, which would be done by one clerk in Singapore, was shared between four. This was vividly demonstrated to me when I went to a Chinese bank, even in the 1980s, to change US$ travellers' cheques into RMB Foreign Exchange Certificates. Four clerks were involved in the transaction.

In 1978, Deng Xiaoping toured the southern provinces of China and launched the "open door" policy. He removed the dead wood of Communist dogma and doctrine. By raising the banner that it is virtuous to be rich, he unleashed the boundless entrepreneurial spirit of millions of his people. In having the political courage to break the iron rice bowl, he set China on its current dazzling phase of economic development.

There has been much debate about whether economic or political freedoms come first. Perestroika or Glasnost? Economic or political opening? In my view, when people are hungry and unemployed, it is moot to debate whether democracy comes before or after economic growth. The Chinese and my fellow Singaporeans are in no doubt that earning a decent livelihood comes before everything else.

However, economic growth thrives only when societies are politically stable. Political stability emerges when there is strong competent and incorrupt leadership. The real question is, "How is the leadership of a country chosen?"

Choosing the Leadership

Basically, there are two models of selection. The first is the model enunciated in Plato's Republic.[2] Peers choose the leader who becomes the philosopher king. He is the first among equals. This is very much akin to the recent election of Pope Benedict XVI, chosen by his fellow-cardinals who were themselves selected by his predecessor, Pope John Paul II.

This is also the model of the Chinese Communist Party, where the Party leader selects the cadres who in turn elect him as the leader. Under this system, a change of regime rarely occurs. Party leaders may change, but not the Party. In Communist idiom, this is known as the dictatorship of the proletariat. The greatest danger is that the Party can become fossilised over time.

The opposite of a closed system, whether Catholic or Communist, is a system for free and fair elections. This is how Singapore has chosen its leaders. Every citizen of voting age, normally above 18 years of age, has one vote. The candidate who wins the most votes is elected a Member of Parliament (MP). The leader of the Party with the most number of MPs forms the government.

One variant that is seen in some other countries is a Presidential system, in which the people elect a President who then selects his own government, whether or not they are elected officials. Whichever way the government is constituted, there is one advantage in having elections. As General Elections have to be held at regular intervals, normally four or five years, the citizens of a country can change their government without having to resort to rebellion or bloodshed.

Yet, I would add some caution. The system of democratic elections only works if the citizens are well informed and educated. It works best when there are at least two or more political parties led by able and incorrupt men and women. Although they may have different ideologies, they must believe in "one country".

Some developing countries that have elected governments struggle with other factors and institutions. One of these is the role of the army and other armed forces. The army must remain above party politics. Its role is to protect and defend the nation, and not to prop up any particular party or group. In reality, however, the army has often intervened in many developing countries, taking over power from behind the barrel of the gun. No economic development is possible in a country prone to coups and countercoups.

After spending forty years engaged in the economic development of Singapore, I am convinced that the most important condition for success is good government. A good government is one led by able, honest, selfless men and women. Though political labels can be misleading, I would stick my neck out and say that Singapore's founding fathers are pragmatic socialists. I

---

2   Plato, *Plato's Republic Book Five* (Agora Publications, Inc, 1996).

believe that Mr Deng Xiaoping and his political colleagues are also pragmatic socialists.

Baking the Cake First

Although China is a socialist state, and Singapore a democracy, the economic philosophy is essentially similar, which is to bake the cake first. The economic strategy of both countries is the creation of jobs and the provision of affordable housing.

When I started work in the Singapore Economic Development Board (EDB) in 1961, our mission was to do everything possible to find jobs for Singaporeans. Ten per cent of a workforce of about 2 million was unemployed. What nearly overwhelmed us were the 25,000 to 30,000 school-leavers entering the labour market each year.

Our first Minister for Finance, Dr Goh Keng Swee, one day told me that he felt depressed every time he passed by a school at the end of the school day at 1 pm, or 6 pm. Because of a shortage of classrooms, Singapore operated a two session school day, 7.30 am to 1 pm, and from 1.30 pm to 6 pm. Even today, many of our primary schools continue to operate on two sessions.

When I asked Dr Goh why he felt depressed, he asked me how we were going to find gainful unemployment for the 25,000 to 30,000 school-leavers each year. Dr Goh challenged and inspired my colleagues and I in the EDB to scour for jobs. In the first ten years of economic development, 1960 to 1970,[3] labour-intensive industries, garments, hair wigs, transistor radio assembly, and ship breaking, saw us through. The label "high tech, low tech" never entered our vocabulary. Any "tech", which could provide our young school-leavers with jobs, would do.

If finding employment opportunities for 100,000 Singaporeans is an uphill task, how much more would it be for our EDB counterparts in China and India? I read recently in the press that some 3 million young people enter the labour market each year in China. India cannot be far behind.

However pressured Singaporeans are from the rigours of global competition today, our economic problems are finite. From a high unemployment rate of over 10 per cent in 1960, we created enough jobs by the mid-1970s, to achieve what economists call full employment, with unemployment rates below 3 per cent.

Similarly, the Housing & Development Board (HDB) cleared slums and kampongs[4] to build enough flats to house 85 per cent of our citizens by the

---

3   Although Singapore became fully independent only in 1965, it achieved self-government in 1959 and thus took responsibility for its economic and other domestic policies.

4   Malay word for village.

mid-1980s. In fact, a strong economy providing high CPF savings[5] led the HDB to overbuild. As of 2005, there are some 10,000 flats lying vacant. Although it will not bankrupt the Ministry of Finance, it is an economic waste.

Singaporeans should count our blessings. But we should not be complacent or, worse, arrogant. In 1980, I accompanied our Finance Minister Mr Hon Sui Sen to Beijing to sign the Trade Agreement with China, to allow for the establishment of trade representative offices in Beijing and Singapore respectively, as a precursor to full diplomatic relations in 1990.

We called on Mr Deng Xiaoping in one of the great Halls of the People. First, Mr Deng complimented Singapore on its high economic growth rate. Our per capita GDP was then around US$5,000. Mr Deng said that China's per capita income was about US$400. His ambition was to raise it to US$1,000 by the year 2000.

Mr Deng then leaned forward in his chair and stated that as a matter of fact, China's GDP would be US$1,000 multiplied by 1.2 billion people. China's per capita GDP today is above US$1,000. She is now the world's third largest economy.

If China continues to grow at 8 per cent a year consistently, China will be able to achieve full employment in 40–50 years' time. On a much smaller population base, Singapore achieved full employment in under 20 years. There are already reports of labour shortages in China's burgeoning industrial cities. Even with strong economic growth, it will take China twice as long to provide China's population with good affordable housing and modern sanitation.

Jump Starting Development

In comparing the economic development process in China and Singapore, as between a big country and a small country, it is easier to jump-start the process in Singapore than in China. Being small in size and socially compact, Singapore can mobilise its resources and align its policies faster than larger countries, such as China and India.

This was vividly illustrated to me in 1996 on a trip to China with Dr Richard Hu, when he served as Finance Minister, as guests of the Chinese Ministry of Finance. After Beijing, we visited several major Chinese cities accompanied by their Vice-Minister of Finance. At every stop while the Singapore guests rested, our Chinese host was out calling on the Mayor and the Party Secretary of the province.

---

5   The Central Provident Fund (CPF) is a comprehensive compulsory social security savings plan, to help provide for workers in their old age. The overall scope and benefits of the CPF encompass retirement, healthcare, home ownership, family protection and asset enhancement. More information available at: <http://www.cpf.gov.sg/cpf_info/home.asp> [10 Jan. 2006].

When I asked the Vice-Minister whether he was just making courtesy calls on the provincial officials, he told me that he had to pay his respects to persuade them to let the central government have a part of the revenue collected. He smiled and said that Singapore Ministry of Finance officials had an easier time. In Singapore, the Finance Ministry collects and receives the revenue the day after a tax law was passed. In China, the process was more complicated and complex.

In a similar context, I overheard a conversation among three Chinese officials who were at the Ministry of Finance to learn budgeting from Singapore officials. One of them said that the difference between Singapore and their own country was that Singapore only had one Lee Kuan Yew, while China had 100. What he meant was that it was a hundred times more difficult for a Chinese Vice-Minister to navigate the power structure in his government than his counterpart in Singapore. The Singapore Permanent Secretary suffers far less stress than his Chinese counterpart.

While it is true that we can get things going faster in Singapore, I need to say that we are only good for short sprints. On the other hand, China runs the marathons. As a nation, China has more people and talent. As a professor friend of mine said, even if the Chinese are no cleverer than other races and assuming that only 0.000000001 per cent of a population are geniuses, China with a population of 1.2 billion people would have 12 potential Nobel Prize babies born each year! The big "if", of course, is whether they will receive enough nurture in their education to realise their potential.

China is a country that reveres education, and so is India: I therefore believe that more and more Nobel Prize winners in the future for science and economics would be Chinese and Indians. Can Singapore ever produce a Nobel Prize winner? With a population of just 3 million, the chances are slim. However, it is not impossible, if Singapore concentrates on educating our people in science, engineering and the arts.

With their vast populations and deep talent pools, China and India have the potential to become global economies. I am confident that they will reach the finishing line and go beyond. However, the economic and political challenges they face are also enormous. Providing employment opportunities, raising literacy rates and increasing life expectancy, are Herculean tasks. Building infrastructure and transportation systems require trillion dollars of investments.

Being big players on the world stage carries its own burden. China and soon India not only inspire respect but also attract fear. Taiwan will continue to be manipulated by the United States and Japan to keep China off balance. A British partitioned India will always remain divided because of two antagonistic religions. Because of the burden of their size, it will take both these Asian giants several generations to go from third to first world.

In contrast, Singapore went from third to first world in one generation. How did we achieve this feat?

Third World to First: Singapore's Experience[6]

Singapore, in 1960, inherited a stagnant entrepot economy and a crumbling city from a dispirited British colonial administration. Though victorious against the Germans and the Japanese in the Second World War, the expenditure of sweat, blood and tears had exacted its toll on the psyche of the British nation.

The British leadership decided to withdraw from territories East of the Suez. The final withdrawal from Singapore came in 1968, leaving 25,000 Singaporeans unemployed. To the great credit of the British government, it left Singapore with the military bases intact. These well-maintained naval and air bases were quickly transformed by us for civilian use. Sembawang Shipyard and Keppel Shipyard were established to repair civilian ships and vessels.

Like other developing countries in the 1960s, Singapore tried to kick-start industrialisation through a policy of import substitution, advocated religiously by academic UN economists. Import tariffs were imposed on the full range of consumer products to give fledgling domestic industries time to grow.

As Singapore's domestic market was minuscule, we sought a common market with Malaysia through political merger. The creation of a Malaysian common market was aborted when Singapore separated from Malaysia because of irreconcilable differences.[7]

On gaining independence on 9 August 1965, Singapore dismantled all its import tariffs. Through force of circumstances, we had to learn very quickly to face frontally the head winds of global competition. Singapore is probably the original global economy even before the concept was conceived by the World Trade Organisation (WTO).

Fortunately for Singapore, we were the exception in a world of infant industry protection. Multinational companies invested in Singapore because we practised a free and open economy, without exchange controls or protected industries. Forty years ago, China and India rejected foreign participation in their economy. Today, China welcomes foreign manufacturing investment. She attracts some $50 billion worth of foreign direct investment a year, compared to India's $5 billion.

---

6 This title is drawn from the publication *From Third World to First: The Singapore Story 1965–2000: Memoirs of Lee Kuan Yew* and is used purposefully as an acknowledgement of Mr Lee whom many acknowledge as the father of modern Singapore.

7 See Ernest Chew and Edwin Lee (eds.), *A History of Singapore* (Singapore: Oxford University Press, 1991). Nancy M. Fletcher, *The separation of Singapore from Malaysia* (Ithaca, NY: Southeast Asia Program, Cornell University, 1969), p. 98.

With the advent of WTO, the world of free and open global competition is upon all of us. All countries have to practise good governance or risk being ignored by the international investment and business community. In the early 1960s, Singapore was one of a few countries that practised economic virtue. Investments poured in, helping Singapore to achieve GDP growth rates of 8 per cent consistently, like China today.

Now in a world where nearly every country is virtuous, how does Singapore differentiate itself to stay on top?

$$\left[\begin{array}{l} \text{JOBS AND HOUSING} \\ \text{IN SINGAPORE} \end{array}\right]$$

In ancient China, there was a special relationship between astrology and the power to govern. It was believed that the Emperor ruled with the mandate of heaven. The mandate is not bestowed, but won through the force of arms. In the modern context, the State governs with the consent of the people, expressed through free elections.

Whichever way power is won, the ruler, whether as an Emperor or as a democratically elected Prime Minister, continues to exercise power if he is able to meet the basic needs of the people. The basic needs are food and shelter, or jobs and housing. When the ruler fails to deliver prosperity and peace, he loses the mandate of heaven.

So it is with Singapore.

The People's Action Party (PAP) government has delivered on both jobs and housing since it won its first General Elections in May 1959. This was the year I graduated from the University of Malaya.[1] Peace and prosperity have however not come easily. Singapore has experienced its share of the ups and downs in its first forty years of existence as an independent nation.

Tackling Communism, High Unemployment and Slums

The PAP swept to power in Singapore's first general election in May 1959. The Party won 43 seats out of 51 constituencies, gaining 53.4 per cent of

---

Seminar on 2 July 2005.

1   The University was the predecessor institution of the National University of Singapore.

the total votes cast. On 3 June, the new Constitution confirming Singapore as a self-governing state was brought into force by the proclamation of the Governor, Sir William Goode, who became the first Yang di-Pertuan Negara (Head of State). The first government of the State of Singapore was sworn in on 5 June, with Mr Lee Kuan Yew as Singapore's first Prime Minister.

A self-governing Singapore had freedom of action in all areas of policy other than internal security and defence. This was just as well, as Britain was obliged to defend and protect the territorial integrity of Singapore and Malaya, which it did when Indonesia launched its campaign of confrontation against Malaysia in 1963.

We now know that the stunning PAP electoral triumph belied a deep underlying struggle for power within the Party itself. The Party was split between the western English-educated, non-Communist democratic socialist wing which formed the administration, and the Chinese-educated communist Left which controlled the party branches.

The government lost no time in tackling the twin problems of high unemployment and slum housing. It established the Economic Development Board (EDB) and the Housing & Development Board (HDB) in 1961 to, respectively, seek jobs and build flats. The outstanding track records of these two key institutions speak for themselves.

By the mid-1970s, just over a decade after we started, Singapore achieved full employment. Statistically, unemployment had fallen from the dangerously high rate of 10 per cent for a city state to under 4 per cent. In other words, anyone who was looking for a job could find employment. Job-hopping emerged as a pleasant surprise, which paradoxically we found hard to manage. So we established the National Wages Council under the chairmanship of Professor Lim Chong Yah to bring about orderly wage increases.

Malaysian Common Market and Swimming the Big Ocean

Singapore, like other developing countries, adopted a policy of import substitution. Politically, Singapore merged with Malaya, Sabah and Sarawak to form the Federation of Malaysia. We had hoped that a Malaysian common market would be formed to provide economies of scale for our manufacturing industries. A common market never came about. There was a lack of political will.

Malaya, led by Tengku Abdul Rahman, allowed Singapore to merge with his country to contain the Communist threat that a hungry and unemployed Singapore would pose. Singapore, led by Mr Lee Kuan Yew, saw merger as a way of bringing about a "Malaysian Malaysia", a multiracial nation to outflank the leftist Chinese wing of his party. The Tengku was alarmed that the PAP's campaign for a "Malaysian Malaysia" was the wedge that would threaten Malay supremacy. No Malay leader can forsake Malay supremacy.

I was a young officer during those tumultuous years, and have no claim to complete knowledge, nor a full understanding of all the events and issues. But I do know that the communist wing of the PAP was bent on fomenting strikes and creating chaos in Singapore. They adopted classic class struggle tactics to win power like communist parties everywhere else, including China.

The greatness of Mr Deng Xiaoping was that he exhorted his countrymen after the chaos of the Cultural Revolution, to seek truth from facts. Singapore was fortunate to have the pragmatic leadership of Mr Lee Kuan Yew and his colleagues. They triumphed over the ideological obsession of the Left. The Singapore Civil Service was never asked by the government to chant slogans. We were asked instead to roll up our sleeves, to seek jobs and build homes for the people.

In political history, Singapore must be the only country in the world that sought survival by merger with a bigger neighbour, only to be expelled to become an independent nation. It could almost be said that Singapore gained independence not by choice, but by chance. It was painful and intimidating at the time. Singapore's independence, although providential, was truly blessed. After two short years of suffocation under Malaysian rule, we regained our freedom of action.

In industrial policy, we made a virtue out of necessity by switching from an inward-looking import substitution strategy to an international export-oriented policy. All at once we had to learn how to swim in the deep oceans of global competition, leaving the small domestic pond of Malaysia behind.

It wasn't easy. Although we did not conceive it as such at that time, Singapore became one of the first states in the world that had to compete on terms that the world now recognises as knowledge-based global competition. We were lucky in one sense — fellow-developing countries at that time stuck to import substitution policies, which in the end proved self-defeating. These countries did not even welcome foreign investment. We did, and benefited from investments and markets brought in by multinational companies (MNCs).

MNCs gave us a relatively comfortable ride to full employment. But this benefit has a potential problem built in. Now that all countries have embraced global competition, opening their markets and welcoming foreign investments, Singapore, no longer unique, finds itself vulnerable. We have depended on MNCs and have failed to grow our own timber, building up our own enterprises and brand names, to compete in international markets. Can we ever?

Housing: From Low Cost to Over Optimism?

Housing was the other basic need for Singapore when it became independent. In the late 1950s, Singapore was a stagnating economy dependent on entrepot trade and the British military bases for a living. Infrastructure was crumbling.

Slum housing dotted the landscape. The first order of business was job creation but, at the same time, the government launched a massive low cost housing programme by the HDB.

Flats with modern sanitation, electricity and piped water were built. In the eyes of the electorate, flats were concrete tangible progress. And more important, they were affordable. No one will need to spend more than 20 per cent of the monthly household income on rent or mortgage repayments.

Initially when household income was low, one-room, two-room and, at best, three-room flats were built. Per capita income rose during the boom years from US$512 in 1965 to US$20,816 in 2001.[2] With this, the HDB went on to build four-room, five-room, and even executive flats. In the optimism of the late 1980s and mid-1990s, HDB lessees were encouraged to upgrade to bigger flats with a second or even a third subsidised mortgage loan. This invariably led to over consumption of housing and, worse, speculation. By giving everyone more than one loan, one bite of the cherry, greed replaced need.

Without a doubt, the HDB low cost housing programme is one of the twin pillars of electoral success of the PAP. The other pillar being jobs which yielded the savings marshalled through the Central Provident Fund to pay for the housing. It was a virtuous triangle of jobs, savings and housing.

Success begets success, and being human we overdid it. The current CPF savings rate of 33 per cent adds to wage cost, which is too high compared with wage level in China, India, and our ASEAN neighbours. Unscrambling the high cost structure to competitive levels will be a challenge the PAP government will have to face once again, this time with a new leadership under Prime Minister Lee Hsien Loong.

The Mandate to Govern

If the government falters, it will lose the mandate to govern. Jobs and housing have always been the underpinning of the PAP. What then is the secret of success? The route to survival for Singapore must be based on education and growth.

---

2 Singapore Department of Statistics, "Historical Data Per Capita GDP at Current Market Prices", Singapore Statistics website. Available at: <http://www.singstat.gov.sg/keystats/hist/gdp.html> [12 Jan. 2006].

[LAND AND
  INFRASTRUCTURE]

Singapore is literally a dot on the world map. With a land area of just over 600 square kilometres, she is not even half the size of a county in China. Yet this little speck of land has to provide space for 4 million people to work, play and live in. How has this been achieved?

Continental countries such as China, India, the United States, and Australia have vast tracts of land and open spaces. But not all the land can be cultivated or inhabited. Much of these continental countries are deserts. Mountains of sand are of no use to anybody. Of course, with luck there may be oil beneath these burning sands. But it requires sweat and investment to extract the black gold from the ground or the sea beds.

Singapore would have remained a virgin tropical jungle if not for the effort of its people to build the infrastructure. Roads, mass rapid transit systems, power stations, water reservoirs, sewerage treatment works, incinerator plants, schools, hospitals and parks, are all investments financed from the savings of the preceding generation.

As a country, Singapore has always practised fiscal rectitude. In other words, we do not spend more than we earn. For most years after our independence on 9 August 1965, we have balanced our budgets. The conventional definition of a balanced budget: that operating revenue from taxes and fees is sufficient to pay the operating costs of administration, largely salaries and wages.

I was appointed the Permanent Secretary of the Ministry of Finance in charge of the Budget Division (spending) in 1987, and the Revenue Division (collection of taxes, fees, levies and other revenue) in 1989. Hitherto, there were two Permanent Secretaries, namely PS (Budget), who controlled spending, and PS (Revenue), who had to find the money to spend. My Minister, Dr Richard Hu, combined the two jobs into one. As PS (Budget) and PS (Revenue), I could only approve as much expenditure as I could collect revenue. Though we did not consciously set out to achieve it, the check and balance of policy and practice was perfect.

You could say that the budget would always balance under such an administrative arrangement. Nevertheless, my colleagues always suspected that my right hand (the taking revenue hand) was longer than my left hand (the giving or spending hand). How else could the Ministry of Finance achieve budget surpluses?

Financing Infrastructure

Most governments in the world borrow from the World Bank, the Asian Development Bank, or raise bonds to finance capital expenditure, such as highways, railways, power stations, reservoirs, sewerage treatment plants, and airports. Even schools and hospitals are built with loans. Singapore was no different from other developing countries. Initially we borrowed modest sums from the World Bank and the Asian Development Bank (ADB) to finance construction of our power stations, reservoirs, sewerage plants, the new airport at Changi, and the National University of Singapore (NUS).

As loans have to be repaid, we only borrowed for productive purposes, not for consumption. HDB flats were built with CPF savings, not with external loans. We borrowed to grow the economy. For only with economic growth could we achieve fiscal and budgetary stability.

No country, including the United States, can borrow its way to prosperity, less so for mini states like Singapore. We borrowed from the World Bank and the ADB to establish our budgetary credentials as a stable and rational government, so that Singapore can attract private investments from MNCs.

One example of this was that we budgeted for a deficit in FY1999/2000 because of the Asian financial crisis, but still there was a small surplus. Indeed, the Singapore government has been able to achieve its budget policy objective of financing total operating and development expenditures from operating revenue since the financial year of 1988 (FY88). This means that the Singapore government has been able to meet in full both its operating expenditure and development expenditure out of its operating revenue. Operating revenue did not include investment income earned on past reserves, as such income is protected under the Constitution.[1]

---

1 Articles 22B, 22D and 148A of the Singapore Constitution prevent reserves accumulated by past governments from being drawn down by the current government without the approval of the

This is a feat which no democratic government in any other country has been able to achieve in recent times. Even among corporations and institutions, the only other example I know of with a similar achievement is Singapore Airlines. In the late 1980s and early 1990s, SIA was able to pay for all its purchase of new aircraft out of current earnings. SIA did not have to resort to borrowing for the growth of its business.

Similarly, the Singapore government hardly borrowed. Today, we have virtually no external debt.

Land Acquisition and Pricing

Land without infrastructure is merely sand. As infrastructural investments to land are largely made by the state, the Singapore government believes that a large part of appreciation in the value of land brought about by public construction of roads, mass rapid transit systems, even schools, should accrue to the State. Hence, when the government acquired land for public purposes, such as for HDB flats and industrial estates, compensation was based on the price of raw undeveloped land without infrastructure. The cornerstone of our industrial and public housing development is the Land Acquisition Act.[2] Private landlords were compensated on the pre-development value, not potential values.

In charging for land in Jurong, the EDB and the Jurong Town Corporation (JTC) adopted what the Japanese know as "sharing prosperity, sharing misery". Under this policy, EDB did not charge industries the full value of land at the outset. The premium was set at 6 per cent of the annual value of the land fixed for five-year terms. In the initial years, land at Jurong had very low annual values. The annual value of industrial land in the first ten years of development did not exceed $1 per square foot.

Industries paid only 6 cents per square foot for their land per year in the first five years of their 30-year leases. Not having to pay a big lump sum premium, scarce capital could be used for purchase of plant and equipment, and construction of factory buildings. Capital was not tied down in land.

The land value was however revised once every five years. As Jurong developed, the annual value of land was raised, but the increase was capped at 50 per cent. In other words, annual value of land in the second five-year period could increase at most only to $1.50 per square foot. Rental in the next five years can only increase from 6 cents to 9 cents per square foot. In

---

President. The reserves that are protected are past reserves accumulated in the government and the key statutory boards listed under the Fifth Schedule. The Singapore Constitution can be accessed at <http://statutes.agc.gov.sg/>.

2 Land Acquisition Act (Chapter 152). Further references: Tan Sook Yee, *Principles of Singapore Land Law* (Butterworths, 1994). Tsuyoshi Kotaka and David Callies (eds.), *Taking Land: Compulsory Purchase and Regulation in Asian-Pacific Countries* (Honolulu: University of Hawaii Press, 2002).

the event, annual values over the five-year period rose by an average of 25 per cent. If Jurong had failed to take off, the annual value of land would have been revised downwards. Misery would be shared.

Fortunately, for the JTC and Singapore, the economy grew and industrial land values steadily increased. Industrialists prospered from their core business of manufacturing and not from the windfall of land appreciation. Steady state was reached in Singapore after the first decade. The JTC phased out the early "sharing prosperity, sharing misery" policy which required goodwill and trust from both the lessor and the lessee to work.

Since our departure from this virtuous policy, land values in Singapore have shot up, and we are in danger of losing our competitiveness to countries with abundant land resources.

Policy makers and administrators from other countries like China may wish to look at Singapore's early land policy and see how the principle of sharing prosperity and sharing misery can be adapted to their own circumstances.

Public tendering of land is a fair transparent way of pricing land. It has been practised in Singapore for sometime, and is being adopted in China and other countries today. Overshooting is always a constant reality in open tendering. Those who do their sums correctly reap rich rewards, while those who misjudge have to endure grievous losses. By and large, I would leave it to the market to reward and punish.

There is, however, a place for intervention by the State in critical areas. In the case of Singapore, it is public housing. Like all cities in poor countries, Singapore, in our early years, had squatter settlements. In the heart of the city, tens of thousands of people lived in fetid slums at low rentals. The Rent Control Act[3] prohibited the landlord from raising rentals. The landlord therefore had no reason whatsoever to repair and improve his properties. On the contrary, he was waiting for the structure to collapse so that his tenants had no choice, but to move out. Even then, there was no way out for him because the Commissioner of Land would compulsorily acquire the property under the Land Acquisition Act.[4] It was fair for the government to acquire the land because it had the obligation to re-house the slum dweller in HDB estates.

State lands in the rural areas were squattered upon by subsistence farmers on temporary occupation licences (TOLs). They reared poultry, grew fruit trees and farmed vegetables. Technically, TOLs conferred no security of tenure; they could be asked to vacate their farming lots at any time, and without compensation. Nevertheless, the HDB compensated them when these farmers were asked to move to make way for the development of HDB new towns.

---

3 Control of Rent Act (Chapter 58) was repealed on 1 April 2001.
4 Please refer to footnote 2.

The rural population was not only given priority in allocation of new HDB flats, but were also paid compensation to tide them over their temporary loss of livelihood. Fruit trees, cemented pig pens, and other structures were paid for by the HDB according to a schedule subject to actual measurement.

Even then, our farmers outwitted the HDB resettlement inspectors by hiring small time contractors to supply fruit saplings rooted in plastic bags and overnight cementing of floors to claim as much compensation as they could. Once the fruit trees were photographed for the record as a basis for compensation by the inspectors, they were moved to the next plots to provide the basis for claiming compensation once again.

Despite this hiccup, it was possible to free land for the development of HDB estates, such as Toa Payoh, Ang Mo Kio, Yishun, Bukit Panjang, Chua Chu Kang, and other suburban estates because of our open, fair and transparent system of compensation.

As countries like China embark on vast new housing schemes in their major and secondary cities, they may wish to make a detailed study of Singapore's resettlement policies and practices. The Singapore experience will not provide all the answers. But the principle of fair, open and transparent resettlement policies should be adhered to and practised. To do otherwise is to expose development schemes to political dissension and turmoil.

⟦ MNCs AND MARKETS ⟧

From Import Substitution to Export-led Industrialisation

When Singapore separated from Malaysia on 9 August 1965, the prospect of a Malaysian common market, however dim, vanished forever. In the years as part of Malaysia, Singapore, like all developing countries at the time, adopted import substitution as industrial policy. By keeping imports out with prohibitive tariffs, planners dreamt of creating mega industries through the consolidation of domestic demand to provide economies of scale. The outcome was the creation of monopolistic, inefficient state-owned enterprises run by rule bound bureaucrats. Private ownership of monopolistic enterprises was no better, leading to what is now called crony capitalism.

Fortunately, or unfortunately, for Singapore, our domestic market was simply too minuscule to make import substitution a viable option. Nevertheless, our first notable indigenous industry, the National Iron and Steel Mills, was a business based on domestic demand for steel bars required by our HDB low-cost housing programme. Low-cost housing also sustained our cement grinding mills, paint factories, and brickworks. The public housing programme helped to mop up our large pool of unskilled construction labour.

On separation from Malaysia, we did a policy about turn. Overnight, we removed protective duties across the board. We plunged into export-led industrialisation that required the free import of raw materials and components from whichever source that is cheap. There was great agony. As EDB officers, it pained us to see the manufacturing businesses of our friends fail — as we brought tariffs down and they struggled to compete with foreign companies — for we had persuaded them to go into manufacturing in the first place.

Competitiveness Counts

The hard truth is that it is not the size of markets that counts. Competitiveness counts. Competitiveness is the sum total of what a country or economy has to offer capital. It is the combination of wage costs and labour skills, educational levels, land and infrastructure, political stability and security, and simply good government, free of corruption and nepotism.

When Singapore, by force of circumstances, plunged into export-led industrialisation, we offered multinational companies (MNCs), and our own people, a large measure of these attributes. And, we welcomed all manufacturing investment — foreign and indigenous, low tech, high tech, or no tech. In the early years, Singapore stood out as a rare exception welcoming MNCs, and Asian companies. The truth is that we made a virtue out of necessity. But I would add, we did so also because of the hard knocks of our adverse experience in searching for a Malaysian common market.

How did Singapore succeed in attracting MNCs? Mr Chan Chin Bock was one of our best investment officers[1] and established an investment promotion network for Singapore, covering North America and Europe. Chin Bock told me that to succeed in investment promotion, we must quickly identify the push and the pull factors.

The push factors are the points Singapore wins by default. An MNC may wish to locate part of its manufacturing facilities abroad because of high labour costs and excessive taxation in their home countries. Or they may wish to position themselves to penetrate markets they are kept out of because of distance or tariffs. But push factors are not sufficient in themselves to attract investments to Singapore.

We had to offer strong pull factors for companies to move operations our way. Inertia and unfamiliarity with the terrain were the greatest stumbling blocks. What were these pull factors that Singapore offered?

First and foremost, in those days, was low-cost, semi-skilled and literate labour. In the initial years of industrialisation, Singapore was able to attract garments, hair-wigs, toys, and simple electronic assembly plants to Singapore, helping to employ thousands of primary school-leavers. Ship-breaking and steel re-rolling was one industry that required both brawn and skills. The value-added was higher than in simple assembly plants.

We soon discovered that low wages alone was not enough. We needed to offer higher skill content for precision engineering industries. The EDB

---

1 See Chan Chin Bock, *Heart Work (心耘): stories of how EDB steered the Singapore economy from 1961 into the 21st century* (Singapore: Economic Development Board and EDB Society, 2002).

persuaded industries such as Rollei of Germany, Phillips of Holland, and Seiko of Japan, to establish joint industrial training centres with us. In two years, secondary school-leavers were trained to be precision machinists and mould makers, able to operate computer-aided machines.

In the next phase, our polytechnics produced disciplined technicians to man our petroleum refining, petrochemical and pharmaceutical, and other process industries. All these industries are fundamentally skill- and even knowledge-based.

Today, more than ever, Singapore and Singaporeans have to compete with the best in the world, in terms of knowledge, skills and innovation. While the individual Singaporean may be equal to the best in the world in most fields of expertise, there are just not as many talented Singaporeans as there are talented Chinese, Indians, Japanese, Russians, West Europeans and Americans.

So how does Singapore continue to compete?

Stable Government and Free Trade

Although Singapore is devoid of natural resources such as crude oil, we have nevertheless developed into a leading petroleum refining and petrochemicals hub. Capital-intensive industries with long pay back periods require good and stable government as a *sine qua non* of investment.

Beyond this, we have emphasised our connections with all major markets, whether they are neighbours or are further away. Transportation-wise, our market reach includes all our ASEAN neighbours,[2] India, China, Japan, Australia, and New Zealand. Although more distant, we are also within sight of the Pacific United States, and South America. The Singapore government is now weaving a net of Free Trade Agreements with all these countries and major markets.

At the fundamental level, the little red dot[3] would have just remained a dot without good, strong government. The PAP has provided Singapore with a quality of leadership unsurpassed anywhere in the world. Singapore is not a miracle. It is a product of hard work and right policies. Singapore will endure if its citizens continue to work at it.

---

2   ASEAN consists of Brunei Darussalam, Cambodia, Indonesia, Laos, Malaysia, Myanmar, Philippines, Singapore, Thailand and Vietnam.

3   The term was originally used in a derogatory sense by the former Indonesian President B.J. Habibe to refer to Singapore at the 4th ASEAN Informal Summit. This phrase however is now used by Singaporeans as a matter of pride. See Tommy Koh and Chang Li Lin (eds.), *The Little Red Dot: Reflections by Singapore's Diplomats* (Singapore: Institute of Policy Studies, 2005).

ASEAN Economic Cooperation

The Association of Southeast Asian Nations (ASEAN) was established on 8 August 1967 at a meeting of foreign ministers in Bangkok. The five founding members were led by Adam Malik (Indonesia), Tun Abdul Razak (Malaysia), Secretary Ramos (the Philippines), Thanat Khoman (Thailand), and S. Rajaratnam (Singapore). As a young officer, I was privileged to be a member of the Singapore delegation to the historic inaugural meeting.

From the outset, ASEAN was conceived to be more an economic and less a political, or security grouping. It was hoped that through economic cooperation, each country would build up its economic resilience, and collectively be strong enough to protect ourselves against a victorious Communist Vietnam, and a Communist China dedicated to exporting revolution.[1]

The devil was in the details. First, the ASEAN Economic Ministers took some time to get going. There was even some initial procedural discussion on whether the Economic Ministers should report to the Heads of Government meetings directly or through their foreign ministers. There was sensitivity because in most ASEAN countries, the economic or finance ministers outranked the foreign ministers in terms of seniority and protocol.

The first ASEAN Summit Meeting was held in Bali, Indonesia, in February 1976. To prepare for this inaugural summit, Indonesia, which considered itself

Seminar on 13 Aug. 2005.

1   A contrary view has been expressed by some ASEAN experts that while economic cooperation was the stated goal, political cooperation was the unstated goal. Tay, Simon S.C., Jesus Estanislao and Hadi Soesastro, *Reinventing ASEAN* (Singapore: Institute of Southeast Asian Studies, 2001).

the first among equals, sent a consultative team to sound out other ASEAN countries on economic cooperation.

Different Perspectives on a Common Market

Indonesia is the largest and most populous country in ASEAN. It is 1.9 million square kilometres in size with a population of 208 million people.[2] In contrast, Singapore is geographically a tiny dot with a land area of 648 square kilometres and a population of about four million people.[3]

Our approaches to economic cooperation are at polar opposites. Without a domestic market of any significance, Singapore suggested that the way forward was the creation of an ASEAN Common Market with common external tariffs to keep foreign imports out, and free competition within ASEAN on a level playing field for all members. At our very first preliminary meeting, Indonesia baulked at the concept of an ASEAN Common Market.

The leader of the Indonesian delegation visiting Singapore to prepare the groundwork for the economic ministers to meet explained to me that even within his own country they would rather forego the benefits of comparative advantage, preferring harmony, even if progress is to be slower. In other words, the Indonesian government, for the sake of political stability, had to ensure that every province developed at the same pace rather than to let say Java or Sumatra streak ahead.

I remembered speaking to the Indonesian official, Professor Mohammed. He was candid enough to tell me that Indonesia could not accept that Singapore should become the highest peak of development within an ASEAN Common Market. I tried to persuade him that the contrary was more likely to be the case. Being the most populous country, endowed with vast human and natural resources, Indonesia would be the most attractive destination for foreign investors within an ASEAN Common Market.

Indonesia would have the economies of scale superior to any other ASEAN member country and, most of all, Singapore. Even in the absence of a common market, Singapore suffered from a shortage of labour by the late 1970s and early 1980s. Job-hopping emerged when demand for labour far exceeded supply. There is no reason why the major Indonesian cities could not achieve full employment as Singapore did. My Indonesian counterpart did not accept these arguments.

As the *primus inter-pares*, the first among equals, Indonesia was unable or unwilling to provide the economic statesmanship necessary for the progress

---

2 Indonesia's population statistic can be found at <http://www.bps.go.id/sector/population/table1.shtml>.

3 Singapore's population in 2005 was 4.35 million according to the Singapore Department of Statistic: <http://www.singstat.gov.sg/keystats/annual/indicators.html#Population%20Indicators>.

and prosperity of ASEAN. Instead, it adopted a very narrow mindset insisting that all decisions must be unanimous.

A very dear friend of mine in the Indonesian delegation reminded me more than once that the obverse side of unanimity is veto. As the first among equals, Indonesia reserves the right to veto any initiative that it considers not in its interest. Singapore learnt this the hard way when we proposed a diesel engine project which was to have been a part of the Industrial Complementation Scheme sponsored with a US$1 billion fund by Japan. This was torpedoed by General Yusof, the Indonesian Minister for Industry at the time.

Development economists in the 1950s and early 1960s were taught and nurtured on the doctrine of import substitution and infant industry protection. Young Singapore economists, including myself, were blind-sided by the siren calls of UN bodies, such as ECAFE.[4]

Unfortunately, the doctrine was quickly hijacked by businessmen, the crony capitalists of the ruling elite, who grew fat and comfortable on infant industry protection. The sad story is that the infant never grew up. And countless poor in developing countries had to pay more than they should have for consumer goods, medicines and other daily necessities.

Except for Singapore, which could be said to be making a virtue out of necessity, all the other ASEAN member states, namely Indonesia, Malaysia, Philippines and Thailand, looked at the ASEAN Common Market as a zero sum game. They all feared that they would lose more markets than they would gain. They could not believe that the whole would be bigger than the sum of the parts.

Each ASEAN nation scrambled for foreign investments in manufacturing. If the five ASEAN markets had been consolidated into one, each country would become even more attractive for the particular investment, without having to offer higher tariffs and more tax and financial incentives to the MNCs.

Without a unified market, ASEAN economic ministries lowered our sights to the next best level of cooperation. The Japanese government, under then Prime Minister Fukuda, offered US$1 billion as a fund to finance one industrial project for each ASEAN member state, provided all ASEAN countries agreed to support the particular project chosen by their ASEAN partner, through tariff protection and equity participation.

On our part, Singapore chose the manufacturing of diesel engines as our ASEAN industrial project. The horse-power range was specified so that our plant would not displace existing diesel engine assembly plants outside the range. From nowhere, out of the blue, the other ASEAN member states

---

4   Established in March 1947, at Shanghai, ECAFE — The Economic Commission for Asia and the Far East was founded to assist in post-war economic reconstruction. The Commission moved its Headquarters to Bangkok in January 1949. The name was changed, in 1974, to better reflect both the economic and social aspects of development and the geographic location of its Members. Department of Public Information United Nations (UN), "UN Regional Commissions", website available at: <http://www.un.org/issues/reg-comm.asp> [12 Jan. 2006].

claimed they have already established, or planned to establish, diesel engine plants of the specified horse-power capacity. It was clear that no ASEAN member state was prepared to concede its market to the products of the other ASEAN economy's industrial project. Low interest loans in yen offered by Japan could not overcome the zero sum mindset of the ASEAN member states.

As Singapore could not have its own ASEAN industrial project, we were allowed to participate in Indonesia's US$250 million urea project with a token 1 per cent, instead of the standard 20 per cent participation. This was given as a concession, much to the chagrin of Thailand which had opposed our diesel engine project. Without a project, Singapore was let off lightly. As things turned out, it was a blessing in disguise for us, as the urea project was only marginally profitable so those who invested more received little benefit. Further, the equity for Singapore was borrowed in yen from Japan.

The Long Road Ahead for ASEAN

Having chosen what we thought was a gentler, gradual road to economic integration, the five ASEAN nations — now joined by Brunei, Vietnam, Cambodia, Laos and Myanmar — have largely spent the last forty years in the international economic backwaters. Other regional economic groupings, such as Mercusor, and now Eastern Europe in the expanded EU, are said to have made more progress in economic integration than the original ASEAN-5, not to speak of the new ASEAN.

Professor Lim Chong Yah, in his meticulously documented and analytical work, "Southeast Asia: The Long Road Ahead" has got it right. For ASEAN, it has been a long road, of what I would describe as timid half-hearted attempts at economic co-operation.[5] The topics range from ASEAN Preferential Trading Arrangement (PTA), ASEAN Industrial Projects (AIP) Scheme and ASEAN Free Trade Area (AFTA). It may be unduly harsh for me to say, but most of this has been an exercise in frustration for most of us. I hope that, with WTO and global competition, ASEAN will begin to feel the heat and find its feet.[6]

---

5   See Lim Chong Yah, *Southeast Asia: The Long Road Ahead* (Singapore: World Scientific Publishing Co. Pte. Ltd., 2004), pp. 200–11.

6   The Declaration of ASEAN Concord II, also known as Bali Concord II, which was endorsed at the just-ended Ninth ASEAN Summit, is a historic step toward regional integration. The Bali Concord II, named after the Declaration of ASEAN Concord, or The Bali Concord, which was produced at the First ASEAN Summit in Bali in 1976, consists of three pillars, namely an ASEAN Security Community (ASC), an ASEAN Economic Community (AEC) and an ASEAN Socio-cultural Community (ASCC) among ASEAN member countries. For more: ASEAN Secretariat, "DECLARATION OF ASEAN CONCORD II (BALI CONCORD II)" ASEAN Secretariat website. Available at: <http://www.aseansec.org/15159.htm> [12 Jan. 2006].

As the Permanent Secretary responsible for economic affairs in the Ministry of Finance in the mid-1970s, I spent five years leading the Singapore delegation negotiating various forms of economic co-operation with our ASEAN fellow members. As the economic doctrine was import substitution and infant industry protection, no headway was made. There were too many exclusion lists of products exempted from competition. The mindset was zero sum.

All member states believed that because we were at different stages of development, any gain in trade for one country must be at the expense of the other. The road was not only long; in fact there was no destination in sight. Fundamentally, we could not agree on where we wanted to go. At best, ASEAN economic cooperation could be seen as a meandering river, moving imperceptibly through the marshlands of nationalism, confounded by crony capitalists.

Lacking patience, I asked to be relieved of my ASEAN responsibilities. I went on to become the Chairman of the Economic Development Board (EDB) in 1975, where I found far greater satisfaction. My colleagues in the Trade Development Board (TDB), led by Mr Ridzwan Dzafir,[7] had to carry the more onerous ASEAN torch. Fortunately, they persisted, for in 1989 a new economic grouping came into being, with the Asia-Pacific Economic Cooperation (APEC) forum.

Although most ASEAN member states[8] are a prominent bloc in APEC, there are also far larger economies, namely the United States, China, Japan, Korea, Australia, Mexico, Canada, and Chile. These larger economies can provide the impetus for economic growth and cooperation. In this way, the slow meandering river of ASEAN now suddenly finds itself plunging into the strong invigorating ocean currents of the Pacific Ocean.[9]

With global economic competition under the demanding and rigorous rules of the WTO, Singapore now finds release from the ASEAN straight-jacket. Will Singapore survive in such a world?

---

7   Mr Ridzwan is currently the Ambassador-at-Large at the Ministry of Foreign Affairs in Singapore and a member of the Council of Presidential Advisers. He is also the Chairman of the Malay Heritage Foundation. He was the Director-General of the Trade and Development Board (now known as International Enterprise Singapore) from 1983 to 1999 where he played a key role in shaping the parameters of the ASEAN Free Trade Area.

8   ASEAN members who are also members of APEC: its five original members (Indonesia, Malaysia, Singapore, Thailand, Philippines), Brunei, and new member, Vietnam. For more see APEC, "Member Economies" APEC website, available at <http://www.apec.org/content/apec/member_economies.html> [12 Jan. 2006].

9   There are also scholars like Hadi Soesastro (Centre for Strategic and International Studies, Indonesia) who noted the weakness of institutions within APEC, and the limited ability to learn because of weak institutional memory in the "Report on International Symposium on Perspective for APEC: 2002 and Beyond". Report can be found at <http://www.asiapacific.ca/about/apec/apec2002.pdf>.

EDUCATION, GROWTH AND OUR FUTURE

Education, in my view, has three imperatives; namely the economic, the cultural, and the political. Over the last 40 years, from 1960 to 2000, the overriding priority of education in Singapore has been our economic growth. Faced with a young and rapidly growing population, our schools, polytechnics and universities were all geared up to teach literacy in English and the mother tongue, technical skills, science and technology.

Literature and the arts, history, geography, were derided as soft options. Even many of those who excelled in law in their professional careers later on in life, struggled to obtain "A" marks in the hard sciences when they were in school.

Now that the world is entering an era of knowledge-based competition, we are unsure whether our hard science education will stand us in good stead. By neglecting the "soft options" of poetry, music and philosophy, have we missed something? What has happened to our imagination? Do we find it difficult to think out of the box? Why are the majority of Singaporeans followers? Is that true of all societies, and not just Singapore?

Politically, do we want to be a Sparta, or an Athens? Ideally, can we be both? Where do our political temperament and instincts lie?

Education has to serve society's cultural, political and economic imperatives. The priority and emphasis depend on a country's time in history and its stage of development. In the case of China, the political imperative was paramount during the period of the Cultural Revolution. In contrast to

Edited from the Inaugural NUS FASS (Faculty of Arts and Social Sciences) lecture, "Education & Growth: The Singapore Experience 1960–2000", 26 Oct. 2004 and a seminar on 8 Oct. 2005, NTU.

Chairman Mao's ideological leadership, Mr Deng Xiaoping, seeking truth from facts, brought the economic imperative to the fore.[1]

What were the priorities for Singapore in the early decades? What are they now?

Colonial Administration and English Education

At the end of the Second World War and on the return of the British colonial administration to Singapore, English-medium schools funded by the colonial government were quickly re-established. During the brief period of the Japanese Occupation (1942–5), the Japanese civilian administration used the private Chinese-medium schools to teach Japanese to youngsters like me. Japanese was taught whenever the Japanese supervisor was around. Teachers and students reverted to Mandarin the moment he was out of sight. In this way, I had one year of schooling in Mandarin.

The British colonial government funded and staffed only the English-medium schools. Vernacular schools in Chinese and Tamil were left to fend for themselves. They were financially supported by the various ethnic clan and community associations. Teachers were poorly trained and poorly paid. Most parents sent their children to English-medium schools, as school fees were lower and facilities better.

Being poorly paid, some teachers in Chinese schools became embittered and taught leftist ideology to their students. The Chinese Middle School Union was a powerful political force, which the PAP government had to contend with in the early years after self-government.[2]

English-medium schools, on the other hand, were apolitical. The aim of the British colonial government was to teach the English language so that young Singaporeans could serve as clerks and bookkeepers, primary school teachers and nurses, and policemen. The British Colonial government, supported by our own philanthropists, established the King Edward VII School of Medicine and Raffles College. The two institutions merged in 1949 to become the University of Malaya, serving Singapore and Malaya. The Law and Engineering Faculties of NUS were established later in the 1960s.[3] The

---

1 For readings on Deng, see Maomao, *My Father Deng Xiaoping in the Cultural Revolution* (Beijing: Central Literature Publishing House, 1993); Kueh Ash, *The Chinese Economy Under Deng Xiaoping* (Oxford University Press, 1996); and Michael Marti, *China and the Legacy of Deng Xiaoping: From Communist Revolution to Capitalist Evolution* (Brassey's Inc, 2002).

2 Singapore Chinese Middle Schools Students' Union, *All-Party Committee on Singapore Chinese Middle Schools Students' Union* (Singapore: Printed at the Government Printing Office, 1956); Chew, Ernest C.T. and Edwin Lee (ed.), *A History of Singapore* (Singapore: Oxford University Press, 1991); and Clutterbuck, Richard, *Conflict and Violence in Singapore and Malaysia 1945–1983*. Rev. ed. (Singapore: Graham Brash, 1984).

3 Lee-Wang Cheng Yeng and Lee Ching Seng (eds.), *90 years of NUS history: a select bibliography* (Singapore: National University of Singapore Library, 1995).

colonial education policy was essentially aimed at oiling the wheels of its administration.

Self Government, Jobs and Technical Education

When we attained self-government in 1959, Singapore had a population literate in English, and this was an advantage over other non-English speaking countries in attracting American and European MNCs. The population however possessed few technical skills. Paradoxically, the Chinese-educated Singaporeans possessed more technical skills that they had acquired through apprenticeship. This skilled labour went on to build complex steel structures that MNCs wanted, such as oil drilling rigs.

The indigenous skills in Singapore at the time, however, were inadequate for the higher end precision engineering and process industries. The EDB was tasked with starting up technical education in Singapore. I remember, when I served at the EDB, how we established joint industrial training centres with MNCs, such as Philips of Holland, Rollei of Germany, Seiko and Yokogawa Electric of Japan.[4] The industrial training systems became models for our five polytechnics today.[5]

In the first three decades of independence, the economic imperative was the driving force of our education policies. In our schools, attention was focused on the teaching of science and mathematics, which were dubbed the hard sciences. All other subjects were derided as soft options.

As a result, fewer and fewer students in English-medium schools studied English Literature. Paradoxically, it was harder to score an "A" or distinction in English Literature than in Maths or Science, simply because English was not our mother tongue at home. Without studying Literature and History, whether in English- or Chinese-medium schools, our literacy in both languages fell.

History has been and still is a neglected subject in all our schools. Politically, we have been an independent country since 1965, hardly 40 years old. In world history, we rate only a comma. Yet our multi-racial and multi-religious society must retain our roots. Without a sense of history, we will become a people lost in limbo.

Yet, in the first half of our short history to date, Singapore had no choice but to embrace science and technology for economic survival and thus to neglect other subjects.

---

4 The overseas training programme was drawn up in 1971. This placed young Singaporean workers in apprenticeship position. Discussions began for Joint Government Training Centres with Tata of India, Philips of Holland, and Rollei of Germany. EDB, "Our History about Us", EDB website available at: <http://www.edb.gov.sg/edb/sg/en_uk/index/about_us/our_history.html> [12 Jan. 2006]. See also Chan Chin Bock, *Heart Work (心耕): stories of how EDB steered the Singapore economy from 1961 into the 21st century* (Singapore: Economic Development Board and EDB Society, 2002).

5 The polytechnics in Singapore are Nanyang, Ngee Ann, Republic, Singapore and Temasek.

At a very basic level, we established industrial training centres to train our young school-leavers in precision machining and mould making, which were core skills for the manufacturing industry. At the polytechnics, students were taught process engineering and technical analysis. They also learnt finance and cost accounting. As our manufacturing and service industries grew and became more sophisticated, there was a great need for trained manpower that could go beyond the "how" to the "why" of things.

When we had achieved full employment in the mid-1970s, our economic advisor at the time, Dr Albert Winsemius, persuaded the then Prime Minister, Lee Kuan Yew, to establish the Nanyang Technological Institute (NTI), to train more practice-oriented engineers. This was to complement engineering science that was already taught at the University of Singapore. The EDB, which had been nicknamed "metal eaters" by Mr Lee, had boldly asked that our university, polytechnics and industrial training centres produce 1,000 engineers, 5,000 technicians, and 10,000 skilled workers annually to meet a surging demand for technical manpower.

The elitist establishment at University of Singapore (soon changed to the National University of Singapore) baulked at the idea. For them, increasing the engineering enrolment only raised the spectre of having unemployed graduates. The professors had little faith at the ability of the EDB to attract high tech jobs to Singapore. They should not have doubted such a need. Even in the recent recession of 2002–3, MNCs still find difficulty recruiting skilled personnel for high tech industries, such as wafer fab plants. As a result, a number of them have been relocating to China.

NTI was therefore established as a university of science and technology. To establish its academic credentials, NTI was initially allowed to award a joint degree with the NUS. Today NTU (Nanyang Technological University) conducts degree programmes in almost every academic discipline, other than medicine and law.

I hope that the NTU will be established as the MIT of Southeast Asia, while the NUS will become the Harvard in this region.[6] The goal of all academic institutions must be excellence in both teaching and research. Simply

---

6   The NTU has a distinguished lineage with roots that go back to 1955, when Nanyang University (Nantah), the first Chinese-language university in Southeast Asia was set up. The NTU was established on the same campus in 1981 with government funding to educate practice-oriented engineers for the burgeoning Singapore economy. Its vision is to be a global university of excellence; steeped in ideals, passion, creativity and entrepreneurship. The NTU web: <http://www.ntu.edu.sg/publicportal/about+ntu/about+us/history.htm> [12 Jan. 2006]. The NUS was officially established on 8 Aug. 1980 as a result of a merger of the University of Singapore and the Nanyang University. This was through recommendation of the Dainton report that Singapore should have a single strong university. Its current vision is "Towards a Global Knowledge Enterprise". For further information: <http://www.nus.edu.sg/corporate/about/vision.htm> [12 Jan. 2006]. The goal of world class education and the analogy of Harvard and MIT were made by Singapore's then PM, Goh Chok Tong. See Goh Chok Tong, "National Day Rally Speech, 1997 Global City, Best Home". MOE website, available at: <http://www.moe.gov.sg/speeches/1997/240897.htm> [12 Jan. 2006].

establishing new faculties and departments because the other university has such a department will just distract the faculty and administration of both universities from the drive for excellence.

Some Things We Have Lost

Out of sheer necessity, we concentrated on the economic imperative in education. Efficiency, rather than effectiveness, was the name of the game. Along the way, we also lost some of our cultural roots and ethnic instincts.

This was the case for Chinese Singaporeans. In the late 1960s, the government decided to drop Chinese dialect programmes over radio and TV. There may be compelling reasons for stopping Hokkien, Teochew, Cantonese, Hakka and Hainanese programmes over the airwaves. One reason given was that we wanted our children of Chinese descent to concentrate only on learning Mandarin, and not have their young minds confused with the various dialects spoken at home.

Whether this hypothesis is true or not, we do not know for sure. But we do know that those grandparents who spoke only dialects and not Mandarin were deprived of one of their few sources of news and entertainment. As less and less Chinese dialect was spoken at home, the communication gap between the young and the old widened. The transmission of cultural values from generation to generation was diminished. Our children and grandchildren of Chinese descent had to learn to speak Mandarin *ab initio*, and to study the Chinese language outside what was our natural cultural environment.

Today, we cannot go back to the *status quo ante*, to what was before. It will be pointless to restore dialect programmes back to our airwaves. The generation of grandparents today do not speak any dialects at all, having grown up under the non-dialect regime. What can be done?

A back of the envelope solution might be to encourage our English-speaking to read Chinese history, literature, and even poetry, in English to enthuse their grandchildren about their Chinese heritage. Though translations will not have the richness of the original, they do give the English literate some flavour. We can also start by reading columns on Chinese literature, like Li Lienfung's "Bamboo Green"[7] columns that used to run in *The Straits Times*.

It is not only Chinese culture that has been affected.

As I remarked earlier, even in English-speaking schools, technical education was preferred over subjects such as Literature and History.

---

7 "Bamboo Green" used to be a column in *The Straits Times* written by Madam Li Lienfung. Madam Li discussed Chinese poetry, major classics and Chinese culture in a simple and witty style. Her bilingual column was very popular and ran for more than ten years. The column was later published in book form: Li Lienfung, *Bamboo Green* (Singapore: Federal Publications, 1982).

With the neglect of English Literature in school, young Singaporeans do not have enough command of English to absorb the essence of western culture. Instead, Hollywood is their western cultural diet.

At the same time, unable to speak to their grandparents, they cannot relate what little culture they are taught in their Mandarin lessons to their daily lives.

My generation, schooled entirely in the English-medium and speaking dialect at home, can at least get a flavour of Chinese history and culture reading the English translations of such classics as *All Men are Brothers*, *A Dream of the Red Mansions*, and Lin Yutang's *My Country and My People*.[8]

In education, as in any field of human endeavour, we have to face reality. Our single-minded pursuit of economic prosperity has brought us to a crossroad. In a knowledge-based global economy, inputs of land, labour, and capital are necessary, but not sufficient for growth and prosperity. We have to learn to apply knowledge creatively.

I was once told that knowledge is power, if applied with wisdom, or with insight and creativity. How do we become a society with insight and creativity?

Holistic Education and Retaining Ethnicity

The short answer is a holistic education system. Such a system will have to serve all the three imperatives of education: the cultural, political and economic. We have successfully established industrial training centres, polytechnics, and universities, to teach the "how" but not — in my view — the "why" of things.

At the risk of being dismissed as an educational Rip van Winkle, may I suggest that the Ministry of Education revisit the grouping of subjects for the GCE 'O' Level examinations?

In 1953, when I sat for what was then known as the Senior Cambridge School Certificate examination, candidates were required to offer not more than nine subjects. These were divided into three groups of English and English Literature; Mathematics and Science; History, Geography and Art. Beyond this, Latin and Religious Knowledge were optional subjects.

A candidate had to pass in at least two subjects from each group, graded into pass, credit and distinction. Your scores determined your overall grading into Grade I, II and III. Only those with Grade I were admitted

---

8 Lin Yutang, *My Country and My People* (London: W. Heinemann, 1935); Shi Naian, *All Men are Brothers*, trans. Pearl S. Buck (London: Methuen, 1937); Tsao Hsueh-Chin, *A Dream of Red Mansions*, trans. Yang Hsien-yi and Gladys Yang (Singapore: Asiapac Books & Educational Aids, 1986).

into the Post School Certificate classes to prepare for university entrance examinations.

The curriculum required competence in both arts and science. In my view, a broader, rather than a narrow, curriculum is likely to produce greater creativity in individuals, and society as a whole. The competition for entrance into university is at the final stage of schooling. Streaming at too early a stage is not only unfair to the individual student, but is also less effective overall in terms of costs to the society as a whole.[9]

The prosperity achieved from pursuing the economic imperative in education comes at a cost. Mr Robert Kuok, the Malaysian entrepreneur whom I know and greatly respect,[10] once told a private gathering at the NUS that to survive beyond economics, Singapore has to retain its Chineseness, and by extension to citizens of different ethnic backgrounds, its Indianness and Malayness. It was not a rhetorical answer to a rhetorical question.

Because of our political history, Singapore embraced English as its *lingua franca*. As English is also the language of international commerce, science and technology, and the language of today's only world superpower, the United States of America, our literacy in English has given us a head start in attracting MNC investments.

Our legal system based on English law is understood and accepted by international banks, shipping companies, fund managers, and the rest of the international business community. As Microsoft dominates the internet, software is largely written in English. So those fluent in the English language have an advantage in writing software than those who are not. Hence, Indians who are more literate in English have an edge over the Chinese.

Our pragmatism has led us to adopt English as our first language, and our "mother" tongue — whether it is Malay, Mandarin or Tamil — as our second language.

But is language facility the only competitive criterion? Or is it the cultural DNA of the Indians, Chinese, and Malays that will count increasingly in the new millennium? I believe that Mr Robert Kuok is correct. It is important to remain culturally Chinese, Indian or Malay.

---

9 "Streaming" is an exercise conducted in primary school to assess students' academic ability, based mainly on their grades, in order that students with similar intelligence and age group are taught together. Streaming takes place at the end of Primary 4 and Primary 6.

10 Robert Kuok Hock Nien is reputedly the richest man in Malaysia. While handing more authority to the next generation, Kuok remains the man in charge, and is advantage of difficult times to train his successors. Kuok was born in 1923 in Johor Bahru, the son of a well-off commodities trader. His ancestral town was in Fujian province, China. An old boy of Raffles College in Singapore, he was a schoolmate of Singapore's Senior Minister Lee Kuan Yew in the late 1940s. After graduation, he helped out at his father's company, and founded the Kuok Brothers Sdn Bhd in 1949. Huayinet, "Robert Kuok Hock-Nien (Malaysia)". The Huayinet website is available at: <http://www.huayinet. org/biography/biography_kuokhocknien.htm> [12 Jan. 2006].

The Future of English and the Rise of Asia

In his memoirs,[11] Minister Mentor Lee Kuan Yew said he sang three different national anthems in Singapore. First, as a schoolboy he had sung "God Save The King in English", in the crown colony of Singapore before the Second World War. Then, for three short years, he sang the Japanese national anthem during the Japanese occupation of Singapore. On the defeat of Japan, it was back to "God Save the King". Finally, when we obtained self-government in 1959 the Singapore national anthem "Majulah Singapura" was composed by the late Mr Zubir Said, a Malay Singaporean, and sung in our national language, Malay.[12]

The origin and language of the national anthem is determined by the political power governing Singapore. Now that Singapore is an independent country, the origin and language of our national anthem is settled. Singapore, however, has still to evolve its own national cultural identity.

Western civilisation has spawned most of the major discoveries in science and technology and has been in the ascendant for the last 500 years. Before then, the Chinese, Indian and other civilisations were at the forefront of the quest for knowledge. Not being a historian, I will stick my neck out and postulate that western civilisation overtook these eastern civilisations because the peoples and societies were more outward looking, and undertook activities such as the conquest and colonisation of foreign lands.

Continental-sized countries, such as China and India, stagnated because they considered themselves to be the centres of the civilised world. China named itself as *Zhong Kuo*, meaning "centre of the world". There is a rock outcrop on the island of Hainan — which is my Chinese ancestral homeland — facing south that is considered as the spot where the civilised world ends.

Similarly, my impression is that Indians consider themselves to be morally superior to other people. Gandhi coined the slogan of simple living and high thinking.[13] But if Indians go on to imply that this is the only way to progress, it falls into the Chinese trap of ethnocentricity.

In contrast, Singapore is under no such impression. We are a small island. This forces an outward orientation upon us and this has enabled Singapore to make progress.

---

11 In an interview with Lee Kuan Yew with the REVIEW's Phil Revzin, Michael Vatikiotis, David Plott and Ben Dolven, interview available at <http://giaodiem.com/FotoNews/interv_lee_singapore.htm> [16 Jan. 2006]. "I've been through the same process. I've sung the British national anthem 'God Save the Queen'; I've sung the 'Kimigayo', the Japanese anthem; I sang the Malayan anthem; and now I sing my own anthem." Also see Lee Kuan Yew, *The Singapore Story: Memoirs of Lee Kuan Yew* (SPH, Marshall Cavendish Editions, 1988).

12 Majulah Singapura was written in 1958, it was formally presented to the nation in 1959, the year Singapore became a self governing state. Upon Singapore's independence in 1965, Majulah Singapura was adopted as the republic's national anthem.

13 Mahatma Gandhi News, "Mahatma Gandhi: embodiment of simple living and high thinking", Mahatma Gandhi News, available at <http://mahatma-gandhi-news.newslib.com/top/2679115/> [12 Jan. 2006].

Japan, like India and China, has supreme confidence in its own culture. I tend to think foreigners can never penetrate Japan's cultural barrier. While Japan can be and has historically been forced to lower import duties, remove quantitative restrictions, or reduce non-tariff regulations, the cultural defence of buying Japanese first is a barrier other countries cannot penetrate. Japan does not promote the study of English. Instead, there is a huge translation industry publishing Western works in Japanese.

Japan, unlike China and India, is not a continental country. It is an archipelago of islands with the sea as the border. Though insular by nature, Japan has no choice but to trade with the world. The orientation is outward. Ezra Vogel, a personal friend of mine and the man who wrote the well-known, *Japan as Number One*,[14] would have done the Japanese a great disservice if the Japanese had believed him. My hunch is that the Japanese were not taken in by the accolade.

In the last 50 years, Japan has become an economic success, one of the few countries in the same league as the United States of America. Now that China and India have begun to embrace openness, how will Japan adjust to compete economically and culturally? And what does this mean for Singapore?

Professor Shih Choon Fong, President of the National University of Singapore, posed a very intriguing question to his North American colleagues:[15] "Will the centre of higher education remain in North America or will it move?" And President Shih meant that if it might move to China and India.

He quoted a Goldman Sachs prognosis that the world in 2050 will face a tectonic change. In 2050, China and India, each with a population far exceeding 1 billion, and the United States with a population under 450 million, could be the largest economies in the world.[16]

In another forecast by an English applied linguist, David Graddol, the English language will probably drop in prominence by 2050, ranking after Chinese, and comparable to Hindi and Arabic.[17]

---

14 Ezra Vogel, *Japan as Number One* (Cambridge: Harvard University Press, 1979). Vogel is a professor at Harvard University and a well-known expert of East Asia.

15 Full transcript of speech delivered on 19 April 2004 at a meeting of the Association of American Universities (AAU), "Plenary Address by Professor Shih Choon Fong, Chairman, Association of Pacific Rim Universities (APRU) and NUS President, at The Association of American Universities (AAU) Meeting", 19 April 2004, Fairmont Hotel, Washington DC. NUS website is available at <http://www.nus.edu.sg/president/speeches/2004/aau1.htm> [12 Jan. 2006].

16 Goldman Sachs, "Global Economics Paper No. 99: Dreaming with BRICs: The Path to 2050", Goldman Sachs website: <http://www.gs.com/insight/research/reports/report6.html>[12 Jan. 2006].

17 David Graddol, Dick Leith and Joan Swann (eds.), *English: History, diversity and change* (London: Routledge, 1996); David Graddol and Sharon Goodman, *Redesigning English: New texts, new identities* (London: Routledge, 1996); and David Graddol, *The Future of English?* (London: British Council, 1997).

Although the United States has been the global education universe in the twentieth century, China and India are now poised to become two of the world's largest economies and may aspire to become the new centres of learning. They will strive for cultural and technological primacy. Can they achieve this?

I attended the Master of Public Administration (MPA) course at the Graduate School of Public Administration of Harvard University in 1963. On arrival at Harvard, mid-career officers such as myself were told that while it was easy to pass, having been carefully selected by Harvard, it would be difficult to excel, as we will be among the best competing with the best.

The teaching method at Harvard was in stark contrast to the then University of Malaya. The professors at Harvard assumed that, as we were learning at a post-graduate level, we already know the subject matter.

I was startled at one of the first American-style lecture when the professor began the course by asking a question. The student he asked responded not with an answer, but with another question! The process was a relay of questions rather than a round of answers. Although strange at first, I soon learnt to navigate this system by thinking of the "whys" rather than the "hows". This is a more stimulating way of learning.

This is something that Asians need to embrace in their quest for further development, beyond the earlier economic paradigm. Without a doubt, the wealth of human talent in China and India can propel these countries to intellectual and technological prominence. But they can do this only if — and it is a big, big "if" — they can break out of the mould of Confucian philosophy of the emperor knows best, and the Indian caste system where some are preordained to be masters while the others are doomed to be slaves.

For such large countries, because of endless cycles of war and famine, stability was prized above everything else. In my view, it will take decades, if not centuries, before Chinese and Indian societies will be ready to embrace openness and risk chaos. Yet, they must.

In the view of some like Mr Robert Kuok, if we lose our ethnicity — our Chinese-ness, our Malay-ness, and Indian-ness — we would have lost everything. Having only western DNA in our blood will lead us to a dead-end in an era when China and India are in the ascendant. Without cultural DNA, our best and brightest, schooled in the leading western universities, will not be stayers. They will rationalise and migrate at the slightest tremor.

Although bright Chinese and Indians also migrate, they have enough cultural DNA to leave their hearts behind. As China and India become more open societies, the best and brightest of their people will return to help build their own countries.

For Singapore, our size and diverse languages leave us in a no-man's land. The present adoption of English as our first language has served the economic imperative of education. But is economics the only imperative? Can national survival depend only on economics?

The Monolingual vs the Bilingual and Bicultural

Personally, I was schooled in the English-medium. English is my master language. In the world of the future, a monolingual person, such as me, will not survive, regardless of whether he is English- or Chinese-educated. Indeed, in a global knowledge-based economy, an individual has to be multilingual and bicultural to survive.

I am encouraged by the recent government announcement of plans to set up a scholarship scheme to nurture a group of Chinese students to have a deeper understanding of Chinese culture and history, so as to be able to engage China in depth. The scheme will groom 100 to 200 Chinese students in every primary school cohort yearly.[18] This will ensure that Singapore could continue to have in depth exchanges and close relations with China.

My guess is that this select group of students will have to study both English and Chinese at first language level. Indeed, some friends of my generation, at the insistence of their Chinese-educated parents, attended English-medium schools in the morning and Chinese-medium schools in the afternoon. They were schooled in both English and Chinese at first language level. As a result, they were comfortable in both cultures.

Although it is tough to achieve, the Singaporean of the future has to be not only bilingual, but also bicultural. It will be a challenge for the Ministry of Education, our society and each family, to bring this about. It is a worthwhile goal. Indeed, Singapore's very survival rides on us being multilingual and bicultural.

Unlike China and India, Singapore has no other choice. Minister Mentor Lee Kuan Yew noted that language and culture were inseparable and the Chinese elite of the new generation had to be like students from the Chinese schools in the past. These students not only mastered the Chinese language but also knew the culture and history of China.

The Future for the Singaporean Nation

I began by postulating that the purpose of education is to serve the cultural, political and economic imperative of a society. Singapore's education system

---

18 See Teo Chee Hean, "PSC Ceremony Keynote Address by Minister Teo Chee Hean". PSD Singapore Government website, available at: <http://app.psd.gov.sg/data/2005 per cent20PSC per cent20Ceremony_Keynote per cent20Address per cent20by per cent20Minister per cent20Teo.doc> [12 Jan. 2006].

The PSC has scholars who have chosen to study in non-traditional countries like China, Japan and Germany. The path less travelled holds unique rewards. The language skills that are picked up and the understanding of the country's culture will benefit the scholars for life. The Singapore civil service hopes to gain from the different and diverse perspectives that Chinese scholars bring to the table, and enable the Singapore government to tap on a wider network.

has focused almost exclusively on the economic imperative. While it is true that man does not live by bread alone, can he live without any bread at all?

Finally, what is the ideal teaching structure? Is it to be prescriptive like Confucius or Plato? Or interactive like Socrates? Or divine like Christ? Learning and teaching will exercise the minds of men forever. A society that stops learning and teaching will be dead and fossilised like dictatorships.

But the worst dictatorship is the dictatorship of the mind. Societies which allow people to be trapped by political indoctrination or religious fanaticism will ultimately self-destruct. Singapore has to change and evolve, breaking out of our present mould and mindset.

Whatever the endowments of a country, the one single aspect that foreign investors will not tolerate is the lack of continuity in public policies, whether economic and financial, social or educational.

I recall a conversation with a senior Chinese Communist cadre in 1985 when I asked him about the Cultural Revolution. He replied with great sadness that, leaving aside the immense personal suffering of individuals, the greatest damage was the loss of a whole generation of students. In the mid-1980s, there was a lack of mid-career cadres with the education, or the experience, to drive the development process that China was then embarking on.

With its vast population and talent base, the wounds were quickly healed. China today is on everyone's radar screen. A tiny city-state like Singapore cannot survive even a mini-cultural revolution, whether in the body politic or in education, in the schools, universities, or society at large.

Yet, we must change. How?

Continuity of policies is only possible if a country enjoys political stability. The post-independence generation, born after 1965, are now young parents themselves and have taken the political stability of Singapore for granted. Without the leadership of Mr Lee Kuan Yew and his first generation founding colleagues, Singapore could well be another sorry third world story.

The older generation of our citizens born during the war years will remember the Singapore of the 1950s and early 1960s, wracked by religious and racial riots, and crippled by left-wing communist inspired strikes. The non-communist English-educated leadership of the PAP fought the chauvinists, racialists, and communists on their turf, and won. It is not surprising therefore that the PAP which came into power in 1959 has won every general election since. The political and economic prosperity wrought by the PAP government has to be jealously guarded. In such an environment, there will be no fertile soil for the opposition to grow.

The greatest danger to the PAP, which has been the governing party for the last forty years, is elitism and complacency. I am glad that our new Prime Minister, Mr Lee Hsien Loong, wants to create an inclusive society, not an exclusive ruling class. Complacency sets in when the administration flies on auto-pilot. This is something that I believe PM Lee must avoid.

The challenge of building Singapore as a nation, and not just a successful economy, is still not fully met. Can it be?

The Jewish nation — which is larger than the state of Israel — is bonded by the Torah, the Old Testament. As a multi-racial and multi-religious society, this is not open to us. My personal belief is that to build the nation of Singapore, we have to value human life and respect the core of the person.

As a Christian, I believe that God has given each one of us at least one talent. In God's eyes, there is no person who is completely stupid. Some of us may be cerebral with abstract thinking skills. Some blessed with motor skills are good practitioners. Artists and great violinists are blessed with both.

So I believe that to become a nation, we — as parents, teachers, siblings and friends — should search hard for the talent that each child has inherently, and help him or her to grow and excel in it. In this way, we can become a people with diversity of skills and temperaments. In time, we will evolve into a nation.

Then, the nation of Singapore will not just be the state of Singapore. It will embrace all who have their hearts in Singapore.

Finding Niches, Seizing Opportunities

What has Singapore done that is right for its development, and that might suggest some examples for other countries? If you were to ask me to sum up Singapore's industrial strategy in a few words, I would say it has been a process of "finding niches, and seizing opportunities". Or, where we have failed, it is because we have been missing these opportunities.

We can see this opportunistic streak in different situations that Singapore faced, and the opportunities that presented themselves.

When we first started our industrialisation programme in the early 1960s, steel was the symbol of a country's industrial prowess. Japan was the leading steel-making nation then, with integrated steel mills of one million tons capacity. What would Singapore do in this context, at that time?

My colleagues and I were in our early twenties when we joined the Economic Development Board under the leadership of our Chairman, Mr Hon Sui Sen, who later became the Finance Minister of Singapore. We were starry-eyed, and like everybody else, our dream was to establish an integrated steel mill in Singapore. Little did we realise then that a one million ton steel mill would spew enough iron and coal dust to cover every square inch of Singapore.

Prime Minister Lee Kuan Yew dubbed us metal eaters. But we were not to be so easily put off. EDB invited a Frenchman through the auspices of the United Nations to advise us on steel. He was Mr Scherechevsky, a former Chairman of Electricité de France. He was an expert on the electric arc furnace process of steel making.

Seminar on 22 Oct. 2005.

Old ships, which were plentiful, were bought and scrapped on the beaches of Pasir Panjang. Their plates were melted in the electric arc furnaces and rolled into steel bars for building HDB flats. Although there was some grumbling from our building contractors that we could have imported steel bars at lower prices, I was not persuaded.

The value added in cutting up ship plates and rolling them into building steel was definitely higher than merely importing finished bars. The vast HDB programme was possible only because of NatSteel, our first indigenous manufacturing plant. Its opening in 1963 was a red letter day for all of us at EDB.

Ship-Repairing, Oil Rigs and Flexibility

Until the early 1960s, there was only the Naval dockyard repairing naval vessels at Sembawang. There was no commercial ship-repair yard. It was Dr Shinto of Ishikawajima-Harima (IHI) of Japan who identified this niche for us. A supertanker took about 24 to 36 hours to de-gas itself after dropping off its cargo of crude oil at a Japanese refinery. This was the time a supertanker leaving Japan for the Middle East needed to reach Singapore, where repairs and maintenance work can be done to prepare it for uplifting its next crude cargo in the Arabian Gulf. Singapore's geographical location at the tip of the Asian continent between the Indian and the Pacific Oceans provided the niche for us to establish a thriving ship-repair industry, and this grew to employ — at the height of this sector — over 20,000 workers.

The skills we learnt in repairing supertankers enabled us to advance into the construction of oil rigs for the major oil exploration companies. Keppel and Sembawang, which followed Jurong Shipyard in ship-repair, are now among the world's largest oil rig builders.

China and Korea are snapping at our heels. When these countries, together with India, undertake their own exploration for oil and gas, the whole competitive landscape for exploration vessels will change drastically. The challenge for Singapore is to find and maintain our niche in this industry. Singapore may have to align itself with construction giants in China, India, Korea, and Japan, contributing value in a rapidly changing industry. We may even build the oil rigs in Texan yards with American companies.

We refused to change in the earlier phase of ship-repair when the Gulf States invited us to help them establish ship-repair yards. They pointed out to us that after all we were using hardy Indian and Bangladeshi workers to do the heavy work in ship-repair. It might be better for our yards to employ them for work in the Gulf States directly.

Our lack of foresight led to a decline in the ship-repair industry because we were too Singapore-centric. We have to be infinitely more flexible in future if we are to exploit the current burgeoning oil rig and exploration industry.

Creating Opportunities

Although we had to settle for an electric steel re-rolling mill, we did not give up our dream of establishing at least one basic industry in Singapore. Working from "chemistry 101", we noted that the three petroleum refineries in Singapore, namely Shell, Exxon and Mobil, produced naphtha, the light end of a barrel of crude. Naphtha could be cracked into ethylene, the building block of a whole host of downstream petrochemical products.

Fortunately for Singapore, the then Chairman of Sumitomo Chemicals, Mr Hasegawa, was then exploring the possibility of diversifying the production of petrochemicals outside Japan. Sumitomo needed to be nearer the source of feedstock. In Singapore, the three refineries could supply the naphtha on tap.

Natural gas would have been a cheaper feedstock, but most of it was to be found in the Middle East and Iran. Mr Hasegawa considered Singapore to be politically stable. Political stability was the *sine qua non* for locating capital-intensive industries with a long pay back period. Indeed, Mitsui Petrochemicals was half way through the construction of its plant in Iran when the Iran-Iraq war broke out. It had to be abandoned.

The Singapore project was not an easy one as our feedstock, naphtha, was actually a semi-processed product from petroleum refining. The breakout of the Iran-Iraq war gave us the market opening. Petrochemical plants were billion dollar investments, and projects had to wait their turn for world demand to grow before a new plant is built.

The Petrochemical Corporation of Singapore (PCS) plants would not have been built, if not for the determination and faith of two men — Mr Hasegawa and Mr Hon. Mr Hasegawa said that the Singapore project was established through divine intervention. His meeting with Mr Hon laid the true foundation for the project. Through sweat and tears, they saw the project through. The naysayers have to keep their silence forever now that PCS had grown into the Jurong Island integrated petrochemical complex, one of a handful of such complexes in the world.

Finding niches is only the first limb of our industrial strategy. Creating opportunities is the second limb of our policy. It is much tougher. We need to create the opportunities. This is akin to the "Blue Ocean Strategy" enunciated by Professors Chan Kim and Renée Mauborgne of INSEAD in their recent book.[1] Today, Singapore has to create opportunities for and by itself. We can no longer just be a niche in somebody's industrial pyramid. It is becoming harder to be part of a value chain that is open to all. We have had some experiences and successes.

One of these has been in forex trading. The Asian Dollar Market is the earliest example of Singapore creating an opportunity for itself in the trading

---

1 Chan Kim and Renée Mauborgne, *Blue Ocean Strategy: How to Create Uncontested Market Space and Make the Competition Irrelevant* (Boston, Mass.: Harvard Business School Press, 2005).

of the US Dollar. Previously, only New York, London, and Tokyo traded the US Dollar on the international markets.

It was Mr Van Oenen of the Bank of America who suggested that Singapore trade US Dollars when London went to bed, and before Tokyo woke up. All we needed to do was to fill in the time slot when no one else was trading. It was a simple, but brilliant idea. Singapore is today the world's third largest foreign exchange trading centre.

A second example was how we got into fruit farming in China. Very few Singaporeans know that "Fuji" apples, "Sunkist" oranges, luscious grapes, pears and peaches, apricots and persimmons, are grown by a Singapore company on 500-hectare orchards in Shangdong, China.

The man behind this remarkable project is Mr Ee Tai Tong, who started life as a pushcart cut fruit seller in Eu Tong Sen Street. His company, Fook Huat Tong Kee (FHTK), is one of the largest fruit importers and distributors in Singapore.

In traditional agriculture, farms in China, India, and Indonesia are postage-stamp sized, tilled by millions of peasant farming families. There was no economy of scale in production or marketing. To remedy the lack of scale, the Chinese Communist government consolidated the myriad of small farming plots into large communes. Economies of scale could not however be harnessed because farmers became employees, all eating from one iron rice pot. There was no sense of ownership or accountability.

Mr Ee's great contribution was to let the individual farmer continue to grow and nurture the fruit trees he is responsible for in two or three hectare lots. His company supplied the root stock and fertilisers. FHTK also guaranteed to take up to 90 per cent of the fruits produced at guaranteed prices. The farmer was free to sell the balance of 10 per cent on the market for whatever price he could get. This was to demonstrate that the prices paid by FHTK were fair and reasonable.

FHTK's pivotal contribution was the marketing and sale of products to overseas markets. By providing access to markets, FHTK is able to combine scale and incentive, making for a win-win partnership between the farmer and the fruit company.

The business model is sound, and FHTK should be able to come out of its current financial difficulties. More inspiring to me is the ability of a humble Singapore company creating opportunities, where none existed before.

A third example of creating opportunities was in prawn farming in Indonesia. In searching for and creating business opportunities where none existed before, an entrepreneur has to understand the business model in depth. Mr Shamjhul Nursalim of Gajah Tunggal and his wife were Indonesian Chinese who studied at Nanyang University in Singapore. They went on to build up their family firm into one of the largest conglomerates with the manufacture of bicycle and car tyres as the core.

The business lesson that I learnt from Mr Nursalim is not about the making of tyres. It is about a more basic activity, namely large-scale prawn farming. I came to know him when I was in DBS Bank. He needed a loan to build cold storage facilities at his prawn farm, which he said was the size of Singapore. Like FHTK with fruits, and indeed before them, he had adopted the system of having individual farming families tending ponds allotted to them. They harvested their own ponds and sold the catch to the central marketing company.

The large-scale decentralised farming of Gajah Tunggal and FHTK are not the insight Mr Nursalim gave me about his prawn business. He told me that in constructing a business model, the key decision is to identify the single most critical factor for success.

In the case of large-scale prawn farming, success or failure depends critically on the fertility of the mother prawn. A mother prawn spawns thousands of fry each time. Mr Nursalim employed a top notch marine biologist from Hawaii to enhance the fertility of mother prawns.

SWOT and Searching for Our Blue Oceans

Professor Chan Kim advocates Blue Ocean strategies where enterprises search for what he calls uncontested space. In other words, companies should move into uncongested markets, not into bloody, shark-infested Red Oceans.

In searching for uncontested Blue Ocean space, I believe that we should begin by assessing our strengths and weaknesses, otherwise known as SWOT analysis in the management idiom of an earlier decade.

Classical economics taught us that land, labour and capital are the three basic factors of production. What is Singapore's limitation? Simply put, it is our physical size. And the man-made one of a declining birth rate. It is not going to be easy. In the first three decades of development, Singapore practised the economic virtue of open markets and welcoming foreign direct investment. The economic and political landscape has completely changed. As a friend of mine said, the changes are seismic. The ground has been cut from under our feet.

All countries practise, or try to practise, good governance. Singapore is not the only virtuous state in the world. All countries, big and small, welcome foreign direct investments. China today attracts US$50 billion foreign direct investments a year. India, starting later, receives US$3 billion to US$4 billion. Soon, Vietnam, and not inconceivably even North Korea, will be competitors for foreign investments.

Multinational manufacturing companies from Japan, the United States, Europe, Hong Kong, and Taiwan brought with them not only their technology, but more crucially their markets. They established plants in Singapore to employ our semi-skilled, low-cost labour. Our administration is relatively efficient and free from corruption. Our policies were consistent and our legislation transparent and clear. Political stability and good governance are the strongest weapon in our armoury for competing in a knowledge-based global economy. Singapore possesses soft power more than hard power.[2]

How do we employ our soft power in the search for blue oceans? In what knowledge domains do we compete in?

Knowledge-based competition is now the norm. This was vividly brought home to me by a German consultant to the Environment Ministry. As Perm Sec (Budget), I visited the new Tuas incinerator plant. This plant cost about S$600 million then. When I arrived at the facility, the consultant shook my hands and thanked me profusely. I remarked that he and his firm must be extremely gratified to receive a consulting design fee of $50 million. He shook his head and said that he was not thanking me for the handsome fees earned. He said that he was grateful for the operational data collected.

As Singapore's climate was wet and humid, the rate of fuel injection to burn the garbage was quite different from the fuel consumption rates in the cold dry climate of temperate countries, such as Germany. The data collected would enable his company to design even more efficient plants for wet tropical locations, such as Kuala Lumpur, Bangkok and Jakarta. He thanked me for this knowledge he gained and would use.

Like him, we in Singapore now need to analyse what we do well and see if they are exportable to other markets and locations. This is especially for markets that share similarities with us, and in which we might have advantages, as compared to multinationals from elsewhere.

Hard Science or Soft Knowledge

A*STAR,[3] our agency for research in science and technology, is embarking on a vigorous PhD programme to educate and train as many of our best and brightest students in the hard science to enable Singapore to be part of cutting edge science, such as stem cell research. We will be competing in the red oceans of hard science alongside countries such as the United States, Russia, Western Europe, China and India, with their wealth of human talent and resources. I am not decrying A*STAR's Herculean efforts. I certainly hope

---

2 Mr Ngiam alludes to the distinction drawn by Joseph Nye between hard and soft power. Professor Nye developed the concept of soft power and defined it as "the ability to get what you want through attraction rather than through coercion". It differs from hard power which is the ability to use carrots and sticks of economic and military might to make others follow your will. This power "could be cultivated through relations with allies, economic assistance, and cultural exchanges". See Joseph S. Nye, *Soft Power: The Means to Success in World Politics* (United States: Public Affairs, 2004).

3 A*STAR is the Agency for Science, Technology and Research in Singapore. It comprises the Biomedical Research Council (BMRC), the Science and Engineering Research Council (SERC), Exploit Technologies Pte Ltd (ETPL), the A*STAR Graduate Academy (A*GA) and the Corporate Planning and Administration Division (CPAD). Its key focus is knowledge creation and the exploitation of scientific discoveries. For more information, see <http://www.a-star.edu.sg/astar/index.do> [7 March 2006].

that Singapore will one day produce a Nobel Laureate. Perhaps however, I can offer a different perspective.

In the 1970s, I visited the Boeing Company in Seattle in my capacity as a Singapore Airlines director. The President of the company received me. When I told him that I was very privileged to visit the world's leading commercial aircraft manufacturing company, he corrected me immediately. He said that Boeing is in essence an aviation marketing research company.

Boeing constantly scans the growth of air traffic between pairs of countries and cities. In-depth market research enables Boeing to decide on the size and range of aircraft for different traffic sectors. Boeing is probably the world's most successful commercial aircraft company. But the key to success is not the technology as much as the marketing fit. Having decided on the size of the aircraft for the different sectors, Boeing aeronautical engineers then set to design the aircraft. It buys 64,000 different parts, including the engine, which its engineers assemble into a Boeing 707. Boeing's technology is in the design of the aircraft to suit the different market segments.

Do we go for cutting edge science? Or soft knowledge?

In pondering this question, I recall a conversation I had with Mr Pieter Gyllanhammer in the 1970s. He was then the Chairman of Volvo, the leading Swedish automotive company. As Volvo at that time operated a motor assembly plant in Singapore, I asked him what he thought were the prospects for Singapore in the world automotive industry. In reply he asked me whether I wanted to know the truth, or just enjoy a cerebral massage. I asked to know the truth.

He told me that by the year 2000, there would be only about ten world-class car companies. To be in the game, a company must produce one million engines a year. Because of the scale of competition, he thought that North America would have two automotive companies, Europe one, China and India with one or two each, Japan two, South America may have one. He said that tiny Singapore and the rest of ASEAN should not even try.

However, countries like Singapore could still participate in the niches of the industry, such as car electronics. Mr Chan Chin Bock, my intrepid EDB colleague, rushed to Kokomo Illinois and persuaded General Motors (GM) to move their car radio plant, Delphi Electronics, to Singapore. This humble plant later grew to produce electronic car control systems for GM vehicles.

In my view, in a global economy, Singapore can best compete in the domain of soft knowledge, rather than hard technology.

The company that I chair, Surbana Corporation, has grown out of the Housing & Development Board (HDB). As HDB's development arm, we have designed and built 28 new towns in Singapore, changing the entire landscape. Modern high-rise towns have risen out of crumbling city slums and unsewered kampongs.

Mr Zhu Rongji, the former Prime Minister of China, and his mayoral colleagues when visiting Singapore have always stopped over at the HDB to be briefed on how we develop new towns and establish communities. They were very interested in the soft knowledge side of the business rather than hard construction techniques.

We have in the last 45 years established a Singapore branding, providing low-cost housing for the middle class. This branding stands Surbana in good stead as we seek business in China, India, the Middle East and South Africa.

We do not have the resources to make and sell hard technology. But we do have the soft knowledge to persuade others to do business with us. Besides housing, there are in my view three other areas where we can compete with the best in the world.

One of them is in teaching and education. Teaching is a soft skill. Good teachers are hard to find. Great teachers are rare. At school and university, we as students are truly blessed when we are taught difficult subjects by mentors who make understanding a subject effortless. It is a joy, not a chore, to learn. Our academic standards are high by international benchmarks. Our school and university students regularly win prizes at international mathematical or literary competitions. Though our middle class background provides the home support, it is our teachers and mentors who bring out the best in our students.

This was brought home to me when I visited the Salk Institute as an Eisenhower Fellow in 1985.[4] Research at the Institute led to the discovery of the anti-polio vaccine, which saved countless children in the 1960s from the dreaded disease. The director at the time of my visit was Professor Hoffman, a nuclear engineer by training. When I asked Professor Hoffman how we can raise the standard of physics and mathematics at the National University of Singapore, he offered to assemble teams of top scholars and, more importantly, great teachers in their domain to teach our students through video conferencing, which he said can be interactive as well. He added that during their summer vacations, these scholars can visit Singapore and give face to face tutorials to our final year students.

While Singapore does not yet have the star scholars to teach hard science and Mathematics, we do have the teachers who can help to develop the curriculum for Mathematics, Science and English at the primary and secondary school level. We can help to draft the curriculum for countries who want to use our methods of teaching and content.

As Singapore has spent the last 45 years honing our teaching skills, we can export these soft skills. Countries can jump-start their educational systems for a knowledge-based world. This is a new field of endeavour which

---

4 Eisenhower Fellowships engages emerging leaders from around the world to enhance their professional capabilities, broaden their contacts, and deepen their perspectives as they exchange ideas and experiences to foster mutual understanding. It is the exposure to businesses, governmental organisations, and civil society institutions that allow the fellows to examine, re-energise, or re-focus their personal and professional goals. Eisenhower website can be accessed at <http://eisenhowerfellowships.org/index.html> [7 March 2006].

will stand Singapore in good stead for years to come. I believe we have the critical factor for success.

A second area that should be considered is in medicine. This is a related area of soft knowledge which Singapore has the competitive edge. Traditionally, our best and brightest students have studied medicine at NUS and its predecessor institutions. Our geographical position, with comprehensive air connectivity, makes Singapore an ideal medical hub. We should develop and promote our cutting edge medical and surgical skills to care for both the seriously ill, and the professional who want a thorough rest and recreation medical check-up in Singapore, such as those provided by the specialist clinics in Switzerland.

A third area Singapore can look at is banking and, especially, financial services and wealth management for Asia's middle class. In my view, Singapore has the potential to be one of the world's great wealth management centres in banking. The middle class of Asia, whether in China, India, Malaysia, Indonesia, and Vietnam, are rapidly growing. As their incomes rise, the Asian middle class, like people everywhere else, will want to buy a car, then a house. They will expect and demand higher standards of education and health care for their children and themselves. After all these needs are met, they will have growing personal savings which they would want to invest for returns higher than bank deposit rates.

Singapore can become the wealth management centre for Asia. We have English and Chinese language skills, the savvy and the sophistication to appeal to the Asian middle class. Good governance, impartial courts of law, our honesty and integrity are the bedrock for wealth management. Our education system has produced a generation who are both literate and numerate, core skills required for banking.

In my personal view, the key factor for success in wealth management is sincerity and genuine friendship for the customer. Our bankers have to put the interest of the customer first. If we can deliver this intangible, there is nothing to stop us in the new blue ocean of banking and wealth management.

We have also honed our skills in consumer banking. These skills can be employed in China and India when our banks enter these markets. Housing loans is one area where we have considerable experience and expertise. Singapore banks could partner Chinese and Indian banks in mortgage loan financing.

Singapore banks are not large enough to compete in corporate banking. Corporate banking is the domain of the world-scale US, Japanese, and European banks. We can of course participate in loan syndications for giant infrastructural projects led by the larger international banks. But in my view our niche in banking is in wealth management for the rising middle class.

Developing our soft knowledge — in education, medicine, and wealth management — is the way to go. We can do hard science, but the rewards will be long in coming. Why not be true to ourselves and use the soft skills we have now?

The way forward for Singapore is finding niches and creating opportunities. It always has been so.

PART 3

LOOKING BACK, NAVIGATING FORWARD

SUCCESS AND FAILURE OF PUBLIC POLICIES: THE SINGAPORE EXPERIENCE, 1960–2000

How many Singaporeans, and What Types?

At a time when Singapore is not even replacing itself, it is difficult to recall that the population growth rate in the early 1960s was over 4 per cent. The rate of birth was 3.6 per cent. From today's perspective, such figures would seem to be a golden age. At the time, however, it was a nightmare. Our stop-at-two family planning policy has to be seen in this context.[1]

In a matter of two decades, our population growth rate leaned towards 2 per cent, and soon fell below that figure. This occurred in the mid-1970s when we achieved full employment, that is, we had an unemployment rate of below 3 per cent. What was known as "job-hopping" was the despair of employers.

How did this happen? Why was nothing done to try to stop it?

While our demographers were tracking the statistics, they failed to think out of the box. If they had, they might have realised that given abundant job

---

Edited from a speech given at "The Economic Society of Singapore Luncheon Discussion Series 2004" held on 15 Jan. 2004, OCBC Centre.

1   The post-independence period of the late sixties and the seventies saw the government embarking on a programme of urban renewal, socioeconomic planning and extensive industrialisation. At that time, the country was beset with an urban housing shortage, large-scale unemployment, and a net population increase as death rates fell and birth rates remained high. The government felt that the achievement on the economic front would be swallowed up by an unsustainably large population, and began a family planning programme to encourage families to "stop-at-two (children)" by offering practical incentives and disincentives. See Wong, Theresa and Brenda Yeoh, "Fertility and the Family: An Overview of Pro-natalist Population Policies in Singapore", in *Asian MetaCentre Research Paper Series* no. 12. Asia Research Institute, National University of Singapore.

opportunities, married women chose paid employment outside the home to having more babies and domestic chores. It is worse that single women chose careers over marriage.

Even as the birth rates were falling, the Ministry of Health and the Family Planning Board continued to fly on the auto-pilot policy of penalising the third child.

In the early years, when numbers were literally drowning us, our immigration policy was to bridge the talent gap. The Trade Department of the Ministry of Finance introduced what was known as the Immigration Deposit Scheme.

For a $1 million deposit, entrepreneurs from around the region could settle their families in Singapore as permanent residents. They are free to invest their funds in industries on a list suggested by us. That was how NatSteel, OG Garments, Malayan Steel Pipes, and a host of other SMEs started in Singapore.

Even when the EDB was scrambling for every job in the international market place, those of us who were at the frontline of job creation realised we did not have the critical mass to be an industrial nation. Our population was then around 3 million.

What was the magic figure? Four million, five million, six million? We compared ourselves to countries like Switzerland, Israel and Sweden. Our physical planners in the Urban Redevelopment Authority (URA)[2] poured over their maps to determine the optimum size of population that Singapore could accommodate.

But were we asking the right questions? If size alone counts, then countries like China and India would have long ago dominated the world, as indeed they now can by opening up their societies and economies.

What then are the options for small states like Singapore?

Competition in the global economy has moved from a resource base of land, labour and capital, to a knowledge driven race in education, technology, skills, and organisation. Sheer population size is no longer decisive, if it ever was. What counts is the average level of academic education of the bulk of the population.

When I was Chairman of the EDB in the 1970s, a former President of the Matsushita Corporation of Japan, Mr Yamashita, told me that Japan was strong in manufacturing because the average level of schooling of the population then was senior high (roughly the equivalent of 'A' levels in Singapore). He also made the point that what counts is to have a high massive plateau of people with a high average level of education.

At that time, Singapore did not have such a high plateau for the mass of our people. Instead, we had high peaks of academic achievement by our President Scholars, our modern day imperial scholars who are of course

---

2   The Urban Redevelopment Authority (URA) is Singapore's national land use planning authority. URA prepares long-term strategic plans, as well as detailed local area plans, for physical development, and then co-ordinates and guides efforts to bring these plans to reality. Prudent land use planning has enabled Singapore to enjoy strong economic growth and social cohesion, and ensures that sufficient land is safeguarded to support continued economic progress and development. See URA website: <http://www.ura.gov.sg/> [7 March 2006].

a matter of pride not only to their families, but also the country. But Mr Yamashita's deeper point to me is that an education system should not be totally dedicated to producing imperial scholars. It is better for the country to achieve high national averages. He preferred massive plateaus to high solitary peaks.

Which should Singapore prefer? Which would be better for our economic development? Of course, we can say "both". But priorities have to be clear. I believe that Singapore has to resolve this conflict in our national psyche. If we prefer to promote high peaks for some, we have to consider a second question: When does meritocracy end and elitism begin?

When we thought we had too many people in the early years, we kept people out except for the $1 million entrepreneurial depositor families. When our birth rate fell below the replacement rate, we panicked. We introduced the landed PR scheme for people from Hong Kong just before 1997, when the territory reverted from British colonial rule to mainland China, and some people felt uncertain.

Other than those with criminal records, at that time, any Hong Kong family could literally obtain PR status on arrival at Changi Airport. Even then, many Hongkongers thumbed their noses at us.

The few who did accept PR in Singapore promptly bought an HDB flat on the resale market, which they were allowed to let out because they did not stay to work in Singapore. When property prices rose, they gave up their PR and sold their flats for a capital gain. Few have stayed.

In a knowledge-based world of global competition, sheer numbers alone are not enough. What counts is the quality of the numbers.

I venture to suggest that the average level of education of Singaporeans should be at least 'A' or polytechnic levels. All PR applicants should be better. Their role is to help raise our average, not just to add to our numbers. We need to build up this critical mass of people as quickly as possible from our own people and selective immigration.

The name of the game is to build up the numbers and quality. If we go about it methodically, we may have 10 to 20 years to build up the critical mass. The critical mass is however a moving target.

Education: Content, Creativity, Substance

Not being a teacher, I am not acquainted with theories of education. But I was privileged to know the late Mr Tan Teck Chwee,[3] an illustrious chairman of our Public Service Commission. Mr Tan was a teacher at

---

3   The late Mr Tan Teck Chwee was the Chairman of the Public Service Commission (PSC). The PSC is a key pillar of the public service. Constituted in 1951 as an organ of state, it serves as the independent custodian of the integrity, impartiality and values of the system. See the PSC website at <http://app. psc.gov.sg/index.asp>.

Raffles Institution in the early years of his career. He told me that before anyone can be selected to be trained as a teacher, the person must have a first degree in a teaching subject. The person must have content before he can teach.

Similar advice was given to Dr Albert Winsemius, our government's economic adviser then, by Dr Pannenberg, who was the R&D head of Philips of Holland. He told Dr Winsemius that his grandson should do a first degree in engineering before he specialises in software and computers for which the boy had a special talent. A person must have a thorough grounding in one intellectual discipline before he can be creative in his chosen field of endeavour.

Singapore is undertaking educational reform. But the point about education made by Mr Tan Teck Chwee is still valid: a person must be deeply immersed in the basic of a subject before one is able to solve problems and be creative. While I am all for fun learning, especially for my grandchildren, I hope that the growing effervescence of spirit in our schools will not be overdone so much so that it turns into froth. In our heart of hearts, we all know that learning is hard work. It is not just play.

By most measures of academic achievement, our schools, polytechnics and universities have done well. Both Singapore and MNC employers acknowledge that our graduates are competent. They know "how to get things done", but when faced with a roadblock, they often cannot figure out the "why".

To succeed in discovering new knowledge you need the spark of brilliance. Eureka does not come at the flip of a switch. Mr Evan Erikksen, President of Sundstrand, is the man who invented the constant speed drive for jet engines. He told me that when he was a young research engineer he could not wait for the sun to rise before rushing off to his research lab. Mr Erikksen held no fewer than three patents, which were the foundation of success of his company.

This reminds me of a demonstration that Professor Shih Choon Fong, the President of the National University of Singapore, once gave with a block of ice. While the ice shatters an impact when dropped from a height, it will remain a solid block when tissue fibre is mixed with the water before freezing. A materials science professor, Professor Shih then compared the qualities of steel, plastics and glass. Steel is the strongest proportional to weight, and plastics, the most malleable. Glass, which at first sight is the weakest compared to steel, and most brittle compared to plastics, turns out to be the best material when pure glass fibres are fused with plastic to produce, say, a strong lightweight car chassis.

What is Singapore made of?

Singapore with a population of 4 million cannot play the "steel" numbers game alongside China and India with their billion populations.

But an educated 4 million population can endure, if we have some of the globally mobile talented (including our own), to be engaged, work, live, and stay in Singapore, perhaps not for a lifetime but in the prime of their lives. In this way, the nation of Singapore will be larger than the country of Singapore. The "little red dot" will grow into a centre of world civilisation, and not fade away into history.[4]

Finances and the Inverted Pyramid of Taxes

In most countries, the public finance structure is a pyramid where the broad based 90 per cent of the population support the poorest 10 per cent. Singapore is an exception. We are an inverted pyramid where the most able 10 per cent support the other 90 per cent. A mere 10 per cent of the population pays all the income taxes. They also pay the bulk of dividend taxes, tax on interest, property and estate. The net balances in the CPF accounts are also saved by this group.

Because of this inverted pyramid character, public finances in Singapore are like a spinning top. So long as the momentum is strong, at an annual GDP growth rate of 8 per cent or better, the social compact prevails. But when the growth rate is halved to 4 per cent or less, the top wobbles and social fissures will appear. There are some signs of unease even now.

Members of the upper middle class who do not enjoy public housing subsidies or conservancy rebates are increasingly frustrated by what they view as populist schemes, such as the ERS share schemes.[5] Cars, housing and education of children are more expensive in Singapore than even in the capital cities of developed countries. The upper middle class feel they must meet these costs without much visible benefit.

There are strong expectations in some quarters that income taxes should be lower for the upper middle class. So when personal income tax rates are dropped, the Goods and Services Tax (GST) on purchases goes up by about one per cent plus one per cent, bringing about a general rise in the retail price index. We have to remember that prices are sticky downwards. This affects all Singaporeans, whether rich or poor, and the government has felt it necessary to give more rebates to the poor to offset the GST increase.

---

4   Refer to footnote 3 on page 107.

5   The Economic Restructuring Shares (ERS) is part of an offset package to help Singaporeans adapt to structural changes in the Singapore economy, especially the increase in the Goods and Services Tax (GST) from 3 to 5 per cent between Jan. 2003 to Jan. 2004. The shares earn dividends every year until the end of 2007. The first lot was issued in 2003, the second in 2004 and the third and final lot in 2005. Information on the ERS can be found at <http://www.mof.gov.sg/budget_2002/offset/faq-ers. doc> [7 March 2006].

As a result, the revenue impact is at best neutral. It may have in fact been slightly negative when we first introduced GST in 1996, at a rate of 3 per cent. I hope my guess at the arithmetic is wrong. But more than this, I would argue that the government ought to cut its own expenditure to make up for the loss of revenue from an income tax cut, rather than to seek to raise taxes from the GST or other sources.

Moreover, the best time to cut income tax is when an economy is booming. A lower rate of tax from an expanding economy will still yield higher revenue. In contrast, if taxes are cut during a recession, a lower rate of tax can only lead to even lower revenue.

In our early struggling years, Singapore offered zero per cent pioneer tax status to companies. The MNCs came and their operations in Singapore were fabulously profitable when compared with operations in their home countries. But I wish to emphasise that this was possible because Singapore then was competitive. Pioneer status was a bonus given to MNCs after they came, and not before.

Being a former Permanent Secretary of the Ministry of Finance, I do not wish to be cast as a gloom monger. But I do believe that "tax gymnastics" shifting from income tax to other tax sources is not a panacea to our problem. Such gymnastics can only pile on the costs of doing business in Singapore. We have to face reality, and tighten our belts. To do otherwise, is to lose the people we need most — the pure glass strands in materials science.

Competitiveness, Currency and CPF Cuts

In the mid-1970s, I was invited by Dr Goh Keng Swee, who was then the Chairman of MAS, to attend its weekly staff meetings, normally held on Monday mornings. The meetings were in effect tutorials that Dr Goh conducted in order to train his officers on how to read interest and exchange rates in the coming week.

Out of this baptism of fire, we have produced men such as Ng Kok Song, who is Managing Director (public markets) of the Government of Singapore Investment Corporation (GIC), and Seck Wai Keong, now with Singapore Exchange (SGX). It was excruciating even for me, a non-combatant from the Ministry of Finance, when forecasts made were way off the mark against the actuals as recorded by another officer Chuang Kwong Yong who had a precise methodical way. Kwong Yong has risen to be Singapore's Auditor-General. He was helping Dr Goh to audit the performance of our young money managers then in training. Dr Goh was however more interested in their reasoning than in the actual results. After university, this was the most intellectually stimulating period for me.

The honeymoon lasted until the day I had the temerity to challenge Dr Goh's exchange rate policy. Under Dr Goh, and to this day, the instinct of the MAS was always for a strong Singapore dollar to the point that it became a badge of honour. The *raison d'etre* is that a strong currency keeps imported inflation at bay.

Has this been carried too far?

By the early 1980s, Singapore's competitiveness in the international markets was rapidly eroded. Dr Tan Kong Yam, who became the chief economist of the Ministry of Trade and Industry (MTI), argued that this was because of what he called "the twin blades" (as in a pair of scissors) of high wages and a "strong", overvalued currency.

Dr Goh would not give way on the exchange rate. Dr Winsemius and I would not budge on our wage adjustment policy which aimed deliberately to raise wages to help restructure our economy. This resulted in a policy tug-of-war between the MAS which is in charge of our currency, and the MTI. This was resolved only when the government accepted the recommendation of the first 1986 Economic Review Committee to cut the employers' CPF contribution by 16 per cent.[6] With this, CPF was slashed from 46 per cent to 30 per cent.[7]

The full burden of this economic adjustment fell on labour. The CPF cut of 16 per cent was, in effect, a wage cut. Weeks before this cut was made, both then PM Lee Kuan Yew, and then DPM Goh Chok Tong, were making speeches to the effect that the CPF was sacrosanct and would never be cut.

I was then Permanent Secretary for the Ministry of Trade and Industry, and I went to see Dr Goh, always the *eminence grise* on economic policy. He told me that there were no sacred cows in politics.

So I pressed this insider's knowledge on Lee Hsien Loong, who was then the Minister for Trade and Industry, to cut the employer CPF contribution by 10 per cent, as recommended by the Committee. In the event, even more — 16 per cent — was cut. Our people swallowed bitter medicine in one gulp. Within two years the economy recovered.

I now know that Lee Hsien Loong, my Minister then, was against a cut. He was wrong then. A CPF cut was the only available policy instrument for the situation in the mid-1980s. However, he would have been right if he had rejected the CPF cut option, recommended by the second Economic Restructuring Review Committee of 2002–3.

What, in my view, are the differences between these two cuts?

The CPF cut in 1986 was bold and decisive. It would have been of lasting value if it had been a permanent cut, a basic structural adjustment. Instead, it was eventually adjusted upwards from 10 per cent to 16 per cent for employers.

---

6 The Central Provident Fund (CPF) is a comprehensive social security savings plan, which has provided many working Singaporeans with a sense of security and confidence in their old age. The overall scope and benefits of the CPF encompass retirement, healthcare, home ownership, family protection and asset enhancement. More information available at: <http://www.cpf.gov.sg/cpf_info/home.asp> [10 Jan. 2006].

7 Currently, it stands at 33 per cent.

The cut of 3 per cent recommended in 2002–3 was even more tentative. We have not been facing up to our loss in competitiveness. Wage increases have been exceeding productivity increases for far too long. We have introduced too much uncertainty into the decision-making process for foreign investors. Investors are prepared to adjust to market pressures, but they will not accept government-mandated wage cost increases.

The CPF is the one silver bullet adjustment to be used in extremis, such as in 1986 when it was reduced to 30 per cent. It should have been a permanent change. Instead, it crept up once again to 36 per cent, before being again reduced, to 33 per cent. The uncertainty introduced is bad for the forward planning that companies and employers need. Most of them are already attracted by China, and soon India, and will vote with their feet.

A fluctuating CPF contribution rate by employers is also bad for the government agencies such as the Housing & Development Board (HDB) and Ministry of Health (MOH). Both of these rely on CPF as a major factor in their own planning. CPF contributions are a key to the affordability of housing and HDB units. Part of the purpose of the overall CPF is also to fund medical care, in terms of the special account for medisave.

When CPF rates rise above 30 per cent, HDB will be tempted to overbuild, as they anticipate more demand. This is not only in terms of numbers of housing units, but also in terms of the size of flats that buyers with more CPF feel they want and can afford. Similarly, MOH will rush in to increase Medisave rates the moment the employers' rate rises.

I believe the MOF has been studying what should be the optimum CPF rate. Let me suggest that my former Ministry adopt what Dr Goh would approve as a robust approach in policy making. I propose that the CPF rate be fixed permanently at 20 per cent for employees' contribution and 10 per cent for employers'. Saving 20 per cent of one's monthly salary to pay the housing loan mortgage is not an unreasonable arrangement. HDB's calculation of affordability will be less optimistic and more concrete. The tendency to overbuild will be curbed.

When I was Chairman of the HDB, then PM Goh Chok Tong had suggested to me that the carrying cost of unsold flats be met from HDB's operating budget. My HDB management was horrified!

Similarly, MOH would have to accept that the Medisave rate would have to be frozen at its current 6–8.5 per cent, depending on age group and sector. Savings for old age, which is a tiny 4 per cent, can only increase if we are able to cut back the portion for housing to below 20 per cent. The political arithmetic is tough, but it has to be done if we are to retain the confidence of investors and employers. Any real wage increase must come from real increases in productivity.

Productivity increases in Singapore have long lagged wage increases. This time around, the adjustment must fall on all Singaporeans, not just labour. The other blade of the policy "scissors", the exchange rate, has to be used.

The MAS under Dr Goh has pegged the Singapore Dollar exchange rate to a weighted basket of currencies. In other words, the exchange rate band is calculated on the balance of trade flows with major trading partners, such as the USA, China, Malaysia, Indonesia, Japan and the European Union. It is a clinical approach giving intellectual satisfaction.

But in the real world, nearly everybody trades in the US Dollar. Two of our major trading partners, China (including Hong Kong), and Malaysia, and one can even argue a case for Japan, have pegged their currencies to the US Dollar. Under the old Currency Board system, the Malayan Dollar was pegged to the pound sterling, and when it devalued, we pegged the new Singapore Dollar to gold. The old Currency Board system did not allow the colonies, such as Singapore, to depreciate their currencies as it has to be fully backed by gold. Gold was and still is a stable store of value. So long as a currency is 100 per cent backed by gold or foreign currencies, it will always be convertible and stable.

The break-up of the Bretton Woods agreement by US President Nixon, resulting in floating exchange rate regimes, made life more difficult for central banks, but not impossible. Instead of fine tuning exchange rate fluctuations, the weighted basket of currencies approach, it would be better in my view to simply peg the Singapore Dollar to the US Dollar, just as Malaysia and China have done. The whole world prices in US Dollar. If the price of exports from Singapore goes up in US Dollars, it is a clear signal that we are less competitive, for whatever reason.

So long as we stick to the straight and narrow road of balanced budgets and do not induce our CPF savers to participate in stock markets, the Singapore Dollar will always be fully convertible, a *sine qua non* of competing in a global knowledge-based economy.

This impacts on how we look at the reserves that Singapore holds. From time to time, when times are hard, there are calls in our Parliament to spend our reserves to "tide us over". The MAS should educate the people to understand that our reserves are our best guarantee for a stable, fully convertible currency. Without such a currency, we will not be able to import anything. Unlike the Americans, we are just too minuscule for anyone to give us any long-term credit. Our real reserves are the budget surpluses and net CPF balances accumulated over the years. Any reserve over this hard core are just temporary funds parked with our banks because the depositors expect the Singapore Dollar to appreciate, or our interest rates are attractive, or both.

MAS, in my view, should not just look at the gross official reserves, but the net core of reserves, i.e., what really belongs to us and over which we have control. Hence, my "kiasu" attitude against MAS' strong Singapore Dollar stance. If the hedge funds sense that our currency is overvalued, they can make a meal of us in a morning's trading.

What Singapore needs is a stable fully convertible currency like the old Singapore Dollar under the Currency Board system.

Land and Transport Policy

In Singapore's context, land and transport policies are intertwined. As early as the late 1960s, the Ministry of National Development established the State and City Planning Office, which evolved into what is now the Urban Renewal Authority (URA).

This institution proposed what is now built as the Pan-Island Expressway (PIE), the spinal pan island expressway, the East Coast Parkway (ECP) as the east west parkway, and the Central Expressway (CTE), the north-south central expressway. Our planners told us that these expressways, which are land-intensive, are just to meet basic needs.

To be a modern dynamic city, we need to invest in a mass rapid transit system to get people to work on time in the morning and to be home in time for dinner in the evening. Such a system has to be rail-based with clear rights of way in the form of tracks. Bus lanes are a second best choice; motorists who pay most of the road taxes have no rights at all when bus lanes are imposed.

Very few of us know that the USSR government offered to build Singapore a mass transit system in the mid-1960s. According to Mr Howe Yoon Chong, who was then Permanent Secretary of National Development, we could have had that system built for less than $1 billion, if we had accepted the Russian offer.

When Singapore decided to build the Mass Rapid Transit (MRT) in the late 1970s, it cost us $5 billion. Such a heavy investment triggered an intense debate, both in private and in public. In one corner of the ring was MOF, led by Dr Goh, who argued for an all bus system. On this occasion, Dr Goh lost the debate.

When I asked him years later after he lost the fight why he was so adamant for an all bus system when it was clear that our roads cannot take the load, he offered the explanation that it was better to make mistakes in small incremental steps, i.e., bus by bus, than to sink in $5 billion on an unknown and untested system. Until today, I still cannot make up my mind whether Dr Goh was serious in his view, or speaking tongue in cheek.

The pro-MRT believers were more numerous, namely Howe Yoon Chong, the late Teh Cheang Wan who was the Minister for National Development, Lim Leong Geok[8] and I, as Permanent Secretary of the Ministry of Communications, from 1970–2.

The then Prime Minister Lee Kuan Yew and Hon Sui Sen, the Finance Minister, were the referees.

---

8   The late Mr Lim Leong Geok was the Chief Planner at the Planning Department of the Ministry of National Development; the Deputy Director of Public Works Department; and Executive Director of Singapore Bus Services Ltd (1978). He was the Executive Director of the Mass Rapid Transit Corporation from 1983 to 1994, and was responsible for the building of the current MRT system in Singapore.

Joe Pillay led the official Finance team. Even then, Dr Goh nearly torpedoed the MRT proposal by asking what I would call an economist's "trick" question. He asked Lim Leong Geok whether it was justifiable to sink about $300,000 per head so that the morning commuter can get to work on time in the CBD.

Unfortunately, I was not present at the meeting when Dr Goh unleashed his killer question. I would have argued that an MRT system, by providing easy access to suburban Singapore, would in itself raise property value. Without raising property tax rates, the increased value of properties would generate increased revenue, which would rise to yield the $5 billion required to build the first MRT east-west line.

Teh Cheang Wan, who was then the Minister for National Development, made the same point, but in a more dramatic way. He said that land sales on the newly-reclaimed Marina Singapore city site would provide all the capital needed to build the MRT lines.

To be fair to Dr Goh, his conviction that an all bus system would serve as well was never put to the test. The younger Ministers adopted a fail safe position. Under the guise of rationalisation, bus services into the city, which paralleled the MRT route, were terminated. Additionally, although the MRT was a superior service, MRT fares were only marginally higher than bus fares, which affectively increased demand for the MRT.

I recall vividly how the then PM Lee Kuan Yew urged his Cabinet to set MRT fares at levels much higher than bus fares. He made the point that if initial fares are not set at fair economic value — for a superior service to command a premium *vis-à-vis* bus fares — we would be stuck with uneconomic fares forever. This has turned out to be the case. By not biting the bullet at the beginning, public transportation fares are held political hostage.

The Singapore Traction Company, a significant bus operator, collapsed in 1970, and the then Minister for Communications, Mr Yong Nyuk Lin,[9] myself as his Permanent Secretary, and Mr Goh Yong Hong,[10] who then head the registry of vehicles (ROV), had to scramble. Our task was to organise the four main Chinese bus companies operating in the north, east and west to take over the STC routes into the CBD.

We swore never again to depend on one major bus company alone. On my return to MOF in 1972, I was therefore startled to read in the newspapers that the government would merge all four bus companies into one sole provider, namely Singapore Bus Services. Wiser counsel prevailed later and Trans-Island

9   Mr Yong Nyuk Lin was the former Minister for Education and Communications.

10 Mr Goh Yong Hong was the Commissioner of Police from 1979–92, and Executive Deputy Chairman of Singapore Turf Club until 2002. He was also Vice President of the National Olympic Council and Singapore Sports Council. He is currently on the Board of Directors of Asia Pacific Breweries Ltd and sits as an independent Director in listed SC Global Ltd, Guocoland Ltd and Dragon Land Ltd.

Bus Service (TIBS) was founded almost as an afterthought to be a second bus company.

Some 30 years on, we are having a similar debate. But the question of whether we should have one company as the sole rail operator in Singapore, or two is not the right question to ask.

As Dr Goh would have insisted, the competitive test is between rail and bus operations. The comparison is not between Singapore Mass Rapid Transport (SMRT) and SBS Delgro. A duopoly in Singapore's small market may be worse than a monopoly.

The root of the problem, as Lim Leong Geok told me some years later, is that after the epic battle to build the first MRT line, it became too easy to go on to build the second, and then the third line. Dr Goh is no longer around to scrutinise the case for rail systems. The administration just flew on auto pilot. Because of their "kiasu" mindset, they made an uneven playing field more so. The Public Transport Council, which is consulted on any fare increase, should take a sabbatical; as should the National Wages Council (NWC), which has been instrumental in increasing wages across the board, regardless of productivity and competitiveness. As Hon Sui Sen would have said, government should learn to leave well alone.

Let buses compete with rail freely. Fare increases (or decreases) should be decided by the respective operators. School bus operators do not need to ask the Public Transport Council when they increase their charges.

Land Policy: Value, Asset Enhancement

Housing 85 per cent of the population in 900,000 flats is no mean achievement by the HDB.[11] Few know that the cornerstone of our vast low cost housing programmes is the Land Acquisition Act.[12]

The Act allows the State to acquire private land for public purpose at pre-development prices. Dr Goh asked me, when I was a young officer, to draft the Cabinet memorandum proposing that the compensation to be paid for land acquired exclude its potential value.

Why should this be excluded?

We saw no reason why landlords should benefit from public infrastructural investment in roads, drainage, sewerage, power and water pipelines, etc. We

---

11 HDB was set up in 1960, at a time when a large number of people were still living in unhygienic, potentially hazardous slums and crowded squatter settlements packed in the city centres. Taking over from the Singapore Improvement Trust, HDB built 21,000 flats in less than three years and by 1965, it had built 54,000 flats. Today, about 84 per cent of Singaporeans live in HDB flats compared with only 9 per cent in 1960. More information available at: <http://www.hdb.gov.sg> [10 Jan. 2006].

12 Refer to footnote 2 on p. 101.

would pay only the market value of raw land before public development. Our policy discouraged land speculation. The development charge imposed for change of use falls within the same concept.

In effect, the State creamed off about half the potential value. Very few governments are electorally strong enough to implement such a robust policy. But the PAP government did.

Sadly the clarity of thought shown by Dr Goh in pricing land has been lacking in more recent years. Relying on the concept of opportunity cost, the Chief Valuer, at the behest of either the Ministry of National Development or the Ministry of Trade and Industry (I am not sure which), has valued land across Singapore using Raffles Place land as the benchmark. The assumption is that every square metre of land in any part of Singapore has the potential to be Raffles Place.

I was in the Ministry of Finance and had no inkling of what was happening until the Ministry of Community Development and Sports (MCDS) came rushing to us to give them a supplementary budget to help voluntary bodies running charity homes to pay their substantially increased rentals on premises belonging to the Land Office.[13] Similarly, EDB asked for more funds to help defray the higher land cost of MNCs setting up wafer fabrication plants in Singapore. We kidded ourselves into thinking that we are the only intelligent island in the world and ignored the fact that other countries would offer cheap land to such companies.

As a result, PSA[14] priced itself out of the market for transhipment. Unwittingly, we gave its Malaysian rival, Tanjong Pelepas, the window of opportunity.

One of the main causes of Singapore's loss of competitiveness in recent years is our perverse land pricing policy. What did it achieve to send prices and valuations so high? It was no more than a muddle headed book keeping exercise. MOF paid out subsidies to MCDS and EDB, which were returned to MOF as land revenue. In one mistaken manoeuvre, overall land price shot up and Singapore lost part of its competitiveness.

Those of us who grew up after the war in the 1950s will recall the festering urban slums of Chinatown and the mosquito-ridden kampongs of Toa Payoh. So when our families moved into high-rise HDB flats from the mid-1960s onwards, it was like paradise on earth. The EDB worked in tandem

---

13 The Land office has merged with the Singapore Land Registry, Survey Department and Land Systems Support Unit in 2001 to form the Singapore Land Authority (SLA) which is a statutory board under the Ministry of Law. SLA's main role is the development and management of state land and the regulation of land use. See SLA website at <http://www.sla.gov.sg/htm/hom/index.htm> [8 March 2006].

14 PSA was formerly the Port of Singapore Authority, a statutory board regulating, developing, operating and promoting the port of Singapore's terminals. In 1996, PSA's regulatory functions were handed over to the Maritime and Port Authority of Singapore. PSA Corporation Ltd was subsequently incorporated in 1997 as the corporate successor to the Port of Singapore Authority to manage and operate its terminals and related businesses. In 2003, PSA International became the investment holding company for PSA's businesses in Singapore and worldwide. PSA International is fully-owned by Temasek Holdings.

with the HDB. The EDB found the jobs, and the HDB built flats at the rate of one flat every 36 minutes. It was a winning combination underpinning the electoral success of the PAP at every general election since. Jobs and housing secured the mandate of heaven for the PAP led by Mr Lee Kuan Yew.

Mr Howe Yoon Chong, the first CEO of HDB, once startled his ministerial colleagues by proposing that we close down the HDB as it had by then housed some 80 per cent of the people. He thought that we should leave it to the private sector to build for the other 20 per cent.

But old habits, particularly success, die hard, and the HDB was not shut down.

So from providing a first home for a family, we went on to give them a second bite of the cherry by giving a second loan to upgrade from a 3- to a 4- or 5-room flat.

As property prices were rising in the 1980s, there was good cheer all round. The HDB thought they had an endless queue for new flats and went into overdrive. But the party had to end.

The Asian financial crisis in the mid-1990s led to a sharp and sudden fall in demand, particularly those who were hoping to make money by upgrading. The queue disappeared, and HDB was left with unsold flats, some 17,000 units. HDB would have gone bankrupt years ago if it had been a private company. But as a statutory board, it was kept afloat by MOF, which picked up the tab.

With falling demand for new flats, the HDB was asked to embark on what is now known as the interim and main upgrading programme, i.e., the IUP and the MUP.

When first conceived, the clear intention was for the lessee to pay 50 per cent of the cost, with the other 50 per cent from the government. But to qualify for these upgrading schemes, there needed to be a 75 per cent majority to vote for upgrading, and to secure that vote, the share of the lessee was reduced from 50 per cent to nearer 20 per cent. It was our "kiasu" way of obtaining the mandate to upgrade. Even then, in one or two polls in recent years, the HDB could not secure the 75 per cent majority to proceed. The reason was simply that the increase in the resale value of the flat after upgrading has of late been less than the cost of upgrading. So much for asset enhancement in property.

Similarly, the dividend yield from discounted SingTel[15] shares bought by CPF members in the Initial Public Offering (IPO) has been less than 2.5 per cent, which is the minimum paid by CPF on members' balances. There was no secondary market for SingTel shares after listing because the share was

---

15 SingTel was incorporated in 1992 and became a public company in 1993 with its Initial Public Offering (IPO), which was Singapore's largest (SingTel is the largest company listed on the Singapore Exchange with a market capitalisation of about S$34 billion as of May 2005). The IPOs were over-whelmingly received as citizens were given the opportunity to share the upside potential and growth

priced at the margin of \$3.60. There was nothing left on the table for anyone except the government shareholder. While the laudable intention of the issue was to enhance the asset value of the ordinary CPF member, the market taught everyone a hard lesson. There was no free lunch.

As Chairman of the CPF then, I had urged the MOF to pay CPF members the government long-term bond rate of about 4 per cent at the time, instead of promoting unit trusts for them to invest in. The CPF minnow would surely be swallowed by the shark in the unequal market place. What pains me most is having invested in the market, the CPF member has nothing left to pay his HDB mortgage when he loses his job.

Famous Last Words

When Mr Lim Siong Guan was Permanent Secretary for Defence, he came to see me one day to discuss the concept of total defence. We both agreed that total defence would have to embrace economic defence, social defence, psychological defence, and from MINDEF's point of view, the bedrock of military defence. Having spent most of my career in the economic ministries, I thought that a strong economy is the bedrock of everything else, including military defence. We agreed to disagree.

I would just end by paraphrasing Lord Keynes, who said that even the wisest statesman is often the slave of some defunct philosopher. In plain English, the politician is often misled by the economist. So, for those of us who profess to be professional economists, heavy is our responsibility. In this spirit, I would urge my fellow economists in government to accept that sometimes we can be grievously wrong.

---

of SingTel through the government's share-ownership scheme — under the scheme, Singaporeans were allowed to purchase designated SingTel IPO shares at discount using their savings in the Central Provident Fund (CPF) accounts. In 2001, SingTel concluded its largest overseas investment, with the acquisition of Optus — the second largest telecommunications provider in Australia. It also invested in Telkomsel in Indonesia and the Bharti Group in India, and increased its stake in Globe Telecom in the Philippines. Today, SingTel is Asia's largest multi-market mobile operator. Temasek Holdings owns 63 per cent of SingTel. For more information, see <http://home.singtel.com/about_singtel/company_profile/default.asp> [8 March 2006].

STATE CAPITALISM AND ENTREPRENEURS

When I was an undergraduate at the University of Malaya, located then at the Bukit Timah campus in Singapore, development economics was a new topic in the curriculum. It was not a full-fledged course. Classical economics rightly was *de rigueur*. Econometrics was a young infant. Development economics, which dealt with the problems of overpopulation and poverty in poor countries, was not yet on the intellectual horizon.

My generation only knew of one economist who wrote on the problems of development in poor countries. He was Professor Arthur Lewis of Manchester University. Originally from Jamaica, he expounded with great clarity and empathy the economic theories underlying economic and social problems in developing countries. His book on economic development is very readable. I would recommend a re-read if we feel overwhelmed by the challenges of a global economy today. Professor Lewis' advice is to stick to basics.[1]

In contrast to Professor Lewis' eloquent prose is the work of another great economist in the 1950s. Professor Walt Rostow's classic work on the

---

Edited from a speech at the "Young Presidents' Organization breakfast talk", 2 July 2004, Marriot Hotel.

1 Lewis wrote several books, including *The Principles of Economic Planning* (London: D. Dobson, 1949); *The Theory of Economic Growth* (London: Allen & Unwin, 1957); *Development Planning* (London: Allen & Unwin, 1966), *Tropical Development 1880–1913* (London: Allen & Unwin, 1970), and *Growth and Fluctuations 1870–1913* (London: Allen & Unwin, 1978). In his early writings, Arthur Lewis challenged the hallowed international division of labour which ascribed to the developing world the role of provider of primary products to the developed world in exchange for manufactured goods. Instead, he prescribed import substitution and the development of self-sufficient economy. If there was a choice between foreign investment and domestic capital, the latter should be preferred. In the absence of domestic capital, foreign investment should favour the domestic economy and contribute to the development of entrepreneurial, management and administrative skills.

three stages of economic growth often serve as the theoretical underpinning of thinking on how countries develop.[2]

According to Professor Rostow, the first stage of economic growth is in agriculture. Only when farmers produce more than they consume, will there be a surplus. When there is an agricultural surplus, farmers will have the purchasing power to buy the manufactures of the craftsmen, such as clothing. When there is buoyant demand for manufactures the craftsmen will have the savings to buy the services of doctors and teachers. The three stages of growth are primary (agriculture), secondary (manufacture), and tertiary (service).

If I may bring Professor Rostow's theory up to date, intellectual property (IP) can be considered to be the fourth stage of growth. But is it the ultimate stage of growth?

Capital Formation and State Capitalism

In Rostow's work, the production of a surplus sustains the next stage of growth. But growth is triggered only when there is capital formation. Who, or what, starts this whole process?

In early history, the sovereign of the land is the only one with the clout to accumulate resources to build palaces, public works, or defences. An indulgent emperor would build palaces or monuments to glorify himself. An enlightened emperor would build roads and canals to link his vast territory, and dams and waterworks for irrigation and alleviation of floods. The current Three Gorges project in China stands as a modern example.[3] A strong emperor would build great walls to protect the state borders. All rulers and governments have to do all three in the right proportions. The Singapore and the present Chinese governments, while not neglecting the arts or other concerns, are right to concentrate on infrastructure and defence.

Public works on their own, however, do not constitute state capitalism. I would define state capitalism as the sovereign participating in risk taking in what are essentially commercial enterprises. The hidden intention however is not totally profit and loss. National military prowess may well be the real agenda.

---

2 Walt Rostow is best known for his book, *The Stages of Economic Growth* (Cambridge: Cambridge University Press, 1960). Other books include: *Theorists of Economic Growth from David Hume to the Present* (New York: Oxford University Press, 1990) and *The Process of Economic Growth* (New York: W.W. Norton, 1962), amongst others. Rostow developed a take-off model of economic growth, one of the major historical models of economic growth. The Rostovian model argues that economic modernisation occurs in five stages of varying length — traditional society, preconditions for take-off, take off, drive to maturity, and high mass consumption.

3 Audrey Ronning Topping, "Three Gorges Dam: A metaphor for changing ways in China", *Earth Times News Service* (12 May 1998); Dai Qing, *The River Dragon has come!: The Three Gorges Dam and the Fate of China's Yangtze River* (New York: M.E. Sharpe, 1998).

Hence, during the period of the Meiji Restoration in Japan, the Japanese sovereign encouraged and partnered the *zaibatsu*[4] to establish steel plants, aircraft factories, and shipbuilding yards for martial purposes. Under the peace constitution imposed by the victorious Americans, the Japanese have transformed their original defence industries into formidable civilian high tech industries.[5]

Did Singapore have a similar experience in its industrialisation?

Dr Goh Keng Swee, our first Defence Minister, established the Singapore Technology Group[6] of high tech defence-based industries. Ever the economist, Dr Goh persuaded the Cabinet to spend the money on reverse engineering as it was too expensive to buy all weapons new. Our Defence engineers would reverse engineer, upgrade and modify tanks, aircraft and weapons. Most of our defence industries are now listed on the Singapore Exchange (SGX), and so far have stood up to the test of the market.

In the group, ST Engineering[7] continues to serve MINDEF requirements. With the base load, ST Engineering is able to compete for non-MINDEF business as well. The other two majors, namely Chartered Semiconductor[8] and ST Telemedia[9] compete entirely in the open markets. The ST companies which began life as MINDEF companies have made a successful transition to civilian production and discipline.

---

4 *Zaibatsu* is a Japanese term meaning "money clique" or conglomerate. It was used in the nineteenth century and the first half of the twentieth century to refer to large family-controlled banking and industrial combines. The leading *zaibatsu* (called *keiretsu* after World War II) are Mitsui, Mitsubishi, Dai Ichi Kangyo, Sumitomo, Sanwa and Fuyo. The decision on the part of these groups in the post-World War II era to pool their resources greatly influenced Japan's subsequent rise as a global business power. See *The Columbia Encyclopedia*, Sixth Edition, 2001–5.

5 Marius B. Jansen (ed.), *The Emergence of Meiji Japan* (New York: Cambridge University Press, 1995); Peter F. Kornicki (ed.), *Meiji Japan: Political, Economic and Social History 1868–1912* (London: Routledge, 1998); Richard Sims, *Japanese Political History since the Meiji Renovation 1868–2000* (London: C. Hurst & Company, 2001).

6 Singapore Technology Group (formerly known as Sheng-Li Holding Company Pte Ltd) is a leading technology-based multinational conglomerate headquartered in Singapore. The Group provides a full array of multi-disciplinary capabilities, spanning research and development, design and engineering, and precision high value-added manufacturing in several core business groups including, technology; engineering; infrastructure and logistic; property; and financial services.

7 ST Engineering is an integrated engineering group providing solutions and services in the aerospace, electronics, land systems and marine sectors. Headquartered in Singapore, the Group is among the largest companies listed on the Singapore Exchange. ST Engineering has 12,000 employees worldwide and over 100 subsidiaries and associated companies in 15 countries and 22 cities. For more information, please refer to <http://www.stengg.com/home/home.aspx> [10 March 2006].

8 Chartered Semiconductor Manufacturing (Chartered) is one of the world's leading foundries in the production of wafers used for diverse applications, including high-end computing and communications. Chartered has forged a technology alliance with Lucent Technologies; manufacturing alliance with Motorola and several marketing alliances. For more information, please refer to <http://www. charteredsemi.com/> [10 March 2006].

9 ST Telemedia, the telecommunications arm of Singapore Technologies, is the second telecommunications operator in Singapore. It is the leading partner of StarHub. ST Telemedia has been involved in the telecommunications industry, both locally and overseas since 1994. Its operations spread over a wide array of activities that include cable television, mobile data, internet, satellite, paging, cellular networks etc. For more information, please refer to <http://www.sttelemedia.com/> [10 March 2006].

Having public shareholders has, however, made management more and not less risk averse. After Dr Goh left MINDEF, the ST Group has not grown. They have expanded by acquisition instead of new startups. Entrepreneurship is visibly lacking.

State Entrepreneurship

An earlier period of state entrepreneurship was also spearheaded by Dr Goh, the first Minister for Finance, together with Mr Hon Sui Sen, his Permanent Secretary. They invested in the National Iron and Steel Mills (NatSteel), Jurong and Sembawang Shipyards, Shangri-La and Mandarin Hotels, and a score of smaller private sector companies.

The government injected some equity to instil confidence and to encourage our commercial private sector to venture into industry. The private sector however operated and managed the new enterprises.

Mr Hon went on to establish the Development Bank of Singapore (DBS Bank) to provide long-term financing. Where the financing was too large even for DBS Bank to provide, the Ministry of Finance invested directly in the $1 billion Petrochemical Corporation of Singapore (PCS)[10] with Sumitomo Chemicals. PCS has become the cornerstone of the Jurong Island petrochemical complex today.

State capitalism, in Singapore's case, has been necessary for the establishment of new promising, but risky, and large-scale businesses. Singapore Airlines was established in 1972, with the Ministry of Finance as sole shareholder. Being 100 per cent owned, it would have been tempting for MOF to want to manage and run it directly. Mr Hon, who was then the Minister for Finance, knew better.

Other than appointing the chairman (Mr J.Y. Pillay) and the Board members, SIA management, led by the CEO, Mr Lim Chin Beng, was left alone to run the business. The original Board, which served from 1972 to 1996, can look back with pride that under our stewardship an airline with nowhere to go developed into a profitable international airline.

Financial Governance, the Ministry and Institutions

As Singapore's first Minister for Finance, Dr Goh Keng Swee was not only the economic architect of Singapore; he was also the financial architect.

---

10 Petrochemical Corporation of Singapore Pte Ltd started as a joint-venture between the Government of Singapore, The Development Bank of Singapore Ltd and the Japan-Singapore Petrochemicals Company Ltd (JSPC). The present shareholders are JSPC (50%) and Shell Eastern Petroleum Pte Ltd (50%). PCS' main role is to supply high quality ethylene, propylene, acetylene, butadiene as well as utilities such as water, steam, compressed air to downstream companies which in turn produce high quality petrochemical products for their customers in the Southeast Asia region and beyond. For more information, see <http://www.jurongisland.com.sg/Companies/Information.asp?Company= Petrochemical+Corporation+of+Singapore+Pte+Ltd> [10 March 2006].

He established the Economic Development Board (EDB) to spearhead the economic development of Singapore. As Finance Minister, he established three institutions for the financial governance of Singapore.

First, the Monetary Authority of Singapore (MAS) was established to manage all of Singapore's foreign reserves. But when we decided to conduct monetary policy through the exchange, rather than the interest rate, Dr Goh set up the Government Investment Corporation (GIC) to manage the government's long-term assets. The foreign assets of the Singapore Board of Commissioners of Currency required to back the issue of currency were transferred for management by GIC. The Currency Board's assets were considered long-term. In contrast, MAS, in managing the exchange rate had to intervene in the foreign exchange markets on a day-to-day basis to achieve a stable exchange rate for the Singapore Dollar. Managers in both GIC and MAS are not required to take entrepreneurial risks. Entrepreneurship was and still is the domain of Temasek Holdings.

The Ministry of Finance has practised, and I hope will continue to practise, state capitalism. In state capitalism, the state or sovereign participates as an equity risk partner with private individuals or companies embarking on high risk high reward ventures or misadventures in the event of failure.

It is said that Queen Elizabeth I of England partnered men, such as Sir Francis Drake, in building and manning men-of-war, which then set out to attack and plunder Spanish galleons laden with gold sailing home from the West Indies. These original venture capitalists were knighted in success, and beheaded as pirates when they failed.[11]

The Ministry of Finance established the Economic Development Board with a grant of $100 million in 1961, a princely sum then. While the income was used for operating expenditure, the principal was to be invested as equity or lent to private enterprises setting up new industries in Singapore. Partnership with the private sector gave them comfort to risk their own capital. When we could, we also introduced them to sources of technology.

The National Iron and Steel Mills (NatSteel), the first modern industry to be set up in the Jurong Industrial Estate, was conceived on the recommendation of a UNDP expert, Mr Schereschewsky, a Frenchman. He was a chairman of the national French power utility, Electricite de France, and a specialist on steel re-rolling.[12]

---

11 Jane R. Thomas, *Behind the Mask: The Life of Queen Elizabeth 1* (New York: Clarion Books, 1998); Wade G. Dudley, *Drake: For God, Queen and Plunder* (Dulles, Va: Brassey's, 2003), p. 39.

12 The Minister in charge, Dr Goh discussed Singapore's economic problems with World Bank, UN development specialists and other experts. He requested that Schereschewsky study particular lines of industrial growth. He was determined to move Singapore from a trading economy to a broader-based economy which would include manufacturing, in the "Biography of Goh Keng Swee", Ramon Magsaysay Award Foundation, available at: <http://www.rmaf.org.ph/Awardees/Biography/BiographyGohKengSwe.htm> [10 Jan. 2006].

Wherever we could, MOF and EDB partnered private enterprises in setting up industries simply because they knew the business, and we didn't. But where the risk was too high, MOF invested directly as sole shareholder, as in SIA and DBS. We also partnered Sumitomo Chemicals in establishing the billion-dollar Petrochemical Corporation of Singapore.

In these undertakings and institutions, Singapore practised pragmatic capitalism. Though MOF was often the controlling shareholder, we studiously resisted the temptation to send civil servants to manage and run the businesses. As the predominant shareholder, we had a big say in appointing the Boards of companies, and in some instances, the CEO. State-owned enterprises (SOEs) are therefore not a dirty acronym in Singapore. And we have to keep it this way, lest we fall into crony capitalism.

The Transfer to Temasek Holdings

When DBS Bank was established in 1968, EDB's industrial loan and equity portfolio was transferred to the Bank. Being a bank, DBS could accept only the commercially viable loans and equity investments. MOF was left with the rest. The rump was a nuisance for us, used to managing the much bigger national budget. But when we established SIA in 1972, it was beyond DBS' capacity to finance, less to be a shareholder. Similarly with PCS, where MOF was the sole Singapore shareholder, subscribing $500 million.

Not being able to do justice to our portfolio of companies, MOF decided in the 1970s to hold all its equity investments under one holding company, namely Temasek Holdings. The MOF was just not organised to provide corporate governance for companies, such as SIA, DBS, NOL,[13] SingTel,[14] and the Singapore Technology Group.

Conflict of interest situations such as tax treatment could also be avoided. The role of Temasek, however, was to go beyond the provision of corporate governance. Temasek was tasked with the function of state capitalism, taking over from MOF and EDB.

It was also to see through the corporatisation of large statutory business entities such as PSA[15] and SingTel.

The initial phase of setting up corporate governance is largely done. Temasek has now to turn to its fundamental role of state capitalism. Temasek has to seek out new strategic businesses for Singapore. And to invest, nurture and grow them just as MOF and EDB did in the pioneering years. When

---

13 The Neptune Orient Lines (NOL) is a global transportation company, with core businesses involved in container transportation and supply chain management.

14 Refer to footnote 15 on page 154.

15 Refer to footnote 14 on page 153.

such businesses mature, Temasek will have to divest, get out, and go on to new frontiers.

However hard it is, the virtuous cycle has to begin all over again. If Temasek does not take the straight and narrow path, blue chip icons (like SIA and DBS) of the future will not emerge.

Divestment Report and the Private Sector

There are those who believe that the government and Temasek are too much involved in the economy, that the private sector should be allowed more space. Letting go is the hardest thing for a parent to do. Divestment of enterprises by the government has been a long-standing issue. When Dr Goh received the first Divestment Report in the mid-1970s, he sighed and asked two questions: If the GLC is profitable, why should the government shareholder sell out? If it is not profitable, how can we as government sell?

He then asked the ultimate question: Sell out to whom? Can we find controlling groups that can take over SIA, grow and run it as profitably as we have? Why should we on ideological grounds sell our strong companies to funds managers to unlock value? Being a small economy, we can only live and die once. Should the state cease to be a capitalist?

These questions continue to be relevant and require debate.

For me, I wish to suggest that, instead of unlocking value within the companies that have already been created, Temasek should go back to its roots, which is to create value with new startups — which NatSteel, SIA, Keppel,[16] SembCorp,[17] DBS, SingTel, NOL and PSA once were.

Knowledge-based competition will throw up hundreds, if not thousands, of new businesses. As EDB did in the pioneering years, I hope Temasek will now lead the charge for Singapore with as much gumption and passion as old warriors of my generation did.

---

16 Keppel Corporation Ltd key businesses focus is on offshore & marine; property; and infrastructure. The Group was one of the first Singapore companies to spearhead investments abroad. Today, it has a global footprint in 27 countries. For more information, please refer to <http://www.kepcorp.com/home/default.asp> [10 March 2006].

17 SembCorp Industries (SCI) is a leading player in infrastructure services in Asia, providing integrated utilities and energy, environmental management services and process engineering services to industrial customers. It is also Asia's largest integrated logistics provider, offering advanced supply chain management solutions to global customers; and a leading global marine and offshore engineering group. For more information, please refer to <http://www.sembcorp.com.sg/> [10 March 2006].

LEADERS IN BUILDING THE SINGAPORE ECONOMY

The role of political leaders and their relationship to civil servants is a key factor in the building of Singapore and our economy. There is a long and distinguished line of Administrative Service officers in Singapore. I am pleased to share some recollections of the political leaders and civil servants who have contributed to Singapore's progress. This progress is all the more remarkable when we consider the situation when the People's Action Party (PAP) first came to rule Singapore.

The PAP swept into power in Singapore's first General Elections in May 1959. The PAP won 43 out of 51 seats, gaining 53.4 per cent of the total votes cast. On 3 June, the new Constitution proclaiming Singapore as a self-governing State was brought into force. Sir William Goode, the Governor under British colonial rule, became the first Yang di-Pertuan Negara, or Head of State. The first government of the State of Singapore was sworn in on 5 June, with Mr Lee Kuan Yew as Singapore's first Prime Minister.

Inheriting a stagnant economy and a crumbling city, Mr Lee appointed his most able minister, Dr Goh Keng Swee, as Singapore's first Finance Minister.

The new Ministry of Finance (MOF) established by Dr Goh was more than the old Treasury under the colonial government. The Treasury in the colonial administration was traditionally responsible for collecting taxes, controlling expenditure, and personnel administration under the Establishment Office.

Dr Goh and the new MOF realised they had to do much more.

Edited from a speech "On being an MOF Admin Cadre", 25 Oct. 2005, Ministry of Finance (MOF) internal staff training session.

Faced with an unemployment rate in excess of 10 per cent, Dr Goh set up the Economic Development Division under Mr Hon Sui Sen as its first Permanent Secretary. As Permanent Secretary, Mr Hon set up the Economic Development Board (EDB). Mr Hon was the founding Chairman of the EDB. We focused single-mindedly on job creation.

By the mid-1970s, Singapore achieved full employment, with an unemployment rate of 3 per cent or lower. Our colleagues in the EDB and Ministry of Manpower (MOM) today have to deal with the infinitely more complex problems of structural unemployment. Even if the unemployed anxiously seek work, they are unable to find any. The reasons for this are diverse: there may be skills mismatch, or whole industries may have relocated to lower cost cities.

During the Ministry's formative years, Mr George Bogaars was Permanent Secretary in the Ministry for Budget, and also the Head of Civil Service. He once told me that under the British Raj in India, the Treasury officer was both respected and feared. Much like the Brahmin, whose shadow would part the way for him through a crowd.

If the MOF in Singapore once enjoyed this image, by the 1960s, the mystique was gone. What protected us was having a stubborn streak in saying "no".

Dr Goh told young officers that when a Ministry asked for a budget, however laudable the purpose, the Treasury officer should instinctively look away and say "no". He said that the supplicant Ministry would not take "no" for an answer and would come back a second time. Again, the answer would be a resounding "no". He would come back a third time. This time you approve half of what he wants. You reward him for his tenacity. He goes away feeling grateful and relieved.

Dr Goh Keng Swee: The Architect Who Said No

As our Minister, Dr Goh Keng Swee urged his officers to adopt a robust approach in administration. Two case studies readily come to mind.

First, he flatly refused the request from the Public Works Department (PWD)[1] for funds to alleviate floods along Bukit Timah Road.[2] In the

---

1 Public Works Department (PWD) was corporatised to form PWD Corporation Pte Ltd in April 1999. It later adopted a new name CPG Corporation in July 2002 to transit the company into a new era of growth. Today, CPG Corporation is one of Asia's leading development and management professionals, providing the complete spectrum of building and infrastructure development services including master planning, architectural, engineering design and consultancy etc. Headquartered in Singapore, CPG Corporation currently has offices in the People's Republic of China, India, Vietnam, the Philippines and Australia. For more information, see <http://www.cpgcorp.com.sg/eng/aboutus/ourhistory/index. asp> [10 March 2006].

2 The government has spent $1.5 billion over the last 20 years to improve drains all over Singapore, greatly reducing flood-prone areas. One of the successful flood alleviation projects was the Bukit

1960s, the Bukit Timah Canal flooded about two to three times a year, stranding motorists and bus commuters. Hence the PWD sought to solve it by re-engineering the canal but Dr Goh told me there was no justification spending millions of dollars just to enable folks to go home on time for dinner!

Second, he also dismissed requests for building public swimming pools. He said that it would be cheaper for people to swim in the sea. In principle, he was prepared to give school children bus fare to go to the beach to swim. It would be cheaper.

Dr Goh, however, was not all head and no heart. He had fine sensibilities. To mitigate the harsh landscape of smoke stacks and chimneys in the Jurong Industrial Estate, he approved funds to build the Singapore Bird Park, and then the Zoological Gardens. He decided on the Bird Park first as birds are cheaper to feed than animals.

When the occasion demanded, Dr Goh could also be as tough as nails. One day, he asked me to see him in his Ministry of Education office, where he was the Minister. I thought he wanted to discuss manpower planning with me as Permanent Secretary for Trade and Industry.

He went straight to the point and asked me to draft a paper recommending that the government close down all the pig farms in Punggol. He argued that if we were to take into account the cost of expensive land and pollution, it would be more cost effective to import all our pork.

Dr Goh was absolutely right. But my heart ached for my younger brother who was then the Director for Primary Production. He and his colleagues had spent years developing pig farms in Punggol.

The Member of Parliament (MP) for Punggol, Mr Ng Kah Ting, known fondly as the "pig MP", was aghast at this sudden change of government policy. Being the seasoned MP, he quickly regained his composure and pressed for the maximum amount of compensation for the pig farms. The lesson to learn in the Singapore political context is that while the government can always change its mind, it has to pay compensation for the after thought. If my memory serves me well, MOF paid about $50 million compensation to get rid of the pig farms. Pig farmers were enterprising people. They turned to farming orchids and ornamental fish for export.

I spent the first 25 years of my MOF career at the EDB, where we promoted investment to help grow the Singapore economy. I remember Dr Goh's words that, as Chairman of the EDB, my fate were to sow, while Mr J.Y. Pillay's *karma* as Permanent Secretary of revenue was to reap the fruits of my labour.

Timah/Dunearn Road diversion canal. Since its completion in the 1990s, flooding has not occurred in the Bukit Timah/ Dunearn Road area. Information obtained from <http://www.pub.gov.sg/downloads/pdf/WaterNet.pdf> [10 March 2006].

In 1986, I was posted to the Budget Division of the MOF to succeed Mr Herman Hochstadt. Two years later, I succeeded Mr Lee Ek Tieng[3] as Permanent Secretary (Revenue), when he went on to be Managing Director for the MAS. I was overjoyed, as I expected that it would now be my turn to reap the rewards of our growing economy.

I was brought down to earth very quickly by Dr Goh. He told me that, when I was a young officer working for him, we made mistakes but they were done on the backs of used envelopes. He said that as Singapore had become more prosperous, I would continue to make mistakes, but only this time on the backs of huge multi-million dollar computers!

This was the best piece of advice I had received as a budget officer. I believe that all permanent secretaries for the Budget should take this dictum to heart.

I am proud to place on record that my colleagues and I practised Dr Goh's robust and austere brand of budgeting and achieved real budget surpluses for eight consecutive years, from 1988–96. I used the word "real" as the surpluses were recorded after we met all expenditure, operating and capital, from current revenue, excluding investment income. This is a feat of budgeting that no other non oil-producing country had ever achieved!

These real budget surpluses underpinned the strength of our currency. When we issued our own currency in 1965, most economic analysts had been dismissive of the value of the Singapore Dollar.

Fortunately, we were honed on the rigours of the Currency Board system, under which every unit of currency had to be backed by a specified weight in gold. Singapore was on the gold exchange standard that American President Nixon dismantled in 1972; a decision by the US that accounted for much of the currency woes of the world today.

Mr Hon Sui Sen: Administrator Par Excellence

If Dr Goh Keng Swee is considered the economic architect of Singapore, Mr Hon Sui Sen, was clearly the administrator par excellence. The late Mr Hon was the builder both of men and of organisations. J.Y. Pillay, S. Dhanabalan, Heng Hong Ngoh and I, were all trained by Mr Hon. We grew and matured under his mentorship.

Mr Hon told me that in managing staff, it is best to identify and use the strength of the individual rather than to dwell on his or her weakness.

---

3 Mr Lee was the Head of Civil Service and Permanent Secretary (Special Duties) in the Prime Minister's Office prior to his retirement in 1999. He was previously the Chairman of the Public Utilities Board, Temasek Holdings Pte Ltd and Deputy Chairman of the Monetary Authority of Singapore. Mr Lee is currently the Group Managing Director of the Government of Singapore Investment Corporation since 1989 and is also on the panel of advisors to Temasek Holdings and a Director at Fraser and Neave Ltd. For more information, see <http://www.fraserandneave.com/fnn/aboutus/board_of_directors. xml> [13 March 2006].

Very early on in my apprenticeship, Mr Hon taught me time management. He said that each morning as piles of files are dumped on the table in front of you, it is best to quickly scan the issues at hand, and deal with those matters that you can do something about first. You can leave the more intractable problems for later. Of course you cannot procrastinate forever. But, as Mr Hon put it so disarmingly, sometimes the sheer passage of time may render matters no longer urgent.

Both Dr Goh and Mr Hon were decisive men. When a file was sent in to either of them, you could be sure that the file would be sent out with decisions made, or instructions given before the working day ended.

If the file was delayed by more than two days, you had better start worrying. The Minister might have decided that you are incapable of understanding the issue or executing his decision. He might have referred the file to a more capable officer. You might have found yourself out of a job.

Today, with the e-mail sending out information and data at the speed of light, we run the opposite danger of responding or reacting without the time to think. There is a lot of motion, but little movement. Our generation thinks only 10 per cent of the time. We spend the other 90 per cent getting things done. There is no room for procrastination.

I am told that Cabinet papers have recently been getting longer and longer. In the past, we worked to a regime of a Cabinet paper 2.5 pages long, clearly setting out the problem or issue faced, suggesting the solutions, and most important, drafting the decisions that you wanted to be made, in clear precise language.

The Cabinet Secretary at the time, Mr Wong Chooi Sen, was authorised to reject any Cabinet paper exceeding 2.5 pages in length and double-spaced, whatever the substance. All Administrative Officers were required to read Gower's Plain English classic.[4] A short Cabinet paper demanded rigorous thinking and persuasive writing. Every word was literally worth its weight in gold!

Dr Goh and Mr Hon were more than mentors to us. They were also our teachers and tutors. When a young cadet, as I was when I first served with them, put up a submission to him, more often than not, Dr Goh would return it with his unmistakable corrections in green ink. His judicious intervention not only polished the language, but also strengthened the arguments that you were trying so desperately to make.

Mr Hon did not correct your language. His own written decisions or instructions were crisp and crystal clear.

---

4   See Sir Ernest Gowers *et al.*, *The Complete Plain Words* (Harmondsworth, Middlesex: Penguin Books Ltd, 1987). Ernest Gowers' *Plain Words* is a guide to effective writing from the 1940s for British civil servants. Over the years it has gone through many editions. The most recent version, *The Complete Plain Words*, still shows its focus on British usage and the civil service with discussions on common writing problems.

From both of them, I learnt clarity of thought, economy of language, and the power of persuasion. In my view, the power to persuade, not compulsion, is the key for success in managing friends and foes. In modern idiom, emotional quotient or "EQ"[5] is as crucial as "IQ".[6] I would like to add that more important than even IQ and EQ is to have a genuine interest and respect for the other person.

The Civil Servant and Entrepreneurship

There is a saying in Hokkien that the civil servant "*jia bo pa, gaw bo si*". Translated from the vernacular, this means that civil servants "eat not full, starve not die". In Chinese culture, the public servant, although feared, is often held in contempt.

I am proud to say that the Singapore Administrative Service has proven the cynics wrong. In the 1960s, when we started the process of economic development, Singapore's businessmen were basically commodity traders, building contractors, commercial bankers, and property developers. Many still are today.

Because of this, there were many gaps if the Singapore economy was to successfully develop, and the government at the time had little choice but to try to fill them.

No private bank at that time would lend long term to a manufacturing company. Development finance was simply not available. Therefore, Dr Goh asked Mr Hon to set up the Development Bank of Singapore (DBS) to provide development finance to businesses.

DBS did not start from scratch. The Bank was given the choice project loans of the Economic Development Board and a substantial line of credit from the MOF. DBS was not considered a commercial bank subject to liquidity requirements. It could not be expected to borrow short and lend long. The backstop was the MOF, the licensing authority itself!

Under the entrepreneurial leadership of its first Chairman, Mr Hon Sui Sen, DBS has grown to become a universal bank, able to compete with the best in the world. I am proud to record that DBS has all along been led by Permanent Secretaries, namely Mr Hon, Mr Howe Yoon Chong, Mr J.Y. Pillay, myself, and then Mr Dhanabalan, a former Cabinet Minister.[7]

Whoever said that civil servants cannot run banks? In the beginning, many of us had to take on a role as state entrepreneurs.

---

5   Emotional quotient (EQ) is a person's ability to understand their own emotions and those of others, and to act appropriately using these emotions.

6   Intelligence quotient (IQ) is a score derived from a set of standardised tests developed to measure a person's cognitive abilities. It indicates a person's mental abilities relative to others of approximately the same age.

7   Mr Koh Boon Hwee became Chairman on 1 Jan. 2006.

Dr Goh, however, was the *primus inter pares* among us as the state entrepreneur. Besides the EDB, he established the Jurong Town Corporation, DBS, Neptune Orient Lines (NOL), the Keppel and Sembawang Shipyards, and even Intraco.[8] His greatest contribution was setting up Sheng-Li Holding, which was later renamed Singapore Technologies.

As Defence Minister, Dr Goh was the driving force behind Chartered Industries, Singapore Shipbuilding, Singapore Aerospace and even Singapore Food Industries. The main defence industries operate today as ST Engineering.

When I served as Chairman of Sheng-Li Holding from 1981–91, I had the pleasure of watching Mr Philip Yeo and his young colleagues of those years build up the defence industries to be what they are today. My only regret is that the defence industries were the last serious thrust in state entrepreneurship. There was just no drive without Dr Goh.

The Can-Do Spirit: Mr Woon Wah Siang

No one epitomised the can-do spirit of the pioneering generation more than Mr Woon Wah Siang. Mr Woon was a colleague of Dr Goh when they were both officers in the Social Welfare Department. When Dr Goh became Minister for Finance, he brought Mr Woon into the Administrative Service to get things done.

His first test was to build scores of community centres to replace the PAP branches, which had been lost to the Barisan Socialis (Socialist Front) when they split from the PAP.[9] This may not seem like much today. But without the simple zinc roofed community centres, the democratic wing of the PAP led by Mr Lee Kuan Yew would have lost the support of the grassroots, the backbone of the PAP.

Mr Woon was one officer who built first and then asked for planning approval later. (The redoubtable Mr Howe Yoon Chong, a former Head of Civil Service and later Minister for Defence, was the other.)

My first contact with Mr Woon was when Dr Goh decided to build a golf course on Sentosa to cater to Japanese tourists. Dr Goh asked me to contact Mr Woon, who was by then the Chairman of the Jurong Town

---

8 Intraco was incorporated in 1968 with an initial role to assist in the creation of export markets for locally manufactured products, the promotion of external trade and to source for competitively priced raw materials, commodities and manufactured goods for the domestic market. It was listed on the then, Stock Exchange of Singapore in 1972. Today, Intraco Group of Companies is involved in commodities trading; projects, i.e. infrastructure; info-communications and semiconductors. For more information, see <http://www.intraco.com.sg/corp_info/corp_profile2.htm> [10 March 2006].

9 C.M. Turnbull, *A History of Singapore 1819–1988* (Singapore: Oxford University Press, 1989); Diane Mauzy and R.S Milne, *Singapore Politics Under the People's Action Party* (London: Routledge, 2002); Leong Ching, *PAP 50: five decades of the People's Action Party* (Singapore: People's Action Party, 2004). Some leftwing PAP members split off in 1961 to form the new Barisan Socialis. They were against an unequal merger with Malaysia and the PAP portrayed them as communist stooges. They included some of the most prominent PAP members the British had arrested for involvement in protests. Many of its leaders were arrested in Feb. 1963 "Operation Cold Store", which crippled its organisation.

Corporation. Known affectionately as the Mayor of Jurong, Mr Woon was famous for his can-do spirit. As Dr Goh put it, if you were to ask Mr Woon to send a man to the moon, he would say "yes" straightaway.

So when the Administrative Service cadet, namely me, conveyed the Minister's request to build a golf course on Sentosa, Mr Woon accepted the challenge without hesitation. Few happy golfers teeing off from the first tee of the Tanjong Course would know that the beautiful Sentosa Golf Courses, rated among the world's most scenic courses, was conceived and built by a non-golfer.

Mr Woon was not a golfer. It demonstrates the credo that if an Administrative Officer puts his mind to a task, nothing is impossible. Mr Woon also developed the Jurong Bird Park.

Building the golf course was a different proposition from operating a golf course. For the latter task, Dr Goh pointed me in the direction of Mr Dennis Lee, an illustrious lawyer and avid golfer. As President of the Sentosa Golf Club, together with his golfing "kakis",[10] he developed the Club into what it is today. His elder brother, Lee Kuan Yew, opened the Club. In a memorable speech, Mr Lee Kuan Yew said that nowhere in the world can golfers, while teeing off, see supertankers bobbing in the distant sea.

In playing this small bit part in the development of the Sentosa Golf Club, Dr Goh taught me a valuable lesson in management. Dr Goh had this unique knack of selecting the right man for the right job.

Dr Richard Hu and the GST Ant Bite

In my entire civil service career, the one major new tax which I had to argue for and implement was the Goods and Services Tax (GST). The economic rationale for the GST is simple enough. Besides taxes on cigarettes and petrol, we needed a major new source of consumption tax. Such consumption taxes were needed to balance the reductions in income taxes, and the tax incentives given to pioneer industries.

We recognised that income taxes had to be reduced to stimulate and incentivise economic growth. This, in turn, would broaden the tax base in the future. But revenue was needed to meet current operating expenditures of government. Hence, the GST.

There are of course arguments for and against such a tax. But what was difficult was the implementation of the GST. Fortunately for the officials, the Minister who steered through the implementation of the GST was Dr Richard Hu, a former Chairman of Shell Eastern.

Dr Hu, schooled in the hard world of business, knew that the GST would be an unpopular tax. He therefore decided to introduce it at an initial

---

10 A colloquial term derived from Malay that means one's regular partners and participants in an activity.

rate of just 3 per cent, like an ant bite. Coverage was only on firms with an annual turnover of $1 million and above. In one stroke of the pen, the MOF thus avoided the high cost of collecting GST from every business entity, and thereby arousing the ire of thousands of shopkeepers.

To reduce the regressive nature of the GST tax as much as possible, MOF paid for rebates on conservancy and other consumption taxes for HDB households.[11] Overall, the GST was initially revenue neutral.

This soft, gradualist approach enabled us to introduce the GST without political heat. Unlike his counterparts in other countries, the Minister for Finance of Singapore did not lose his job introducing the GST!

Swallowing Medicine in One Gulp

A Minister for Finance, however, cannot always adopt a soft approach as Dr Hu did with the ant bite of the initial GST. An earlier Finance Minister, Mr Hon Sui Sen, faced with the sharp increase in oil prices in the first oil crisis in 1972, and he did not flinch.

Supported by the then Prime Minister, Lee Kuan Yew, Mr Hon decided that Singaporeans would have to swallow the medicine in one gulp. Oil and fuel prices were allowed to rise to market levels. The inflation rate that particular year was well over 20 per cent.

The painful economic adjustment was made in one gulp. Singapore never looked back since. This is sound economic strategy. Countries not prepared to face reality suffer in the long run.[12]

This, by and large, has been the Singapore approach: to bite the bullet, to swallow the medicine in one gulp. But it is not a single approach that has been used, without exception, in all areas of policy.

Imposing levies on work permit holders in the construction industry has been one such aberration. Without such levies, such workers would be even cheaper to employ and might out compete Singaporeans for such jobs. In this case, the government has not made citizens swallow the medicine in one gulp.

---

11 GST is a regressive tax on domestic consumption. It was first introduced in Singapore on 1 April 1994. The GST rate was increased from 3 per cent to 4 per cent in 2003 and from 4 to 5 per cent in 2004. A regressive tax as a percentage of income falls as income rises, thus proportionately placing more of a burden on those with lower income. For the lower income people, the government has introduced a comprehensive package of measures, including the Economic Restructuring Shares, rebates for Services and Conservancy Charges and HDB rental to offset the increase in GST. These offsets will be enough to cover the increase in tax for all lower income households for at least five years and those living in one- or two-room HDB flats will be covered for ten years. Information is available on the Ministry of Finance website: <http://www.mof.gov.sg/taxation/index.html#gst> [10 Jan. 2006].

12 Responding to rising demand in Asia and the volatile situation in the Middle East, oil prices have increased drastically in 2004–5. This has affected the national budget in many countries and fuel subsidies, as in the case of Indonesia where the oil subsidy amounted to 2.5 per cent of GDP (CNA, 2005) has cost the state about 60 trillion rupiah. Available at: BBC News, 1 March 2005: <http://news.bbc.co.uk/2/hi/Asia-pacific/4307433.stm> [16 Jan. 2006].

Since there is a shortage of workers in the country, such workers' levies to me seem akin to imposing import duties on goods; in this case, the "good" of labour that goes into the production of construction work.

While it is true that the driver of every government policy is essentially political, the Prime Minister should resist the temptation of overriding the Finance Minister in major economic or financial matters. As the government is now managing more and more by KPIs (key performance indicators), the human tendency is for every Minister and every Perm Sec to set his own agenda and for every Ministry to go its own way. Taken to the extreme, KPIs will undermine the cohesiveness and coherence of the public administration.

The Prime Minister, being the first among equals in the cabinet, has to take very balanced positions on major political and economic issues. He, or she, has to decide in the overall interest of the government and the country. This is easier said than done.

As an MOF cadre, I would like to think that in economic and financial matters, the Minister for Finance is *de facto primus inter pares*. I remember vividly Prime Minister Lee Kuan Yew telling a minister who was complaining about an obdurate Finance Ministry, that he would be convinced if the particular minister convinced Dr Goh first!

In my view, a Prime Minister should never allow a minister, however politically compelling his programme, to go over the head of the Finance Minister and make his plea directly to him.

My reasoning is very simple. The primary duty of the Finance Minister in any government is to balance the budget. Simply put, the Finance Minister's job is to collect enough revenue to pay for the expenditure of the entire government, without having to borrow, or worse to depreciate the currency. The Finance Ministry, which I served with pride, was such a Ministry.

Very early on in my career, I realised that an administrative officer cannot fly solo. You have to fly in formation. This was vividly put to me by Mr Hon Sui Sen, my first Perm Sec.

When I joined the then newly-created Economic Development Division of MOF, there were only four of us; namely the Minister (Dr Goh), the PS (Mr Hon), the Admin Cadet (myself), and Sani, the office assistant. Mr Hon told me that Sani was as much a member of the team as myself. Sani held literally the keys to the office.

Being the sole Admin Assistant, I was the man Friday. There was no EO, or HEO reporting to me. Unlike the more established Treasury Division, where older EOs and HEOs would put up crisply written draft memos for the young AO to sign off. I was left to do everything myself.

Very fortunately for me, I had two great mentors, Dr Goh and Mr Hon with whom I worked directly. They were more than my bosses. They were my teachers and tutors. They taught me to think clearly and to act decisively. Without them, my admin career would not have prospered.

Chairman EDB

When Mr Hon became my Minister and I his Perm Sec, I asked him which was the more interesting job. He smiled and told me that he envied me. By then, I was also concurrently Chairman of the Economic Development Board (EDB).

As Minister, he had the burden of making decisions, which as he puts it, was just on the tip of his pen. As Chairman of the EDB, I had all the fun of getting things done. Mr Hon said that EDB was a more fulfilling mission.

It was in the front line, attracting multinational companies to set up manufacturing industries in Singapore, and creating tens of thousands of jobs for our young school-leavers.

By the mid-1970s, Singapore achieved full employment, and had to deal with what is really the phenomenon of "job hopping". There was great mobility for labour. This was a pleasant problem to have.

Of course, nothing stands still. Today, the EDB has to find jobs for older workers stuck in structural unemployment. It is a more daunting task. As Chairman of the EDB, you have to be not only a farsighted thinker, but also someone with high-octane energy. Like top entrepreneurs and tycoons. The Chairman EDB plays centre forward for Team Singapore in the great game of global competition. The epic quest for economic prosperity is not for the faint hearted. Only the brave and the bold "EDBians" will score the goals for Singapore.

I like to think that those of us in MOF are playing full back and goalkeeper, making sure that goals are not scored against us. Or making sure that, worse, no one is kicking the goal into our own net. Mercifully, these occasions are rare.

In 1979, the Economic Development Division (EDD) of MOF became a full-fledged ministry. The new Ministry of Trade and Industry (MTI) became the economics ministry. Unlike the MOF, the new MTI was given greater latitude. Under Dr Goh, and later Mr Hon, EDD and MTI officers were expected to help other ministries align the economic thrust of their own policies for economic development.

MTI and EDB officers were sometimes considered pushy by our colleagues in other ministries. We provided much of the intellectual content and impetus for labour and wage policies, education and manpower planning, tax incentive policies, housing, and even sports and recreation. Only matters of defence were off limits.

The Defence Ministry

When Dr Goh became the Defence Minister in 1965, he found himself on the other side of the table. Probably fearing the nit-picking and bean counting mindset of MOF, he persuaded PM Lee to set aside a certain percentage of the GDP of the preceding year as the budget allocation of the Defence Ministry.

Only the Defence Council, chaired by the PM, knew what the money was being spent on. The budget applications of all other Ministries were scrutinised with a fine toothcomb by MOF's Budget Division. MINDEF was the first ministry to be given what was to become known as a "block budget". With such a block budget, the Ministry concerned can spend as it thinks best so long as it stays within the given budget. The PS himself has to arbitrate and balance all the competing demands within his Ministry. The Ministry's mission is set by the national priorities as decided by the Cabinet.

In the first decade of self-government and then independence, 1960–70, the pressing problems were jobs and housing. A large chunk of the Singapore government budget went to physical infrastructure, industrial training, and low cost housing.

When Singapore became an independent nation in 1965, defence and internal security demanded immediate attention. Hence, MINDEF was given well over 25 per cent of the national budget. By the early 1980s, Singapore had achieved both political and economic security. We turned our attention to education at all levels. From then on, the education budget equalled the defence budget.

When other ministries fail to get their budget requests in full, some of them will disparage the Budget Division as "bean counters". Having been on both sides of the table, I would say that counting the beans carefully is the only way to ensure everyone will have some.

To do his job well, the Perm Sec (Budget) has to be absolutely fair and objective. In making his budget recommendations to the Minister for Finance for Cabinet, he acts without fear or favour. He should resist the temptation to second-guess the Cabinet or worse, allow his personal prejudice to creep in. It is the Cabinet that approves the Annual Budget, including tax policies. As civil servants, we should leave it to the ministers to make the political judgment.

Having been a civil servant for some 40 years, I have come to the conclusion that the underpinning of every policy is political. This is even more so in a democracy. By this, I do not mean "pork barrel" politics. Just remember that before a government spends, it has to tax. The voters who you favour are likely to demand more and more.

During my stewardship as PS (Budget) from 1986 to 1999, I tried to be as even handed as possible. No Ministry was neglected. No one had to be Cinderella, impoverished while favoured sisters got all the attention and resources. I considered myself a "landscape gardener" in my approach. Some may consider an entire garden planted with roses as absolutely beautiful. I prefer a garden with greater variety. My personal budgeting philosophy is to nurture every aspect of our society and economy. Of course, there are priorities depending on the challenges of the period. The Cabinet decides on the priorities with the Prime Minister as *primus inter pares* or "first among equals".

The NWC Wage Adjustment Policy

The NWC wage adjustment policy of the late 1970s was one area of policy with which Dr Winsemius, Singapore's early Economic Advisor, and I were closely associated. We were, in fact, the main protagonists for raising wages rapidly over two or three years as an instrument of economic restructuring.

To make our life more difficult, the press and those unconvinced dubbed it "Singapore's High Wage Policy". Critics pinned the 1985 recession on what they considered a mistaken policy. From the distance of years, I can now sit back and ponder what went wrong. I am still convinced that the policy analysis was sound.

It was only that the execution was flawed. The EDB, in the first decade of development, 1960–70, did our job so well that by the mid-1970s, we enjoyed full employment and suffered the phenomenon of job hopping. MNC employers complained that they just could not get enough workers.

Because of NWC's prevailing policy of wage restraint, what economists call the "return to labour" was declining as a percentage. Return to capital was rising. As a result, demand for labour far exceeded the supply of labour. A few farsighted employers relocated their labour-intensive industries to neighbouring countries where low cost labour was plentiful. The miracle of economics was working, but because of the problems with labour shortages and trying to keep wages low, some regarded it as a bane rather than a boon.

So Dr Winsemius and I, as the EDB member on the NWC, persuaded both the employer and union members on the NWC to change gears. We switched from the previous years of wage restraint to three years of rapid wage increases. This helped to bring up labour's share of GDP to be on par with capital. We were hoping that laggard employers, who could not pay the higher wages, would disgorge their workers to employers who could afford such wages. That was the theory.

Things, however, did not turn out the way we pure economists expected. Freed from NWC restraint, wages shot up. The public sector, not subject to the rigours of the market place, raised wages effortlessly. There was no link to performance. Productivity stagnated.

The problem was that the NWC's recommendation was for a single rate of wage increase for the year. Though NWC religiously urged employers to consider it only as a guideline, most human resource managers just paid what was recommended, including those in the government. Being the largest single employer, the government set the benchmark for the rest of the economy. The recommendation became, in effect, a one-size-fit-all instrument.

Able employers paid less than what marginal productivity justified. Their managers could clear the hurdle easily without feeling the pressure to raise the performance of the company until it is too late. It was a classic case of the frog feeling comfortable in lukewarm water, complacent to the gradually rising temperature until it is boiled.

On the other hand, workers in industries whose wages were higher than their marginal productivity were protected by the levies imposed on foreign workers. The Foreign Work Permit (FWP) levy, in my view, is a mistaken (if not a perverse) policy, which the NTUC[13] insisted on. For political reasons, the government concurred. Critics were convinced that the high wage policy introduced in 1979 led to the 1985 recession.

Looking back, we need to ask ourselves: Was the NWC an unmitigated disaster for Singapore? The answer is a ringing "no". We introduced the NWC in 1972 when Singapore had achieved full employment. Learning from his experience in the Netherlands, Dr Winsemius advised us that we need to put in place a system of orderly wage increases. Otherwise, as in the Netherlands, there would be a wage explosion.

The NWC was created as a tripartite council of employers, unions and government, which — when it started — would meet one week a year, after the GDP and inflation numbers came. During my years in civil service, I remember Mr Devan Nair, Secretary-General of the National Trade Union Congress (NTUC), would lead the unions.[14] Mr Desmond Neil, the President of the Singapore Employers' Federation, represented the employers. The Head of the Civil Service, myself as Chairman EDB and PS of Trade & Industry, and Perm Sec for Labour were the government representatives. Professor Lim Chong Yah, then the Head of Economics at the University of Singapore (later NUS), was then the Chairman.[15]

Professor Lim, being an economist, would insist that the rate of wage increase, taking one year with the next, should not exceed the productivity increase of the previous year. I would support that approach. When inflation

---

13 The NTUC is the national federation of trade unions in Singapore. Set up in 1961, the NTUC's main objectives are: to help Singaporeans stay competitive and workers to remain employable for life; to enhance the social status and well-being of workers; and to build a strong, responsible and caring labour movement. As of 2004, there are 63 trade unions and four associations affiliated to the NTUC. They collectively represent more than 425,000 union members. For more information, refer to NTUC's website at <http://www.ntuc.org.sg/default.asp> [13 March 2006].

14 Mr Devan Nair was the President of the Republic of Singapore from 1981 to 1985. Prior to this, he helped to form the Singapore National Trade Union Congress (NTUC) in 1961 (he was the pro-term Secretary-General and was then elected NTUC's first Secretary-General), which he was able to transform it into a well knit and forward looking force under the principle of joint labour, management and government partnership. All this was not without a struggle between the communist and non-communist forces back in the 1960s. He passed away in Dec. 2005 at the age of 82. More information can be found at: <www.istana.gov.sg/history.html> [10 Jan. 2006].

15 Professor Lim Chong Yah is the founder and Chairman of the National Wage Council (NWC) from 1972–2001. He joined the University of Singapore in 1969 and was appointed Dean of the Faculty of Arts and Science in 1971. He later founded the Federation of ASEAN Economic Association (FAEA). In 1992 he retired from NUS and became Emeritus Professor. He is a professor of Economics in NTU. Professor Lim has published several books; his latest is *Southeast Asia: The Long Road Ahead* (Singapore: World Scientific, 2004), a concise study of various important economic aspects of Southeast Asia.

was higher than the norm, lower-paid workers were given a fixed dollar amount, over and above the recommended rate of wage increase. Otherwise, since their base wages were lower, a mere percentage increase might not be enough on its own.

By and large, the NWC wage adjustments worked in this period. There was consistency and fairness. Singapore enjoyed a long period of labour stability. We were able to attract enough foreign investments to provide full employment.

The NWC however was not effective enough to accelerate the pace of economic restructuring. Structural growth depended very much on the upgrading of skills and educational levels. Training and education, as we all know, are long-term processes. The opening up of China and India in the last 10 to 15 years has left some of our industries and businesses stranded on the shoals of high cost. MNCs have relocated their labour-intensive industries to lower cost locations.

Paradoxically, the new industries which EDB continues to attract to Singapore simply cannot find the better trained and higher skilled labour required. We continue to bring in high school graduates from China and India to man our more sophisticated manufacturing and service industries.

It cheered me to hear PM Lee Hsien Loong's National Day Rally speech in 2005 that we will increase enrolment in our five polytechnics to provide the mid-level technical manpower required by modern industry and businesses.[16]

Our education system should aim at giving everyone as strong a foundation as possible in Science, Mathematics and languages, to enable them to be trained and retrained as industrial demands change.

In the early years, EDB was able to partner MNCs, such as Philips and Seiko, to train school leavers into skilled machinists and cad-cam programmers. The enduring lesson that Singapore must bear in mind is that skills and aptitudes have to change as rapidly as technology. The one lesson that I take away from my NWC experience is that higher wages can only be sustained by higher skills and productivity. Knowledge is the new weapon of competition.

MOF as Team Captain

I have earlier used the analogy of different economic agencies in Singapore being part of a football team. When I described the MOF, I suggested it was

---

16 PM Lee spoke on the boost for polytechnics and ITEs addressing opportunities for all people, "we are aiming for a mountain range, not a pinnacle". Poly students are the biggest cohort (40 per cent of Singapore student population). "They are close to industry, they can response to industry needs as the needs change and they provide practical and useful training to the students". Transcript of Prime Minister Lee Hsien Loong's speech at National Day Rally 2005 on 21 Aug. 2005, NUS University Cultural Centre. Speech can be found at <http://app.sprinter.gov.sg/data/pr/2005082102.htm> [10 Jan. 2006].

either the goalkeeper or fullback; a defensive role. But I wish to add that the MOF's role in the football team goes beyond guarding the goalmouth. The MOF as fullback is in fact the team captain. The MOF initiates the moves for the mid-field, winger and the centre forward to run with the ball and score the goals.

It is easy for EDB to propose tax incentives to attract foreign investments into Singapore. The cost of incentives is revenue foregone. So while the EDB can ask, the hard part falls on the MOF, which has to control expenditure stringently to balance the budget. No country can run budget deficits year in and year out without running the risk of depreciating its currency. A depreciating currency causes inflation. Wages rise and the economy goes back to square one.

The Singapore government eschewed the soft delusional option of a cycle of subsidies, borrowings, and inflation. We adhered to the tough discipline of spending within our means. Expenditure would have to be met by tax revenue. We were therefore able to achieve balanced budgets for most of the years until the late 1990s.[17]

A stable currency combined with wage restraint was the secret of success. I hope that MOF will continue to steer the economy by these true and trusted rules of navigation. The alternative soft option is not open to Singapore. As Dr Goh often reminded us, the effects of flawed policies in a small open economy like Singapore will be felt within months, rather than years.

Land, Gold and Savings

As an Admin Officer, I have written hundreds of papers during my time. Most of them were routine, such as the annual economic report, back to office situational conference reports, budget submissions, project proposals, manpower planning papers, even National Day award citations.

Now and then, the Minister, in particular Dr Goh, would challenge us to draft policy recommendations to Cabinet. One of the earliest papers I helped to draft was the Cabinet paper proposing the enactment of the Land Acquisition Act.[18] Much of the land in rural Jurong that was required for the development of the Jurong Industrial Estate was privately owned, and it would have cost the State a bomb if we had followed the Western concept of the potential value of land as a basis for compensation.

As an economist, I argued that the land should be acquired at pre-development, and not post-development, value. The argument was very

---

17 Singapore experienced budget surplus from 1988 to 2001, extracted from MAS paper "Singapore's Balance of Payments 1965–2003: An Analysis". For more information, see <http://www.mas.gov.sg/masmcm/upload/mm/MM_75E5D63E_6295_5312_4F0D658B1397AC36__75E5D64E_6295_5312_411433D27608A4B8/StaffPaper33BOP.pdf> [16 Jan. 2006].

18 Refer to footnote 12 on page 152.

simple. As the landlord has done nothing to raise the potential value of the land, it would be unfair to society at large to give him the accretion of value arising from investment in infrastructure, such as roads and highways, public utilities, drainage, sewerage, etc. It was the State that invested in infrastructure out of public funds. The increase in the potential value of land should justly accrue to the government.

Land in Jurong and elsewhere was acquired at about 10 cents per square foot. After putting in infrastructure and resettling squatters, the land was leased to industries and the HDB at about 50 cents per square foot.[19]

The Land Acquisition Act laid the framework for the rapid development of industrial estates and HDB new towns. There was provision for the revision of the basic land values but this would lag behind the market by five years. The same economic justification was and still is used in the levying of development charges for higher density development of prime sites in the city. The cost of the MRT system is partially paid for from such development charges. For road and rail infrastructure, in contrast, the Certificate of Entitlement (COE) is the main source of revenue for such improvements.

The Land Acquisition Act is a powerful tool for development. But it has to be used with care. It can be abused by unscrupulous politicians. Internal safeguards are absolutely necessary to ensure that acquisition does not amount to confiscation.

In Singapore, any proposal for land acquisition by an executive ministry has to be concurred to by the Ministry of Law before it can be submitted to Cabinet, for decision. The Ministry of Law has to be satisfied that the proposal for acquisition is clearly for a public purpose, such as the building of roads, schools, public hospitals, MRT systems, HDB public housing, and industrial estates. Owners of land not satisfied with the rates of compensation can appeal to the Valuation Board of Appeal.[20]

A second policy paper, on which I recall being involved with great satisfaction, was the paper on gold. A few months before US President Nixon de-linked the US Dollar from gold, Dr Goh asked me to study gold to ascertain whether or not the American President could uphold the long standing Bretton Woods Agreement that had made the US Dollar the lynchpin of the world currency system. The US Dollar was pegged to a fixed amount of gold. In turn, all other currencies were tied to the value of the US currency. The Americans were obliged to redeem its currency for gold on demand by holders of the US Dollar.

After studying gold output and gold reserves, I told Dr Goh that if I were the American President, faced as he was with a recession and slow growth, I would find the burden of upholding the value of his dollar in gold

---

19 The equivalent of 0.46 cents per square metre (1 foot is 0.3048 metre).

20 The provisions for the Valuation Review Board can be found in the Property Tax Act (chapter 254) part IV.

too much of a strait-jacket. Weeks before President Nixon moved, Singapore bought its first ton of gold to serve as currency reserve at about US$40 an ounce. As the price of gold has stayed above US$300 an ounce since then, our first purchase of gold was probably the best investment the Government Investment Corporation (GIC) has ever made.

After President Nixon abandoned the gold standard, managing currency in a floating regime became far more complicated. As an MOF cadre, I still believe that a balanced budget is the best assurance of the stability of the Singapore Dollar. It pains me every time highly-paid economists in investment banks tout the line that Singapore is saving too much.[21] In my economic dictionary, there is no such thing as over-saving. Singaporeans, proud as we are of the level of our foreign reserves, should understand that any concerted attempt by the hedge funds of the world can undermine over just one day the value of the Singapore Dollar grievously.

If you were to ask me what gives me the greatest satisfaction as an Admin Officer, I would have to say that prescient analysis leading to correct policy recommendations, which are acted upon, are the best rewards in my career. Admin Officers do not just administer, they can and must also think.

---

21 Singapore's high economic growth and the ethos of fiscal rectitude, have led to budget surpluses averaging 5 per cent of GDP (surplus of $1,180.7 million in 2005), in the past years. Singapore's prudent fiscal policy has contributed to its high saving rate. Gross national savings rose from a modest 11 per cent of GNP in 1965 to over 50 per cent since 1995. Information can be found at the Monetary Authority of Singapore's web: <http://www.mas.gov.sg/masmcm/bin/pt1MAS_Staff_Paper_No_33_Aug_2004.htm> [10 Jan. 2006]. Criticisms that Singapore has excess savings and investments suggest that this is dynamically inefficient.

GRAND MONUMENTS, BRIGHT MINDS AND FLEXIBLE POLICIES

I was a Lands and Estates Officer in the Industrial Facilities Division (IFD) of the EDB in the mid-1960s. The IFD was the predecessor of the Jurong Town Corporation.[1] It was a very small division with only about three or four officers. The Civil Engineering Division was our much bigger cousin. One of the IFD officers was Robert Teng, who was from Penang and popularly known as Texas Teng because he was one of the few Malaysians in those early days who had graduated from the University of Texas. Another IFD officer was S. Sadavison from Kuala Lumpur, who rose to be the Director-General of the Malaysian Investment Development Authority (MIDA), which was, after separation, the Malaysian counterpart of Singapore's EDB.

As for me, on my return from Harvard University, I went from the sound and glory of the Investment Promotion Division to the nitty-gritty of the Jurong Industrial Estate. I must confess that inwardly I was disappointed.

After Harvard, I expected to be catapulted into the management ranks. My Chairman at the time, Mr Hon Sui Sen, knew better. To be an able administrator, one has to be "hands on", and "to walk the talk", as they say in modern management jargon. To the uninitiated, an estate officer's job is routine and mundane. On looking back, it was anything but dull.

Excerpts from a speech at "JTC Alumni dialogue", 27 Feb. 2004, JTC.

1 JTC was formed in 1968 and tasked to develop and manage industrial facilities in Singapore. During those days, the overriding objective was to kick start Singapore's industrialisation programme and Jurong was picked as a prime area for development even though laying the foundation stone was difficult. Chan Chin Bock, *Heart Work — Stories of how EDB steered the Singapore economy from 1961 to the 21st century* (Singapore: Singapore Economic Development Board and EDB Society, 2002).

One evening, as I was arriving home, I got a call from Mr Ong Leng Chuan who ran the Bridgestone tyre company in Singapore at the time, and was also Chairman of the Singapore Manufacturers' Association, the main association for industrial companies. He rang me urgently to say that his workers were up in arms because the water pressure was too low for them to have their baths. The reason was the small size of the pipes.

Apparently, the then PUB[2] refused to lay larger pipes until EDB signed a "take or pay" contract with them that guaranteed a certain level of demand. The same condition was imposed for power supplies. The PUB did not think that EDB could pull off "Goh's folly" and were sceptical of Dr Goh Keng Swee's aim to develop an industrial park and indeed a manufacturing base for Singapore. As the EDB was in the Ministry of Finance family, it gave the guarantee to the PUB. In the event, the guarantee was never invoked and the industrial project in Jurong grew from strength to strength.

Lest stones are thrown at PUB, I remember Mr Tan Beng Lay, who was then the Chief Financial Officer of PUB, calling on Joe Pillay and myself late one evening at our EDB office at the Fullerton Building. He was there to seek MOF's approval to obtain an overdraft from OCBC Bank to pay wages due the following day. Funding was tight for all government agencies at the time and PUB had their reasons to be cautious.

Flexibility and Sharing Misery

This story reminds me of the importance of having civil servants who are thinking and willing to be flexible in their actions. Most civil servants hide behind the Instruction Manuals (or "IMs") as an excuse for not having to think. If you do not decide or exercise your discretion, then you are not thinking. You have to think even when you say "No". Otherwise, you are just flying on auto-pilot. A "No" decision should have to stand up to public scrutiny as much as a "Yes" answer. The Auditor-General should check for acts of omission as much as he scrutinises acts of commission.

Let me illustrate this with an example from my Estate Officer days at EDB. We had built some shops at the light industries section near the flats to provide shopping and other amenities. In accordance with the IMs, we had put out the shops for public tender. As to be expected, the banks made the highest bids for space.

---

2   PUB is a statutory board now under the Ministry for the Environment and Water Resources. It is the water agency that manages Singapore's water supply, water catchment and sewage in an integrated way. PUB is involved in water resource planning and development; water production; catchment and reservoir management; water distribution and demand; and used water collection and treatment. For more information, please refer to PUB website at <http://www.pub.gov.sg/home/index.aspx> [13 March 2006].

There was one shop left when an old barber approached us to say that he could not compete with the banks as cutting hair was not a high margin business. He offered us $400 a month. It was less than what the banks tendered but, in the late 1960s, it was not a sum of money to be sniffed at.

So I brought the case to Mr Hon who was Chairman of the EDB. I suggested that we allocate the shop to the barber, for haircuts were an essential trade. Mr Hon agreed, but stipulated that the lease was to be for only three years. The barber should not expect to be subsidised forever. In any case, his business would grow with Jurong and the lease could later be renewed, at higher rentals.

Mr Hon Sui Sen was Perm Sec and Commissioner of Land before he was appointed Perm Sec (Economic Development) and Chairman EDB. He had introduced the Torrens system of land registration to Singapore.[3] In charging for land at Jurong, he practised what I would later learn from the Japanese as a policy of "sharing prosperity, sharing misery".

Under this policy, EDB did not charge the full premium for land on 30-year leases. Instead, we charged rental at 6 per cent of annual value per square foot. This could be revised once every five years subject to a cap of 50 per cent. The lease of 30 years would be extended for another 30 years if the EDB or JTC as landlord was satisfied that the lessee was making good economic use of the land.

In this way, manufacturers did not need to tie up too much of their capital on the land. Instead, they could invest more in machinery and equipment. Conversely, those who wished to only speculate on land were not welcome. Speculation is a zero sum game which we discouraged. But those who need to give priority to their operations were welcome. They were the ones, we knew, who would help Jurong succeed.

In the 1980s, the JTC and HDB were instructed by the MOF to return all undeveloped land that was surplus to their immediate needs, to the Land Office. Yet while the same policy applied to both agencies, the financial impact on JTC and on HDB was totally different.

While both bodies were made to pay current market rates to repurchase the land for development, the HDB enjoyed a bottom line subsidy. In effect, whatever the Land Office charged for land, HDB received a subsidy to offset it. This was justified by the government's decision to subsidise public housing for citizens. This made the repurchase by the HDB a bookkeeping exercise.

---

3   The land law, which applies in Singapore is based on English common law principles overlaid with the Australian Torrens system of land registration. The Torrens system is a registration system of title adopted by Singapore from Australia since 1954 when the Registry of Land Titles was established to administer the system. The Torrens system is widely acclaimed as a much simpler means of delivering an indefeasible or unimpeachable title. For more information, see John Baalman, *The Singapore Torrens System* (Singapore: Government Printing Office, 1961).

But when JTC repurchased land, it paid current market rates. This meant that it had no choice but to charge as much as the lessees could bear. Is it any wonder then that industrial and other land costs shot up in Singapore?

This has a direct impact on the finances of the JTC and HDB. But there was and is a more serious long-term structural effect on the economy. In effect, we are subsidising consumption (i.e. housing) and penalising production (i.e. industry). This is not a healthy road to take. Mr Hon's policy of sharing prosperity and sharing misery is no longer feasible, as JTC does not own any land stock anymore and cannot afford to be flexible and charge anything other than the highest rate for the land. The policies have become rigid.

Monuments and Bright Minds

How has the MOF treated other agencies and projects?

Most MOFs treat ministries of the arts like they were Cinderella, preferring other sisters. Or, like Oliver Twist, they stand last in the queue for budgetary funding. The mindset is such that schools and hospitals always have priority over concert halls and theatres. So it was with the Ministry of Culture and its successor, the Ministry of the Arts (MITA).[4] Then, in 1991, BG George Yeo[5] was appointed the Minister for MITA.

BG Yeo is a Cambridge-trained engineer. He can weave magic with words. He is a person of the mind and spirit. He has effervescent energy and is truly a renaissance man, a rarity in Singapore where we know the price of everything and the value of nothing.

So I told the Minister that at long last MOF is prepared to look at MITA's budget requests without prejudice, and on their own intrinsic merit. This change of mindset did not prepare MOF for the bombshell budget request that soon arrived on our desk. It was a request from MITA to build the Esplanade theatres and concert halls for $600 million. We were shell shocked.

Before this, the highest ever request from MITA had been for $50 million to reconstruct and refurbish the Victoria concert halls, and even this was only approved because Dr Goh Keng Swee himself placed his considerable power of persuasion behind the proposal.

After the initial shock, MOF soon recovered our composure. As Finance scrutineers, our habit is to start by scrutinising the small print, before admiring the big picture. We discovered that the operating cost of the performing

---

4 With effect from 13 Aug. 2004, the acronym of the Ministry has been changed from MITA to MICA (Ministry of Information, Communications and the Arts).

5 BG George Yeo began his political career in 1988. He was the Minister for Information and the Arts (1991–9), Minister for Health (1994–7), and Minister for Trade and Industry (1999–2004). Since 2004, he has been the Minister of Foreign Affairs.

theatres and concert halls would amount to $50 million a year. Jaspal Singh,[6] who was then my Deputy Secretary (DS), made a quick back of the envelope calculation and concluded that the Esplanade has to sell every seat every night of the year at $300 a seat just to break even on operating costs. From our MOF perspective, this seemed a winning argument. Government would have to insist that the capital costs be recoverable, at least on a reasonable projection. When we put this uncomfortable fact to MITA, there was only silence — no arguments no remonstration. We thought that was the end of the matter. How wrong we were.

Little did we know that the intrepid BG Yeo had appealed to the then Prime Minister Goh Chok Tong, who decided that the Singapore Totalisator Board or Tote Board would finance the capital expenditure. Moreover, this funding was to be outside the budget and below the line.

Strictly speaking, the Tote Board is only the agent for MOF and its revenue was to be credited to Finance at the end of the financial year. But as the Esplanade was to be financed out of future revenue streams, the MOF had no jurisdiction over how the money was to be spent, as it had not yet been received.

MOF was defeated by this ingenious procedural innovation. But personally speaking, I am glad MITA won, for without Tote Board financing we would not have the Esplanade Theatres on the Bay, shimmering in the noon day sun, and glowing on full moon nights.

How different this is from our early and austere days. I remember that the MOF invariably turned down the requests of the then Ministry of Community Development to build public swimming pools. We had calculated that it would cost $2 a swim if we have to build the pools and maintain them.

Our Minister, Dr Goh Keng Swee, considered it more cost-effective to give a schoolboy 50 cents for bus fare to go to the beach to swim. This is an example of what Dr Goh considered a robust approach to budgeting.

If we applied the same cold logic of Dr Goh's robust approach to the Esplanade, we would not have built it, and would instead have given every Singaporean a $150 subsidy each to attend concerts when visiting the great cultural cities of London, New York, or Beijing. This is purely a tongue in cheek proposal. I very much hope that the Esplanade will sell enough tickets a year to pay its operating cost. Otherwise, if and when times are hard, we will likely suspend spending on culture and the Esplanade and other similar projects will suffer.

I have had the privilege of visiting Beijing on several occasions. The most memorable visit was my first in 1979, before the opening up of China. There were few cars. As our motorcade went through the vastness of Tiananmen,

---

6 Mr Jaspal Singh was the former Deputy Secretary of MITA (currently Ministry of Information, Communications and the Arts). Prior to that, he was Deputy Secretary in the Ministry of Finance.

my mind flashed back to centuries of Chinese history when envoys from tributary states made the same journey to the Imperial Palace to pay tribute to the Emperor. The vastness of the square alone would have awed the envoys with the power and reach of China.

The imperial palace was the seat of imperial power. But to me, it is not the architectural icon of Beijing. In our recollection, one does not associate Beijing with the Imperial Palace. To me, the architectural essence of Beijing is the beautiful perfectly proportioned Temple of Heaven. The temple served as the imperial examination hall. Imperial examinations were presided over by the Emperor himself. Based on the results, the Emperor personally selected the ruling elite for the empire. He also offers the hand of his princess in marriage to the *chuang-yuan*, the top imperial scholar of the year.

The Temple of Heaven is built entirely of timber, without a nail being used. It is the product of a soaring imagination and the work of countless loving skilled hands crafting out the entire structure. Cost wise, it must be a fraction of the cost of building the Imperial Palaces. So, monuments do not need to cost a bomb.

In Singapore during our years of budgetary abundance, we have often mistaken form for substance. Our institutions of higher learning, including polytechnics, research laboratories, and even community clubs, headquarters of ministries and statutory boards, have been built to heights of elegance — beyond what their functions require.

Dr Melanie Ng Chew, who wrote the "Pillars of Fullerton", a history of that building,[7] described the old Fullerton Building as being dark and dim. Its saving grace was that there were some bright minds working in it. As I drive by so many of today's gleaming glass palaces, I often wonder whether the learning, teaching and research conducted inside the buildings do justice to the grandeur of the buildings.

It is not just the capital cost. Maintenance is higher. A robust measure that MOF can immediately impose is to charge real, not notional, rentals to be paid out of operating budgets. As operating budgets include wage costs, my hunch is that there will be an immediate reduction in the space required. And ministries may even volunteer to move out to cheaper quarters.

If you read Japanese economic history,[8] you will discover that when Japan rebuilt its economy and industry after the Second World War, they spent whatever precious capital they had on machinery and equipment, and the purchase of technology. They spent as little as they could on buildings, which were then old but functional.

---

7 Melanie Chew, *Memories of the Fullerton* (Singapore: Fullerton Hotel, 2001).

8 Claude Lonien, *Japanese Economic and Social System: From a Rocky Past to an Uncertain Future* (Amsterdam: IOS Press, 2003); Marius B. Jansen, *The Making of Modern Japan* (Cambridge, Mass: Harvard University Press, 2000); Masahiko Aoki and Ronald Dore (eds.), *The Japanese Firm: Sources of Competitive Strength* (New York: Oxford University Press, 1994).

China today is going through this early Japanese phase of industrialisation. Is it any wonder then that China, and soon India, can manufacture goods and provide services cheaper than anybody else in the world? As Lee Kuan Yew has urged, Singapore has to reduce costs across the whole spectrum to compete, even the cost of education and government.

Mr Lee once remarked that on his visits to various countries, he found an inverse correlation between the grandeur of the country's Parliament House and its per capita GDP. In plain English, the more grand the building, the poorer the people will be. I would like to add that the grander the building, the lower the quality of democracy practised. As our new Parliament House, although elegant, is of modest dimensions, Singapore is unlikely to suffer from one or both fates.

Nevertheless, the public sector should forever be vigilant of the cost of providing public services and not be seduced by monuments, concrete or intellectual.

LEADERSHIP AND LEARNING FROM OTHERS: LEADERS, NEW COMPETITION AND THOSE WHO LEAVE

Leadership is an abstract concept. It is difficult to define, yet we can all recognise leadership when we see it. Leadership is an unforced, indefinable quality. It is manifested through deeds, not words. Let me give three examples of what I am trying to convey.

The first example I wish to mention is Mr N.I. Low who was the principal of my alma mater, the Serangoon English School. I remember that long before our national, "Keep Singapore Clean" campaign, Mr Low would simply go around the school picking up litter. This was even before the bell rang for the start of the school day. Very quickly, one, two, three, and then a whole bunch of boys followed after him picking up litter. That was the start of the "Keep the School Clean" campaign. Our beloved principal led by deeds, not words.

The second example of leadership I learnt from was a rank and file union leader of the Singapore Traction Company (STC). As Perm Sec (Communications), I was with the then Registrar of Vehicles, Mr Goh Yong Hong, when we were given the onerous task of shutting down Singapore's major bus company, which was facing bankruptcy. We were neither prepared nor trained to shut down a bus company.

How do you tell hundreds of bus drivers, conductors and mechanics that they were losing their jobs, and yet expect them to drive their buses to Kallang Stadium, and have them parked in orderly lines? How indeed? Tempers would rise and hotheads may smash the buses.

This selection is an edited version of an address delivered at the "Far East Organization Leadership Speakers Series", 24 July 2004.

We were at a loss. Then a rank and file union leader, Mr Lee, came along to help us. Being trilingual in English, Malay and Chinese dialects, he quietly persuaded the former STC employees to park their buses, hand over the keys, and walk across the road to register for jobs at the recruitment booths set up by the four Chinese bus companies who were taking over the STC routes. There was no flag waving, clenching of fists, or shouts of anger.

Mr Lee showed quiet effective leadership of an order I have not seen again. It is a matter of great regret for me that I did not keep in touch with him. Ever since, I have nothing but the greatest respect for the rank and file union leaders.

The third lesson in leadership I have learnt is from my mentor, whom I served under when he was Permanent Secretary and later Minister, Mr Hon Sui Sen. When I joined the Economic Development Division of the Ministry of Finance as a young cadet officer, there were only four of us, namely the Minister, Dr Goh Keng Swee, Mr Hon, then the Permanent Secretary, myself as an administrative service cadet, and Mr Sani, the office attendant.

Lest I be arrogant, Mr Hon told me quietly one day that I should treat Mr Sani with consideration. Holding the key, he may just lock me in the office, should I be working late! Mr Hon was telling me that every one of his staff was valuable, and we should treat each other with respect, without pulling rank.

Mr Hon always showed a genuine interest in the progress of his officers and staff. As my handwriting was notoriously bad, Mr Hon one day offered to buy me a typewriter out of his own pocket.

But the lesson in leadership taught me by Mr Hon is that to be a leader you must not spare yourself. He likened a Permanent Secretary to the chief surgeon of a hospital surgical unit. The chief surgeon has to operate more often, and on the more difficult cases. So has a Permanent Secretary. He (or she) has to draft personally all the important memoranda for submission to Cabinet by his Minister. It was hard sound advice from Mr Hon that I practised to good effect. In other words, the Minister and the Permanent Secretary, as leaders of their ministries, do not spare themselves. They lead and teach not by words, but by deeds.

From these examples, we can look more broadly at our society and the kind of leadership we need for the future.

The Way Ahead: *Quo Vadis*, Singapore?

I believe that we need to emphasise knowledge for the future of our country. Singapore has virtually no natural resources. One resource that we do have is our location on the cross-roads between east and west; this is not only in the physical sense, but also in the cultural sense. Even then, there are dangers ahead. Long-range jets can now bypass Singapore on the Australia to Europe route. A terrorist attack on a super tanker in the Straits of Malacca can close, or at least restrict, access for world shipping to our port. As an interlocutor between China and the West, our falling standard of Chinese and English in our schools can only diminish our usefulness to both worlds. To be a friend of both the East and the West, we need to be rooted in their cultures.

Language proficiency and knowledge of their literature and history are the keys to understanding these nations. While we can reach out to India with English, we cannot depend on English to cultivate China and Indonesia. Only Malaysia, at least until now, is still on the same English wavelength as we are.

Venice was the most famous city state of its time in Europe. It was the centre of culture and commerce. It thrived in the world of ideas. Commerce provided it with the wealth to support the arts. It attracted the brightest and the best.[1] It was the shining star of Northern Mediterranean. But it did not survive the test of time.

In the end, the power of Venice was destroyed by internal dissension and indolence. Today, Venice is known as a city of canals, a charming and, to some, romantic city of love.

Fast forward six hundred years. We have another living and breathing city-state, our Singapore. Singapore became a city state not by choice, but by the force of circumstances.

The self-governing state of Singapore merged with the British colonies of Sarawak and Sabah, and the Federation of Malaya to form the Federation of Malaysia in 1963. We had hoped and believed that our chances of survival would be better by being part of a larger whole. It was a dream in vain however. Irreconcilable differences of ideology and beliefs tore us apart. Singapore was forced to separate from Malaysia to become the independent state of Singapore on 9 August 1965.[2]

For us who were then young men and women in our twenties and thirties, it was freedom regained. We do not know how precious freedom is until we have lost it. Singapore became the world's only city state in modern times. Can we survive in freedom?

Through sheer tenacity and dint of hard work, pioneering Singaporeans, under the strong and outstanding leadership of Mr Lee Kuan Yew, have built up a social and economic infrastructure that older and bigger countries have learnt to respect. Through rational economic policies, Singapore achieved full employment by the mid-1970s. But nothing stands still.

We invested in the education and training of our young to levels where they have the confidence to compete with the best in the world. We are

---

1 David Chambers and Brian Pullan, *Venice: A Documentary History* (Toronto: University of Toronto Press, 2001), Chambers, D.S., *The Imperial Age of Venice, 1380–1580* (London: Thames & Hudson, 1970).

2 Turnbull, *A History of Singapore 1819–1988*; Ernest Chew and Edwin Lee (eds.), *A History of Singapore* (Singapore: Oxford University Press, 1991).

leaving behind the disappointment of economic cooperation within ASEAN and forging free trade agreements with the rest of the world under the aegis of WTO to give us more economic space.[3]

Because of our minuscule size and small population, Singaporeans of my generation have always this sense of insecurity. As Mr Lee had said, the world does not owe us a living. As we grow older, this angst grows in us. In spite of the vicissitudes of their history, Indians and Chinese know with absolute certainty that there will always be an India and a China, unless of course planet earth explodes. Will there always be a Singapore?

Those of us who worked in the early EDB instinctively felt that a population of 3 million does not provide the critical mass needed to develop a self-sustaining economy. We studied successful small economies, such as Sweden, Norway, Switzerland and Israel, and concluded that a population double our size to six million will be more viable. Our town planners in the URA assured us that with some stretching, the physical size of Singapore of some 600 square kilometres can comfortably house a six million population.[4]

New Economics and the Individual

We were, however, thinking in terms of old economics that land, labour and capital are the only factors of production. In other words, potential GDP cannot exceed the sum total of the productivity of land, labour and capital. Training can raise skill levels and productivity of labour. But there is a sound barrier that technology cannot crash through. In what I would call the new economics, knowledge, besides land, labour and capital, is the key dynamic. With the application of knowledge, output can be increased beyond the potential of the three classical factors of production. Knowledge is therefore the key to Singapore's future.

Professor Joseph Nye, former Dean of the Kennedy School of Government at Harvard University, has enunciated the concept of "soft power" in contrast to "hard" power in the pursuit of American foreign policy.[5] The policy of the present Defence Secretary, Mr Rumsfeld, is summarised by the policy of "shock and awe" and is hard power. Winning the hearts and minds of the people is soft power. In classical Chinese thinking, this is the combination of

---

3 Singapore has concluded bilateral FTAs with the following countries and regions outside ASEAN Free Trade Area: Australia, European Free Trade Association, Jordan, India, Japan, Korea, New Zealand, Panama and the United States.

4 The URA concept plan 2001 maps out Singapore's physical development for the next 40–50 years. The plan is based on a population scenario of 5.5 million. According to the URA, long-term planning can help ensure that there is enough space for the competing needs of housing and recreation, industry and commerce, defence and infrastructure. URA Concept plan 2001 can be found at <http://www.ura.gov.sg/skyline/2001/03_May_Jun/draft_concept_plan_2001.pdf> [10 Jan. 2006].

5 Refer to footnote 2 on page 134.

"wen" and "wu", the pen and the sword, or the scholar and the warrior. The Chinese ideal is a combination of the scholar and the warrior in the same individual.

In peaceful competition, we can replace the word "power" with the word, "knowledge". Doffing my intellectual hat to Professor Nye, I would like to apply his useful concept to distinguish between hard and soft to knowledge.

"Rocket science" requires heavy investment in jet propulsion research and has been a short form term for all the technically difficult knowledge in what I would call hard knowledge. In contrast, researching demand for luxury cars in developing countries require soft knowledge.

Although our best minds in Singapore compare favourably with their peers in larger countries, we lack the numbers to research hard knowledge. Similarly, we do not have economies of scale of production for hard technology.

Our comparative advantage is in conceptualising things, more than design and blueprints, and more than production. This does not mean that we can simply conceptualise without having to design, or produce without blueprints. All four stages require thought and imagination. Mastery of the scientific principle involved is a *sine qua non*.

The challenge for Singapore is indeed daunting. Not having the numbers, we have to excel at the upstream conceptual and blueprint stage of knowledge. For us, the competition is between cities, not with countries. Singapore has to compete with London and New York, Paris and Milan, Shanghai and Beijing, Tokyo and Kyoto. At the level of cities, the competition is intensely individual. The individual counts. On a small population base of 3 million, how do we get the critical mass of the hundreds and thousands of talented individuals we need to make a difference for Singapore?

First, scarce as they are, we have to provide space for the creative and talented to think. Our teachers at schools and universities have to learn to respond to disconcerting, even rude, questions from their pupils. Our government and political leadership have to learn to accept alternative views on public policies and resist the temptation to rule uncomfortable questions out of order.

I would say that having "OB markers"[6] is to put a cap on thinking. With one crucial caveat. In a multiracial, multilingual and multi-religious Singapore, there will have to be OB markers on matters of race, language and religion. Not to place OB markers on race, language and religion is to

---

6 The term "Out-of-Bounds (OB) markers" started in 1994 after events such as the "Catherine Lim affair" which suggested a great divide between the PAP and the people, in an attempt to more clearly delineate what was and was not acceptable in terms of political dissent. "OB markers" mark the boundaries of engagement with the state and this has generated heated debates particularly among civil society groups which point to a lack of mutual trust between civil society and the government. See Izzuddin, Mustafa, "What are the Prospect of Civil Society in Singapore" in Workshop on Singapore/ Southeast Asia and the World, National University of Singapore.

invite disaster. This is true of Singapore as for all societies. We need not look far to see how religion and ethnic politics have destroyed countries such as Sri Lanka.

Outside this caveat, there will be no creative Singapore without the freedom to think. As a society, we need to allow the articulation of different points of view. Ideally, as a society we should agree to disagree. Only a free contest of ideas can give rise to the effervescence of creativity. Singapore needs creativity to survive and prosper. Without creative thinking, Singapore would have lost the competition between cities, even before we start. It is a farce to consider bar top dancing as a manifestation of the freedom to think.[7]

Competition between Cities

The competition between cities differs from competition between countries in one crucial aspect. Cities compete on ideas, and ideas spring from the mind of the individual. Unlike oil from the ground, ideas derive from knowledge. And knowledge is acquired from learning. Without natural resources, and a large population base, Singapore can compete only on the basis of knowledge. Knowledge resides in the individual mind. More than in any other society, in Singapore the individual counts. Truly, the individual makes the difference.

As Singapore globalises, more and more young Singaporeans will seek tertiary education abroad. They are likely to be the children of upper middle class professional parents. With thorough grounding in their school years in Singapore, most Singaporeans graduate at or near the top of their class when they are abroad and compete with foreigners. Our talented young are identified by their professors and offered PhD fellow-ships while abroad. Others are recruited by MNC employers. Hopefully, they meet and marry fellow Singaporean spouses. Hopefully, when they are more settled in their careers, they will return home and raise their families here.

Our best and brightest who graduate from NUS, NTU and SMU are also talent-spotted by MNCs, our banks, transport and logistic companies, and a whole host of specialised businesses, which the indefatigable EDB attracts to Singapore. As the world globalises, employers recruit talent not just to meet their local Singapore needs, but for their international business. There is a

---

7   In July 2003, Singapore lifted the restrictions against bar-top dancing. In the National Day Rally speech in Aug. 2003, PM Goh explained that this was to signal a shift in the government's mindset to being more relaxed and open-minded, and less strait-laced and Victorian. The move was to encourage Singaporeans to be self-reliant and robust. Speech can be found at <http://www.gov.sg/nd/ND03. htm> [10 Jan. 2006].

global hunt for talent. Competition between cities is competition between the imaginative and the talented.

In a knowledge-based global economy, the defining characteristic of a person is his individual talent and skill, not his citizenship, race or creed. Although there may still be barriers to the free flow of labour, most countries now realise that they have to welcome talent and skills. Singaporeans, with their fluency in English and hard science education, will be in demand not only at home but also abroad.

Spread out across the world, there are now scores of Singaporeans and foreigners who have worked in Singapore holding CEO or very high management positions in Fortune 500 companies.

In Singapore too, there is world-class talent, even if this is not abundant. There has been an unfortunate impression created in the foreign talent debate that you cannot be a talent if you are a Singaporean.[8] This perception is demoralising and corrosive.

Labelling Singaporeans as "stayers" and "quitters" is also divisive.[9] With a small population and a narrow talent base, we have to take care not to alienate our best and brightest. They are the most mobile in today's knowledge-based world. As a society, Singapore should never quit on anyone, and neither should Singaporeans quit on Singapore.

In the global competition for talent, we will need to appeal to the emotions, the heart more than the mind. Attracting a Singaporean to return with a top job offer is only a matter of dollars and cents. Getting him or her home to start and raise a family however is a matter of the heart. We need to try. The alternative is extinction. *Quo Vadis*, Singapore?

The Majulah Connection

A small group of us have established the Majulah Connection. It was initiated by two young Singaporeans, Dr Richard Lim and Mr Ong Peng Tsin, who found success in Silicon Valley. They could have easily chosen to leave Singapore and live in the West. But their hearts were still at home. I have

---

8 "Foreign talent policy" is part of the labour market policies to encourage foreigners to work in Singapore. It is in the belief that foreign talent is needed to boost the economy, create jobs and strengthen the country's competitiveness. MM Lee has also believed that Singapore with its small population could not produce enough talent and foreigners were needed. This became a highly controversial issue among Singaporeans and the governmental leaders.

9 The term "stayers" and "quitters" originate from a discussion of ideas by then PM Goh Chok Tong. "Fair-weather Singaporeans will run away whenever the country runs into stormy weather. I call them 'quitters'. Fortunately, 'quitters' are in the minority. The majority of Singaporeans are 'stayers'. 'Stayers' are committed to Singapore. Rain or shine, they will be with Singapore." National Day Rally Address by PM Goh Chok Tong, University Cultural Centre, 18 Aug. 2002. Speech can be found at <http://www.gov.sg/nd/ND02.htm> [10 Jan. 2006].

persuaded Dr Richard Hu, former Minister for Finance and Chairman of Shell Eastern, to be the Chairman of the Board of Trustees.

Dr Hu is the archetypal Singaporean we want to have. He rose to the top in a prominent international oil company and came home to serve as our Finance Minister, indeed our longest serving Finance Minister.[10]

The goal of the Majulah Connection is to connect Singaporeans at home to Singaporeans abroad, and Singaporeans to Friends of Singapore (FOS). FOS are non-Singaporeans who have worked and lived in Singapore and have now moved on. Though they have left Singapore, we hope they will leave a corner of their hearts for Singapore, and will remain our friends always.

Singaporeans living abroad and FOS form what we will call the diaspora of Singapore. "The diaSporeans", together with sturdy Singaporean "stayers", will in time form the larger nation of Singapore defined not by citizenship, but by a bonding of the heart. We very much hope that once a Singaporean, we will all remain Singaporean. No one quits on Singapore. Neither should we quit on anyone. Majulah Singapura!

---

10 Dr Richard Hu was Singapore's former Minister for Finance from 1985 until his retirement in 2001. He is currently Chairman of the Government of Singapore Investment Corporation (GIC) Real Estate Pte Ltd. He is also a member of the Board of the Singapore Investment Corporation Pte Ltd (GIC). Prior to his ministerial appointment, Dr Hu held the posts of Managing Director concurrently in the Monetary Authority of Singapore (MAS) and the GIC from 1983–4. He was with the Shell Group of companies in 1960 and his last position was as Chairman and CEO. Dr Hu was also elected Chairman of CapitaLand in 2004.

MINDS AND MINDSETS:
THE CIVIL SERVANT AND THE BUSINESSMAN

I was a career civil servant from my graduation until my retirement in 1999. Over 40 years, I have served in the economic ministries of Finance, Trade and Industry, Communications, National Development, and the Prime Minister's Office (PMO). I also served as Chairman of several statutory boards and government-linked companies, including the Economic Development Board (EDB), the Development Bank of Singapore (DBS), and Housing & Development Board (HDB).

More than my colleagues in non-economic ministries, I had greater contact with businessmen and entrepreneurs in the private sector. Civil servants and businessmen may look at the same set of facts or data, yet draw different conclusions. When looking at a half empty glass of water, the civil servant looks at the half that is empty, and concludes that there is a gap. A businessman, on the other hand, will see the half filled with water and conclude that there is an opportunity.

The difference in perception is because of the difference in their mindsets. The calculus of the civil servant is cost and benefits analysis, taught in schools of public administration. The abacus of the businessman is profit and loss, taught in business schools. My guess is that the civil servant and the businessman march to different drumbeats. The public sector strives to produce goods and services at the lowest possible cost so that the most number of people can afford them. Quality is consistent, but dull. There is no product differentiation.

Based on speech at the Pontiac Land-IPS, Thought Leaders Lunch held on 10 May 2005 at the Regent, Singapore.

Product Differentiation

As Chairman of the HDB, I showed a group of private developers from the Real Estate Development Association of Singapore (REDAS) around three blocks of newly completed design and build flats at Jurong West. The intention was to sell them en bloc to private developers for conversion into private apartments with condominium facilities.

The President of REDAS, an old friend from DBS Land,[1] took one look at the newly built flats and told me that my proposal will not fly because the flats had the "HDB look"! I was very upset because these flats, under our design and build schemes, were actually designed by private architects.

I could not understand why HDB flats designed by private architects should have the same look and feel of HDB flats designed by our own architects. Why is there no product differentiation?

On returning to the office, HDB management patiently explained to me that the look of privately or publicly designed HDB flats has to be similar because HDB or private architects have to design to the same set of cost parameters; which is another way of saying that HDB flats have to be "affordable".

To be honest, I am not totally convinced by HDB management's rationale. On becoming Chairman of HDB, I found it hard to accept that HDB flats built on prime sites still had to wear the same HDB look. The acid test will soon come with the introduction of HDB's Design, Build and Sell schemes (DBSS).[2] Under the new DBSS scheme, the successful tenderer for HDB sites will design, build and sell at prices that the developer sets for itself. The HDB will not set the selling prices.

This liberalisation is to be welcomed. I hope the stage will be reached when HDB developers can sell to all Singapore citizens, and not be confined to citizens who qualify under the household income ceilings, which is currently set at $8,000 a month.

---

1 DBS Land Ltd merged with Pidemco Land Ltd in 2000 to form CapitaLand Ltd. Today, the CapitaLand Group is one of the largest listed property companies in Asia, with international operations in 17 countries. The company is listed on the Stock Exchange of Singapore. The company's core businesses in property, hospitality, and real estate financial services are focused in key cities in Asia, Australia, Europe, and the Gulf region. More information can be found at <http://www.capitaland.com/en/index.html> [13 March 2006].

2 The Design, Build & Sell Scheme (DBSS) was announced in March 2005. This scheme involves the private sector in the development of public housing so as to bring about greater innovation in building and design and more housing choices. It enables public housing to be more responsive to the needs and aspirations of Singaporeans. Under the DBSS, private developers will be responsible for the entire flow of the public housing development process — from bidding for the land, designing the project, overseeing construction and eventually, selling the flats directly to eligible buyers. For more information, please refer to <http://www.hdb.gov.sg/fi10/fi10201p.nsf/WPDis/Buying%20An%20Apartment%20Under%20Design,%20Build%20And%20Sell%20SchemeOverview?OpenDocument> [13 March 2006].

Business Leaders

The 28 March 2005 issue of *Fortune Magazine* featured the affable genial face of Mr Warren Buffet on its front cover. The lead story was entitled, "The Best Advice I Ever Got": advice received — not given — by Warren Buffet, Jack Welch, Richard Branson, Peter Drucker, Meg Whitman, Andy Grove, Vivek Paul, and 21 other business superstars. Their personalities are as far apart as the North and South Pole; just compare Buffet with Branson.

Yet reading between the lines, one common quality shines through. That is, all these outstanding business leaders listen more than they talk. They take to heart advice given by their fathers, their bosses, their spouses, friends, and peers. But, they make up their own mind. They are leaders, not followers.

In my civil service career, I was privileged to know and enjoy the friendship of seven outstanding business leaders. Although none of them has a doctorate degree, they were men with sharp intellects. They valued education and have given generously of their wealth and their time to our schools, polytechnics and universities. What makes them stand out is their immense energy. They are always on the go, prowling and pouncing on business opportunities. You could say that they have the energy of the great cats of the animal kingdom. They are however not predators. They run businesses that do not exploit human weaknesses.

I have the greatest respect for them. That feeling is all the more notable since I am a member of the Singapore administrative service, which has been identified as a "priesthood" by none other than Dr Goh Keng Swee, our former Deputy Prime Minister and a great public servant.

I recollect the conversations I had with these nine business leaders. Although I was a younger man — not only in years but in wisdom — each of these leaders took me into their confidence and gave me very sound advice on business and on life.

"Nothing but the Best"

The first leader I recall was Mr Robert Kuok.[3] I met him first in the early 1960s when he and a group of fellow rice and sugar traders decided to enter an entirely new business — owning and operating hotels. They had bought a large piece of land in the then largely residential Orange Grove Road.

Mr Kuok came in to see me, then a young officer in the Ministry of Finance at the Fullerton Building, still wet behind the ears. I asked Mr Kuok what type of hotel he proposed to build. He told me his group was considering whether to build a super luxury 5-star hotel. At that time, visitor arrivals

---

3   Refer to footnote 10 on p. 121.

to Singapore were only around 400,000, as compared with our current 8,000,000 visitors per year, I demurred and wondered whether they should reduce their risk by building a more modest hotel.

Mr Kuok laughed and told me that although the visitor arrivals were relatively low, those who arrived at our shores were likely to be people of means and substance, and would want nothing but the best. That was the basis for building the first Shangri-La flagship hotel in Singapore, and has proven to be the right decision, judging from how well the chain has become.[4]

Fortunately, the right strategic decision was made by the businessman, not by the civil servant in me.

"Get the Business First"

In the mid-1970s, I was excited when I read in the morning papers that Robin Shipyard had won a contract from the People's Republic of China to build two oil rigs. As I was then Chairman of the EDB, I was wondering how Mr Robin Loh, who had never built oil rigs before, could clinch a contract to build not one, but two, oil rigs. I was concerned that Robin Shipyard might not be able to deliver, putting Singapore's reputation at risk. So, I invited Robin in for a chat.

When I popped the burning question, Robin looked at me, exasperated. He told me that as a businessman, he has to get the business first and worry about how to do it later. He pointed out to me that as a civil servant I would worry how to do the business for so long that we end up missing the boat.

With the contract in hand, Robin hired an American naval architect in Los Angeles to design the rigs. The rigs were built in Singapore under Chinese supervision! His advice to wannabe entrepreneurs was always, "To get the business first."

"Build a Circle Line"

Mr Brian Chang hailed from South Africa and, after graduating in mechanical engineering from the Imperial College in London, came to Singapore in the late 1960s hoping to work for EDB. Fortunately for Brian, the colleague who interviewed him turned him down as, "he was too good for EDB".

---

4 Shangri-La Hotel, Singapore is the flagship property for the award winning Shangri-La group. The hotel was founded in 1971 in Singapore. Today, Hong Kong-based Shangri-La Hotels and Resorts is the largest Asian-based deluxe hotel group in the region. It is regarded as one of the world's finest hotel management companies, garnering international awards and recognitions. Its chain comprises 47 deluxe hotels and resorts in key cities of Asia and the Middle East. More information can be found at <http://www.shangri-la.com/aboutus/company/en/index.aspx> [13 March 2006].

Brian went on to establish the Promet Shipyard and became an outstanding entrepreneur.[5]

He rang me up one morning when I was Perm Sec (Communications), and in the midst of planning and battling the Ministry of Finance to build the MRT. He had seen the proposed route configuration in the morning papers, and told me that it was all wrong. Brian said that an east-west/north-south configuration would only serve to carry traffic into the city in the morning and out of it in the evening. Only half the capacity would be used in the morning and in the evening. There would be little traffic in between the morning and evening peaks. Brian urged me to go for a circle line. Conceptually, a circular configuration would carry traffic through the day.

Instead, we configured the routes by linking up HDB new towns already built in a north-south and east-west direction.

Dr Goh Keng Swee made the same point in a different way. He said that it was too expensive to build rail systems just to carry the morning and evening peaks. This was the same analysis as Brian Chang's. But Dr Goh differed from Brian in thinking it better to develop bus routes, which are more flexible. As he puts it, when mistakes are made the marginal cost is only the cost of the last bus. The rail system requires putting $5 billion at risk.

Both Dr Goh and Brian Chang were right in their own way. Having built the MRT, Singaporeans are now more mobile and can access almost every part of Singapore by rail or bus. Singapore is now a more liveable city. Property values have moved up.

In the great MRT debate, I was for building the MRT, as higher property tax revenue would pay for the full capital cost. As Perm Sec (Finance), my main concern was that fares should be set at levels enough to pay the full operating costs and provide for depreciation. I hope the Public Transport Council would take this to heart in deciding on future fare increases.

"Just Follow the HDB"

The late Mr Kwek Hong Png built a property empire out of a hardware business, and spoke only Hokkien. Although my own Hokkien is elementary,

---

5 Mr Brian Chang was formerly owner of the Promet Shipyard in Singapore. He is now the CEO/Chairman of the Yantai Raffles Shipyard which has a 40-year history of creating offshore vessels for both the Chinese navy and the marine industry worldwide. Within the last couple of years, Brian Chang has acquired a majority interest and has made a major investment in creating one of the most modern sophisticated shipyard in the world. For more information, see <http://www.rafflesyacht.com/about.html> [13 March 2006].

I decided one day to ask him about his business strategy in building up a land bank for the Hong Leong group.[6]

He looked me straight in the eye and told me that he adopted a very simple strategy. He said that whenever and wherever the HDB acquired land for building new towns, he would buy whatever odd lots that the HDB left behind. The zoning did not matter. Mr Kwek figured out that if the Chief Planner allowed change of use from, say, rural green zone to suburban residential for HDB acquired land, by the same token the Chief Planner would have to allow change of use for privately acquired land in the vicinity.

Mr Kwek was a shrewd businessman who understood the mindset of the civil servant. What the civil servant failed to see was that when the HDB acquired the bulk of the rural land, whatever remained in the private domain was scarce, and therefore more valuable. It was public policy that created private scarcity and value for shrewd entrepreneurs, such as Kwek Hong Png of Hong Leong.

"Enjoy your Birds' Nest, before the Chinese do"

The late Mr Lien Ying Chow was a man of boundless energy and tenacity. He established a fledgling Overseas Union Bank[7] in war torn China and moved it back home to Singapore when the Second World War ended. He had very high emotional quotient or "EQ", and built OUB to be one of the "Big Four" banks[8] in Singapore.

I recall a conversation with Mr Lien at a National Day reception held in the Singapore Conference Hall. This was back in the late 1970s, well before China became an economic powerhouse.

He believed in birds' nest as a health tonic and advised me to enjoy birds' nest before, as he put it, the Chinese priced us Singaporeans out of the market. Mr Lien was very prescient. Today, a *tahil* of birds' nest is worth more than its weight in gold.[9] Looking back, Mr Lien in his inimitable way gave me a lesson in global competition that no amount of statistics can ever convey.

---

6 The Hong Leong Group is one of Singapore's largest local private sector conglomerates with about 510 companies, including 9 listed companies engaged in property, hotels, financial services, trade & industry, and e-business in the Asia-Pacific, Europe and North America with gross assets of over S$20 billion. For more information, see <http://www.hongleong.com.sg/hl.nsf/index.htm> [13 March 2006].

7 Founded by Lien Ying Chow in 1949, the Overseas Union Bank (OUB) grew to become the fourth largest Singapore bank and the fifth largest commercial bank in Southeast Asia in terms of shareholders' equity. OUB had 3,000 staff and was ranked 119th in a survey of the world's top 1,000 banks. In 2001, United Overseas Bank (UOB) successfully acquired OUB with a US$5.7 billion offer, and OUB legally became a single entity under the UOB name from 2 January 2002, turning into Singapore's largest bank in terms of domestic customer loans, credit cards and market capitalisation.

8 The "Big Four" banks in Singapore were the Development Bank of Singapore (DBS), Overseas Chinese Banking Corporation (OCBC), Overseas Union Bank (OUB) and United Overseas Bank (UOB). In 2002, OUB was merged with UOB.

9 A *tahil* is a traditional measure of weight used in Singapore and the surrounding region. It is equivalent to 1 1/3 ounces (37.8 grams).

"Lukewarm Water is Best"

Mr Teo Soo Chuan, as the eldest son, heads See Hoy Chan,[10] one of Singapore's leading rice and sugar traders, which was founded by his father Dato' Teo Hong Sam.

Soon after General Suharto came to power as the President of Indonesia, he sent a message to Singapore asking whether our government could send 10,000 tons of rice to a province in Indonesia on the verge of starvation. Dr Goh, who was our Finance Minister, decided that we would do so as a good neighbour. There was no need to enter into any memorandum of understanding. See Hoy Chan shipped the rice on our account.

It was a humane response to a neighbour's request for help. This gesture of goodwill on the part of Singapore paid handsome dividends in our relationship with Indonesia under the stewardship of President Suharto. For the record, Indonesia returned the 10,000 tons of rice to Singapore some years later. Teo Soo Chuan told me that the rice returned was of a higher quality than the rice we gave.

Out of this relatively unknown episode, Mr Teo told me that, in dealing with Indonesia, the best water temperature for Singapore is lukewarm. If the water is too "cold", and Indonesia is as efficient as we are, there will be no role for Singapore. But neither should the water be too "hot" so that Indonesia descends into chaos. If the water is too hot, Singapore would be boiled in it. Teo Soo Chuan summed up in a nutshell what could be our Ministry of Foreign Affairs' policy on Indonesia.

Doing "Chinese" Business on Expat Cost

Mr Goh Tjoei Kok came to Singapore from Djambi, Sumatra, in the 1950s. His Tat Lee Company[11] grew to be a major rubber and palm oil trader with plantations both in Indonesia and Malaysia. He and his business partners established Singapore's first steel re-rolling mill. The National Iron and Steel

---

10 The See Hoy Chan Group is a diversified group with business interest in information technology, asset management, financial services, general insurance, property development, property investment, facilities management, skills training, productivity management and engineering.

11 The late Mr Goh Tjoei Kok is the founding Chairman of the Tat Lee Bank Group, Mr Goh ventured into the rubber trade in 1937 and set up the company Tat Hoa in 1945, making a great fortune from the business. He migrated to Singapore in 1947 and started the trading firm Tat Lee dealing with the import and export of goods. He later ventured into the iron and steel industry and owned 40 per cent of the National Iron and Steel Mills Ltd (the company is a joint venture between the Singapore government and a group of local investors) and was the Vice-Chairman from 1961–86. Tat Lee Bank was set up in 1973 (the first Singapore registered bank to be launched when the government started promoting Singapore as an international financial centre in the 70s). Tat Lee Bank later merged with Keppel Bank to form Keppel Tat Lee Bank Ltd which is now taken over by Overseas Chinese Banking Corporation (OCBC). For more information, see <http://www.ntu.edu.sg/DO/Home/Professorships/Goh+Tjoei+Kok.htm> [13 March 2006].

Mills (NISM) produced steel bars from ship scrap for Singapore's HDB housing programme.

I got to know Mr Goh well when he became the non-executive Chairman of Intraco Limited. Set up by Dr Goh, our hope was to grow the company into a trading conglomerate.

Alas, we got off on a wrong footing. Mr Goh was a quiet man who seldom had harsh words for anyone, least of all a civil servant. But one day, he asked to see me urgently and told me bluntly that Intraco would never succeed because, in his words "the company's management was earning expatriate salary and doing small Chinese business".

In today's idiom, Mr Goh implied that, while we expected to enjoy world class pay, we were not delivering world class performance. As Singaporeans aspire for world class lifestyles, we need to remember that we have to deliver world class performance.

Dr Goh Keng Swee and Bird Seed

Dr Goh Keng Swee was Singapore's first Finance Minister. According to Professor Silcock, who taught economics to Dr Goh in Raffles College, and myself at the then University of Malaya, Dr Goh was the best economics mind he had taught.

As Defence Minister, he established what is now known as the cluster of defence industries grouped under Singapore Technologies Engineering. He did it without purchasing technology, which would have been prohibitively costly. Instead, he adopted what is called "reverse engineering", which was the process of engineering backwards from the final product to the parts and components. Reverse engineering is the approach of the public service manager faced with resource constraints.

A more vivid example of this cost conscious mindset is embodied in his decision to build the Jurong Bird Park first, rather than the zoo. On our return journey from the IMF/World Bank meetings in Washington in September 1968, Dr Goh asked me to draft a project paper to set up a bird park in Singapore.

When I asked him why not a zoo, he gruffly replied that birds only eat bird seeds, which is a fraction of the cost of meat to feed carnivorous animals at a zoo. For the record, Dr Goh approved the setting up of the Zoological Gardens later. In reality, both the bird park and the zoo have had to be subsidised by the Ministry of Finance.

This story outlines one way of summing up the difference between the mindset of the businessman and the civil servant. The businessman wears a demand side mindset, always striving to sell at the highest possible price. The civil servant, on the other hand, works on the supply side to provide a service or a product at the lowest possible cost.

The civil servant, not being attuned to the market as well as the businessman, often has to sell below cost, incurring subsidies at public expense. Of course, when he guesses wrongly, the businessman incurs a loss. But when he gets it right, he makes private profit. Another difference that results from this is that the civil servant is rewarded for output. The businessman is rewarded for the outcome, which is profit.

What Keeps Me Awake At Night

What keeps me awake at night? Having served as Chairman of the Economic Development Board from 1975 to 1981, I have become a chronic worrier on the state of health of the Singapore economy.

The front page of the *International Herald Tribune* (IHT) of 12 August 2004 carried an article with the compelling and provocative headline: "Singapore's economy: Has it passed its peak? Country struggles to sustain its growth."

The IHT journalist raised the right question. I was, however, disappointed that the body of the article was more political rhetoric than economic substance. The heading will serve us Singaporeans well as a wake up call. I will re-phrase the headline as: "Can Singapore Survive?" As a true blue Singaporean, I would say that it is not in our nature to accept preordained fate. If we have to die, we will go down fighting.

The recent economic history of Singapore is a part of most of us born before 1959. When the PAP government first assumed power that fateful year, it inherited a stagnant entrepôt economy with an unemployment rate exceeding 10 per cent. There was a small educated group literate only in English, but largely without any technical skills. Singaporeans were mostly clerks, teachers, nurses, personal drivers, and *amahs*.[12]

Competing with Other Countries

As a young EDB officer, I recall visiting Hong Kong with Mr Lien Ying Chow and Mr Eric Meyer who was from Israel and served as our first EDB director. We called on a Teochew entrepreneur who manufactured metal stampings for alarm clocks. We tried to interest him in setting up shop in Singapore. He turned us down in a condescending way, saying that Singaporeans, who are just small traders, could never manufacture consumer products such as clocks. At the time he was right.

This drove us in EDB to promote industrial training. Fortunately for Singapore, we were able to attract pragmatic multinational companies, such as Philips of Holland, Rollei of Germany, Seiko of Japan, to establish joint industrial training centres with EDB, to turn young school leavers into skilled technicians.

---

12 The term "Amah" refers to a household maid or servant, often one whose job involved looking after children. An *amah* frequently remained with a single family for a long period.

Another man, Dr Pannenberg from Philips was our first Science and Technology Advisor. He told us that basic research was not an option for Singapore. Instead, he urged us to raise our level of competence in science and technology. Dr Pannenberg was confident that if there are competent engineers and scientists in Singapore, we would be able to attract high technology MNCs to establish manufacturing plants here.

EDB therefore pushed for the expansion of engineering enrolment in what is now NUS, and enthusiastically supported the metamorphosis of Nanyang University into the Nanyang Technological Institute. A*STAR, our agency for Science, Technology and Research, ably led by Mr Philip Yeo is basically following the game plan laid by Dr Pannenberg nearly three decades ago. This is to raise the level of competence of our engineers and scientists.

Our three universities, NUS, NTU and SMU, have added IT and soft skills necessary for Singapore to compete in finance, banking, publishing and advertising, and other media services. In essence, our investment in education is to acquire the knowledge that we can use to leverage on the greater resource base of land, labour and capital of our neighbours and trading partners.

Singapore has to find a niche in the economic pyramid of every other country. Because of our limitation of size and talent, we can never achieve an integrated self-contained economic pyramid on our own. In fact no country can, in today's global economy.

I believe that we can leverage on our expertise and experience in fields such as ship repair, port management, housing and township development, transportation and logistics, education and health services, IT networks, retail banking, and other new emerging service sectors.

Our strength in oil refining and petrochemicals, advanced electronics, pharmaceuticals, can be exported to other countries with greater resources to help establish industrial clusters or hubs in countries such as China and India. Knowledge is a platform for win-win cooperation.

The old mindset of a zero sum game in competition is obsolete. What our competitors cannot take away from us is good government.

Finally, Singapore should never opt for quick fixes, such as a casino resort in whatever form or name.[13] We have not done so in the past. Today, Singapore is a far stronger economy and healthier society than, say, Macau.

---

13 After extensive consultations and Parliamentary debate, the government decided to build two integrated resorts with casinos by 2010 at Sentosa and Marina Bay. A Casino Control Bill which regulates the gaming industry and sets out social safeguards was passed in Parliament in early 2006. The Ministerial Statement by PM Lee on "Proposal to Develop Integrated Resorts" dated 18 April 2005 can be found at <http://app.sprinter.gov.sg/data/pr/2005041803.htm> [10 Jan. 2006].

Instincts and Foresight

In facing the future, our current generation of political and business leaders will do well to learn from the instincts, foresight, and grit, of our pioneering business and political leaders. There are many lessons to be learnt. After all, who could have imagined that from a single hotel in Singapore, Mr Robert Kuok and his business partners could have gone on to establish a global chain of Shangri-La hotels?

JAPAN IN SINGAPORE: AN ECONOMIC PARTNERSHIP

Early Help

When the history of industrial development in Singapore is written, the record will show that the whole process was kick-started by two Japanese companies in the early 1960s. The first was Maruzen Toyo, an oil trading company from Tokyo. This upstart company proposed to build an oil refinery in Singapore.

Shell, which had been operating in Singapore for over a hundred years distributing kerosene and petrol from the offshore island of Pulau Bukom, was shocked into immediate action. The Managing Director of Shell Eastern rushed to my office in Fullerton Building and told the Singapore government that Shell too planned to build a huge refinery in Bukom.

Before then, Shell had always considered Singapore as a centre for distribution, and not for refining. In the event, Shell was awarded Pioneer Certificate No.1 for its refinery.[1] The fact remains that Shell would not have developed Bukom into a world class refining centre if not for Maruzen's bold, if not outrageous, move.[2] Being a much smaller oil company, Maruzen built

This is edited from Remarks at the Japanese Chamber of Commerce on 6 Oct. 2004.

1 Shell was established in Singapore in 1891 and is one of Singapore's largest foreign investors. Shell's long standing relationship with Singapore includes the setting up of Singapore's first oil refinery for which the company was awarded "Pioneer Certificate No. 1" by the Singapore government in 1961. For more information on Shell, see <http://www.shell.com/home/Framework?siteId=sg-en&FC2=/sg-en/html/iwgen/leftnavs/zzz_lhn1_0_0.html&FC3=/sg-en/html/iwgen/welcome.html> [13 March 2006].

2 Yeo Ai Hoon, *Enterprise in oil: the history of Shell in Singapore: 1890–1960* (Singapore: Department of History, NUS, 1989).

a more modest refinery in a Pasir Panjang estuary. It was later sold to British Petroleum.

Once Shell was in, Esso and Mobil followed soon after. Singapore today is an international refining, petrochemical, and oil trading centre. For this, we must thank Maruzen Toyo. As it was a small company, it could not succeed as an oil trader in the league of giant oil companies. But Maruzen showed the way forward in Singapore.

The second Japanese company, which showed its faith in the struggling Singapore of the 1960s, was Ishikawajima Harima Heavy Industries (IHI). Dr Shinto, a world famous naval architect and CEO of IHI, decided to establish a modern ship repair yard at Jurong. It is one of three repair yards in the world to service IHI's Freedom vessels.

Dr Shinto sent Mr K. Sakurai, a young naval architect, to Singapore to set up and run Jurong Shipyard. Mr Sakurai spent almost his entire professional career in Singapore and became a Singapore Permanent Resident. Sakurai-san truly became a friend of Singapore.

Singapore's next phase of development in the petroleum sector was again spearheaded by a Japanese company. In 1975, Sumitomo Chemical of Japan, led by its redoubtable Chairman, Norishige Hasegawa, proposed to build a modern petrochemical complex in Singapore on Pulau Ayer Merbau.

It was conceived as a national joint venture project between Singapore and Japan. Although our refineries produced naphtha, the raw material for the production of ethylene, it was not as cheap a raw material as natural gas, which Middle East countries produced in abundance. Ethylene is the building block for a whole host of downstream petrochemical projects.

It was a daunting challenge for Sumimoto's President, Hijikata-san, and his team, which included the young Yonekura-san as the only English-speaker. There was an equally young Singapore team, namely Joe Pillay, Ngiam Tong Dow, Lee Yock Suan[3] and Daniel Selvaratnam from EDB. Yonekura-san subsequently became the President of Sumitomo Chemicals.

The Singapore project had to compete against Mitsui's project in Iran. There was no dearth of armchair nay-sayers in Singapore, including *The Straits Times*. As Mr Hasegawa had committed Sumitomo to build a petrochemical plant in Singapore, the Sumitomo team gritted their teeth and pressed on resolutely. Often, there was agony in their eyes.

In his memoirs, Mr Hasegawa said that the Petrochemical Corporation of Singapore (PCS) was established by divine intervention. He explained that

---

3 Mr Lee Yock Suan was the former Minister for Labour (1987–92), Education (1992–7), Trade and Industry (1997–9), Environment (1999–2001), Information and the Arts (1999–2001) and the Prime Minister's Office (2001–4). He was with the Economic Development Board as a Division Director from 1969–80. He is currently a Member of Parliament. CV obtained from <http://www.parliament.gov. sg/AboutUs/Org-MP-currentMP-CV-40.htm> [13 March 2006].

when he, a Roman Catholic from Japan, met our Finance Minister, Mr Hon Sui Sen, a fellow Roman Catholic, he felt at ease. He found in Mr Hon a partner he could count on, in embarking on what was then Singapore's largest manufacturing investment.[4]

Mr Hasegawa had studied political science at university. He decided on Singapore because of our political stability. Mr Hasegawa's political judgment was vindicated when the Iran-Iraq War broke out in 1981. Mitsui aborted its half-completed project in Iran, giving Singapore the opportunity to build the world's next petrochemical complex. Mr Hasegawa was right in thinking the PCS in Singapore was built through divine intervention.

Singapore broke Mr Hasegawa's heart when we sold our half share of PCS to Shell, when the plant was already running profitably. As a member of the Singapore team that brought about the establishment of PCS as a joint Singapore-Japan national project, I too felt betrayed.

Singapore breached the trust of our Japanese partners. I cannot again meet Mr Yano, MITI's Administrative Vice-Minister, who in a ten-minute interview with me, when I was Perm Sec for MTI, satisfied himself that PCS was indeed a national project for Singapore, as it was for Japan. Without the courage and foresight of Mr Hasegawa, there would have been no PCS. Without PCS, there would be no Jurong Petrochemical Island, of which we are proud of today.

Encounters and Insights

As Perm Sec for the Prime Minister's Office, I accompanied our then Prime Minister, Mr Lee Kuan Yew, on official visits to Japan in the 1970s and 1980s. One of the highlights of these visits was the luncheon hosted by the Keidanren, the top business organisation in Japan. The captains of Japanese industry, in their very polite ways, asked sharp questions of Mr Lee in the Q&A over coffee after an excellent three-course Western lunch.

Their questions on the economic and political conditions of Southeast Asia were short and penetrating. Their staff had done their homework well. I had a faint suspicion that some of the questions were inspired by Gaimusho, the Japanese Foreign Ministry. Some of my Japanese acquaintances became my good friends. We were able to engage in conversations beyond the "business" agenda.

Even further back, in the early 1960s, when I was a young administrative cadet, I accompanied Dr Goh Keng Swee, my Finance Minister, for dinner at the home of Mr Tabata. Mr Tabata was the first representative for JETRO (Japan Export Trade Organisation) in Southeast Asia, based in Singapore.

---

4 Norishige Hasegawa, *Zaikaijin Kara no teigen, do suru Nihon Keizai, Aipekku* (Japanese, unknown binding).

Mr Tabata was one of the very few Japanese then who could speak English, although haltingly. If I recall correctly, Mr Tabata represented a major Japanese steel company besides being the JETRO representative. He visited us at the Economic Development Division of the Finance Ministry often.

One day, I asked him what his role was as the JETRO representative. He smiled and said that he could do what MITI could not do. He could also do what Mitsubishi could not do. In making trade representations to the Singapore Ministry of Finance, depending on the circumstances and the context, Mr Tabata can on occasion speak on behalf of MITI or, if the situation demands, speak on behalf of Mitsubishi.

I now realise that my MITI colleagues had conceived of what we in Singapore now know as strategic pragmatism or, in American terminology, strategic ambiguity. I have a lot of respect for MITI and its officials. In the mid-1970s, Singapore MTI and Japan's MITI exchanged study visits in alternate years "to learn from each other". On our visits to Japan, our Japanese host was Mr Miyamoto, MITI's Director-General of Industrial Policy. Mr Miyamoto later went on to become the President of JETRO.

Mr Miyamoto told me that in visiting Japan, it was best to learn the software, rather than be awed by the hardware. He said that the key to industrial growth was productivity. He pointed out that although Japan could consider itself an industrial nation, Japan's productivity growth could not exceed 4 per cent a year consecutively for ten years. Japan showed Singapore the way in promoting productivity.

The WITs[5] movement in Singapore was conceived out of MTI's exchange visit with MITI. Singapore however did not derive as much success from WITs as Japan did. There are a whole host of reasons. Temperamentally, the Japanese are a group-centred people. Singaporeans are too individualistic, which in itself is not a bad trait. Entrepreneurs are individualistic.

Unfortunately, the Singapore Civil Service bureaucratised the whole process. The participation rate became all important. Because of the lack of spontaneity, the outcomes of WITs efforts were pedestrian. There was no sense of evangelism in the upper ranks of management. Unless we can raise our productivity, Singapore's sustainable GDP growth rate is at best in the 4–6 per cent range.

I then asked Miyamoto-san what was Japan's industrial Research and Development (R&D) policy. Before arriving at MITI, I imagined that MITI

---

5 The Work Improvement Team (WIT) Scheme is a team-based approach to solving problems or creating new value in work-related areas. Starting in the 1980s as a productivity movement, it sank roots rapidly in the Civil Service. The philosophy behind WITs is that all officers at all levels know best the problems in their area of work, and they should be empowered to make a difference to the way work is done rather than wait for the management to drive changes. A WIT is made up of a group of public officers (of any grade) from different departments which meet regularly over a period of time to find new solutions for a work-related topic. It encourages teamwork, cross divisional interaction and work efficiency.

would have drawn up a grand R&D master plan to ensure that Japan stays ahead in the technology race. He told me simply that Japan had no such plan. He said that MITI officials read the same scientific and technology journals as anybody else. He said that Singapore would know as much about progress in advanced electronics, biotechnology, and in today's context nanotechnology, as anyone else.

All that MITI did was to secure as much research funds as possible from *Okurasho*, the Japanese Ministry of Finance. Grants would then be given to say six or more leading companies in each industrial domain. It was up to the companies to research and develop new products for the market. As he puts it, MITI's policy was to bet on every horse in the race. Hopefully, one of the horses would turn out to be a world-beater.[6]

He then looked at me in the eye and said that Singapore's problem was that we did not even have one horse in the race. A*STAR is acutely aware of the paucity of Singapore horses. It is doing the next best thing, which is to import foreign horses to run the race for us.

Miyamoto-san would not have supported such a strategy. It will be far better for A*STAR to identify potential Creative Technology, Hyflux, and super babies yet unborn, and support them whatever it takes. Singapore may yet produce a world champion.[7]

The key is to have as many Singapore horses as possible in the race. Ironically, in one area of endeavour, namely banking, we have tried to have as few horses in the race as possible. The policy of the Monetary Authority of Singapore (MAS) has been to force the five Singapore banks to merge into three and, perhaps in future, into two, if not one, Singapore bank. This is totally misguided.

MAS should ponder what would happen to Singapore banking if the one horse remaining turned out to be lame! I believe however that better counsel now prevails. The challenge is to turn the three Singapore banking horses into regional, if not international banks. After all, HSBC (The Hongkong and Shanghai Banking Corporation), with roots in the Far East, has been transformed into "the world's local bank".

In my last conversation with Miyamoto-san, I remember he asked me whether I had heard of this quotation, "knowledge is power", from an Englishman, Francis Bacon. He said that the Japanese would add, "if applied with wisdom". This conversation took place in the early 1980s, well before the term "knowledge-based economy" entered our economic vocabulary.

---

6 Hiroshi Shimizu and Hitoshi Hirakawa, *Japan and Singapore in the World Economy: Japan's Economic Advance into Singapore 1870–1965* (New York: Routledge, 1999), p. 205. At that time, the Japanese government adopted an economic policy with a view to developing the manufacturing sector in Japan, and therefore encouraged manufacturing firms to invest abroad.

7 See page 23.

Like all other countries, Singapore has to embrace knowledge, which is the foundation of the new economics. If Singapore continues to follow the old economics based on land, labour and capital as the factors of production, our economic growth will be very limited indeed. With our fluency in English, Singapore is well placed to run this race of knowledge.

Similarities and Differences in Education

I have met the chairmen and presidents of many Japanese multinational companies, and also the CEOs of their Singapore businesses. I remember one of my most interesting conversations was with Mr Yamashita, who was then the President of Matsushita.

When he called on me in my EDB office, I asked him what he thought of the Singapore education system. Being Japanese, he was initially very polite and complimented us on our relatively high educational standards. I probed him further and asked him whether there was any structural problem standing in the way of Singapore's industrial development.

After careful thought, he said "yes". He told me that Matsushita found the educational quality of its Singapore workforce very uneven. As he puts it, our educational structure had some brilliant individuals perched like eagles on high peaks. However, the average educational level of the rest was not high. He said that Singapore should concentrate on educating the mass to raise the average level and not just focus on the top scholars. He told me that the average in Japan then was senior high, probably equal to our junior college level. He said that to advance, we need high broad plateaus, not solitary peaks.

All the Japanese ambassadors to Singapore I have known were erudite and cultured men. But only two of them that I knew, namely Ambassador Nara and Ambassador Kikuchi, spoke English well enough to communicate freely with Singaporeans like myself who, unfortunately, could not speak any Japanese.[8]

Over lunch one day, Ambassador Kikuchi asked me where I received my undergraduate university education. I told him that Singaporeans and Malayans of my generation in the 1950s were all educated at the University of Malaya, then located in Singapore at the Bukit Timah campus. The University of Malaya served both Singapore and Malaya and was the predecessor of both the National University of Singapore for Singapore, and the University of Malaya for Malaysia.

One course later in our meal he asked me the same question. So I told Ambassador Kikuchi once again that I was educated in Singapore. Over

---

8 Ambassador Nara served in Singapore from 1969–72, while Ambassador Kikuchi served from 1977–9.

coffee, he again asked me where I was educated! By then I was visibly angry, and asked him whether he was deaf.

Ambassador Kikuchi, in his usual affable way, smiled. He said that I had not understood his question. He said that in Japan, the elite were all educated at home at Todai and Keio, and so he found it strange that our young elite were all educated abroad, at Cambridge, Oxford and Harvard. Observing this, he wondered how I, who as a Permanent Secretary was equivalent to a Japanese Administrative Vice-Minister of the Ministry of Finance, was educated in Singapore, and not in Britain or the US, as were the new elite of Singapore.

Every society will have its own elite. This is not harmful so long as the elite are the leaders who emerge naturally through superior performance and demonstrable qualities of leadership, from the meritocratic system that Singaporeans uphold. It will however be a mistake for elites to practise elitism. Elitism, unlike meritocracy, is exclusive and divisive.

This subtle difference was brought home to me by the president and founder of a Japanese precision engineering company, who visited me at the EDB where I was then the Chairman.

When I talked about Todai and the leadership its graduates provide Japan, this gentleman leaned back in his chair and told me curtly that I was wrong. He said that post-war Japan was rebuilt by men such as himself. He was not from Todai. At the end of the war, he, a naval lieutenant, returned home defeated and dejected. Hungry and jobless, he and a few friends collected scrap metal and fashioned them into cooking utensils for sale. Workers were paid in rice, not cash. Meeting basic needs built up team spirit. His fledging company grew to be a strong precision engineering company.

He challenged me to name a post-war Japanese company founded by a Todai graduate. Instead, Matsushita, Honda, Sony, and a whole host of smaller companies were started by non-graduates. When companies, such as his, succeeded, they hired Todai graduates to manage them; but these Todai elites did not start these companies.

Is there a lesson in this story for us in Singapore? Our three universities: NUS, NTU and SMU, produce about 20,000 graduates a year. Secure jobs in the Civil Service, MNCs, banks, and the professions, are no longer so readily available. Although higher education prepares a person for a job, it does not guarantee one these days. My guess is that the Singapore economy will have to grow at 6 per cent or more a year, if there is to be employment for our graduates. And more and more of the jobs will have to be found overseas. In China, India, Indonesia, Singaporeans will have to compete with the citizens of these countries who are as competent as we are. Our young people educated in the West have to compete with Americans, Europeans, Chinese, and Indians, for jobs in their host countries. This is the reality in a global knowledge-based economy.

How do we open up to this new economy and yet retain something for ourselves? Does the example of Japan's industrial policy hold lessons for us?

The best exposition of Japanese industrial policy that I have read was in *Japan Echo*.[9] The Japanese economic historian who wrote on Japanese industrial policy said that after World War II, a defeated Japan had no choice but to impose high tariff walls to protect Japanese industry as it struggled to rehabilitate and restore itself.

Post-war Japan however realised that it could not close its markets to other countries while expecting to export to them. After a period, Japan had to reduce its import tariffs. When this occurred, the next line of defence was to impose quantitative restrictions and non-tariff barriers. Even this could not be sustained forever.

The final unbreachable barrier was the cultural defence of the ingrained belief of the ordinary consumer to buy only "Japanese". Being unable to read English, the Japanese man in the street had no access to knowledge of foreign products. Though competition in the domestic Japanese market is fierce and cut throat, there was no window to the world when it was time for Japan to export its industrial capacity. So Toyota and Nissan, the two pioneer Japanese automobile companies, sent their best marketing research teams to Hamburg in Germany to find out in detail what is in a car that the German motorist wants to have. The Germans, as we know, are no nonsense demanding customers.

The two research teams returned home after three years and drew up the specifications, the quality standards and price range their production engineers had to deliver, initially in the protected domestic markets, and ultimately world export markets.

The Chinese today, though in joint venture with international automotive companies, are following the same rigorous path of market research to deliver what the customer wants.

In my view, the weakest link in Singapore's industrial structure is our neglect of market research. We have no patience to find out what the customer wants, and what the competition provides. Our dependence on MNCs, including Japanese MNCs, to grow has handicapped us.

The natural instinct of Japan, as of continental countries such as China and India, is to be self-sufficient in food production. When they progressed from the agricultural to the industrial age, this instinct continued to hold. Hence, Japan installed high tariff and non-tariff walls to keep food and other imports out. China suffered from the Middle Kingdom syndrome. Yet, when Japan became a giant international trader by exporting in the late 1960s and 1970s, MITI and the CEOs of Matsushita, Hitachi, Sony, and a whole host of household brand names realised that to compete in international markets, they must produce from the lowest cost location.

---

9 Okazaki Hisahiko and Sato Seizaburo, "Lessons from the Twentieth Century", *Japan Echo* 26, 4 (May–June 1999).

This enlightened self-interest of Japanese companies gave Singapore the opening for rapid industrialisation in the 1970s to 1980s. Singapore offered a relatively well trained labour force, responsible unions, and efficient logistics to Japanese and other MNCs from the US and the EU, to establish internationally competitive industries in electronics, pharmaceuticals, miniature ball-bearings, TV screens, refrigerator compressors, and a whole host of industrial components and parts. These were assembled in our ASEAN neighbours with even lower labour costs for export.

Because of our lower cost structure and political stability, we were able to attract some basic processing industries, such as petroleum refining and petrochemicals. We tried but failed to attract a basic steel mill.

It was just as well because the pollution produced by steel mills could not be absorbed by a little island such as Singapore. We also did not have cheap hydroelectric power, like Brazil. In any event, with advances being made in nanotechnology, heavy basic industries are unlikely to shine again, as they did in the 1950s and 1960s.

Japanese and other MNCs, which invested in manufacturing in Singapore, always introduced the latest technology and industrial processes. It could not be otherwise, as they have to export.

When circumstances changed, MNCs in Singapore did not cut and run. When they moved their more labour-intensive industries out of Singapore, they upgraded their existing plants, introducing new products and technology. Singapore's relatively higher educational levels enabled the MNCs to transit and transform their businesses.

The freeing up of world trade through the WTO has changed the whole landscape of competition. We have now entered a world of global knowledge-based competition. Continental countries, such as China, India, Russia, Brazil, with their vast populations and deep talent pools, will be asserting themselves. All they need is political stability.

Countries, such as Japan and Singapore, with traditions of stability in political leadership and respect for learning, will have to survive both in cooperation and competition with these new economic powers.

Japan in Singapore is our best economic partner. We will make progress together in the spirit of sharing prosperity and sharing misery.

CHINA AND SINGAPORE

My first visit to China was in 1976. I was a member of the Singapore delegation led by our Prime Minister, Mr Lee Kuan Yew.[1] We arrived in Shanghai on a wet dreary evening, and stayed at the Peace Hotel. Our Chinese hosts received us very warmly. In fact, too warmly.

The hotel management turned on the heating in our room to over 30 degrees centigrade, which was the day time temperature in Singapore. We realised that the Chinese, being good hosts, were only trying to please us, having checked the mean temperature in Singapore from their meteorological department. We politely asked that the thermostat be set at 22 degrees, which was below our night time temperature and comfortable for us Singaporeans.

Our visit in 1976 was just before the passing of modern China's greatest leader, Mao Tse-tung. China was then operating under a command economy. To buy a drink from a street vendor, one had to not only pay cash but also hand over a sugar ration coupon. Coming from Singapore, a free market economy, it was an alien practice.

Yet a command economy has its own economic logic. All Chinese then were dressed either in black, blue, or grey fabrics. The senior Chinese cadre accompanying us explained that being such a vast country, it was not practical to let the individual have his choice of colour in fabrics. By limiting choice to three basic colours, great economies of scale could be achieved. In this way everyone could be clothed.

This is edited from Ngiam's speech given to I Globe at the 4th Annual Partnership Meeting on 31 Aug. 2004 at the Marriott Hotel in Shanghai.

1   Ngiam was then the Chairman of the Economic Development Board.

My next visit to China was in 1980. I accompanied my then Finance Minister, Mr Hon Sui Sen, to Beijing for the signing of the agreement to set up trade representative offices. Trade offices preceded the establishment of full diplomatic relations between Singapore and China in 1990.

We were privileged to be received by Mr Deng Xiaoping in the Great Hall of the People. Mr Deng shook hands with us warmly. I noticed that his hand was soft and gentle, the hand of a scholar. He complimented Singapore for having a per capita GDP then of US$4,800 compared with China's per capita GDP of only US$400.[2]

Mr Deng said that his ambition was for China to achieve a per capita GDP of US$1,000 by the year 2000. He then leaned forward and told us that China's GDP would be 1.2 billion people times $1,000. Mr Deng was truly a great mind, a Mandarin in the fullest sense of the word.

During the period 1991–2001, the 10-year average GDP growth rate of China was 9 per cent, exceeding Singapore's rate of 6 per cent, a much smaller economy. My fellow Singaporeans should take to heart Mr Deng's conversation with the Singapore Ministry of Finance Delegation in 1980. China is no longer emerging, but is a world economic power. How has this come about?

I was privileged to be a member, once again, of Singapore's delegation on our official visit to China led by Mr Lee Kuan Yew in 1985.[3] On this occasion, we were accompanied by another senior Chinese cadre. This gentleman in his 60s was a very educated and cultivated man. On our long journey together through the various provinces, we became friends. We gained enough mutual confidence to discuss political issues.

When we asked him about the Cultural Revolution, he told us that, leaving aside the immense human suffering, the greatest damage was the loss of education for a whole generation of students. By the mid-1980s, Chinese institutions were staffed by very old or very young cadres. There was no middle tier with the education, and the experience to drive the development process.[4]

Certainly, the Cultural Revolution set back the Chinese people and the economy, but China is a vast country with very deep talent pools. There is a hunger for learning — whether it is the English language, business, science or technology. The wounds of the Cultural Revolution have quickly healed.

---

2 Per capita GDP in Singapore in 1980 was US$4,854 (Statistic Singapore, <http://www.singstat.gov.sg/keystats/hist/gdp.html> [10 Jan. 2006] while per capita GDP in China was 460 RMB (China: National Bureau of Statistic, <http://www.stats.gov.cn/english/statisticaldata/yearlydata/index.htm#> [10 Jan. 2006].

3 Ngiam was then the Permanent Secretary at the Prime Minister's Office and the Chairman of Sheng-Li Holding Co Pte Ltd (currently known as Singapore Technologies Holdings Pte Ltd).

4 Peng Xizhe, The Changing Population of China (Oxford: Blackwell Publishing, 1998), p. 116. China's basic education experienced rapid expansion during the 1970s but the quality of education deteriorated as a result of the general social disturbances caused by the Cultural Revolution.

The Cultural revolution would have been fatal for Singapore, I realised, but not for China.

China's Future

The Chinese cadre and the Singaporean then went on to discuss Hong Kong. We talked about the vitality and enterprise of the British colony. I told my Chinese friend that China could have a hundred Hong Kongs. He sighed and asked rhetorically: "Yes, but would China want to have a hundred Hong Kongs?"

The answer came from the redoubtable Deng Xiaoping. He decided to open up the southern coastal provinces to open competition with the world. Shenzen and other free trade zones have not looked back. Without this crucial decision by Mr Deng, China could not have been ready to join the WTO some 20 years later.

When he was the Chief Executive Designate of Hong Kong, just a few months before June 1997, Mr Tung Chee Hwa visited Singapore. I was privileged to be at his table for dinner. I told Mr Tung that Singapore envied Hong Kong. By becoming a member of the Chinese family once again, Hong Kong would have access to the vast Chinese market and, more critically, China's rich talent pool. The Pearl River Basin is a huge regional economy in itself.

Under the "one country, two systems" structure, Hong Kong would enjoy autonomy in economic policy for another 50 years. With China's accession to the WTO, the convergence of the Hong Kong economy into China would take place much sooner than that. Indeed, there would soon be 100 Hong Kongs of enterprise in China: Shanghai is already a greater commercial centre than Hong Kong. China's financial centre will inevitably gravitate to Shanghai.

All this has occurred because of the vision of one man. Mr Deng is known in the western media for his "black cat, white cat" aphorism.[5] But in my view, his greater contribution was his exhortation to his countrymen to, "Seek Truth from Facts, Not ideology".

I remember that an MIT professor studying the Singapore development experience has said that Singapore practised "strategic pragmatism". I would say that China is doing the same.

Today, China is on the radar screen of every nation. Its huge economy is still growing at nearly 10 per cent a year. Its consumer products are well designed and low priced, selling in developing and developed markets. Earlier,

---

5 The "black cat, white cat" aphorism is a reference to Deng Xiaoping's quote which expresses a pragmatic rather than an ideological approach. The translation means "It doesn't matter if the cat is black or white as long as it catches mice."

rather than later, cars and other motor vehicles made in China would be as ubiquitous as cars and trucks made in Japan selling throughout the world.

Is China unstoppable? Yes it is, provided it does not stop itself. How do I come to this conclusion? Inspired by the Silk Route of China, I decided to recreate the journey, but not on camels. Some three years ago, we flew to Chengdu to commence our Silk Route adventure. We travelled by plane, coach, and train, from Chengdu to Urumqi. I would not attempt to describe the journey from a tourist perspective. I would leave that delightful task to more able travel writers. Since my professional career was spent entirely in the Singapore Administrative Service, I tend to look at things with an administrator's eye, wherever I go.

These are some of my observations, of small and daily things, that add to my belief that China will continue to grow.

First, to my pleasant surprise, there was hardly any litter on the streets of the six cities we travelled through. Secondly, we were able to use relatively clean toilets. This was a great relief after so many horror stories about China's toilets. Indeed, clean and air-conditioned toilets were available at the famous tourist locations, at the charge of RMB 1 (or 20 Singapore cents) which we were more than happy to pay.

This China that I saw is a far cry from the China I had visited earlier in the 1970s and 1980s. How has this been achieved?

My guess is that a nationalistic appeal was made to the people to keep the streets clean, so that China can be a good host for the 2008 Olympics. Secondly, air-conditioned toilets were built by private enterprise and operated as a business.

Leaders, Corruption and Change

Clean streets and clean toilets are the bright side of China. But there are other aspects. In a Chengdu restaurant, a waitress told us that she and her husband were apple farmers. She only worked in the restaurant during the off season. When the harvest was in, she and her husband would hire a small truck and cross over to other provinces to sell their apples. At every provincial border, they had to pay levies to the customs officers. By the time they sold the apples, there was hardly any money left for them. China was not a unified market. It was fragmented by the custom hordes.

This was bad enough until a relative of mine told me that in China one has to pay the appointing authority a fee "bribe" to get a job in the Civil Service. And each year, during the Lunar New Year, one has to present gifts to one's superiors to retain the job.

It then dawned on me why the apple farmers were shaken down by the customs at the provincial checkpoints. The customs needed the bribes to pay for New Year's gifts for their superiors. In other words, corruption was not just the act of a single individual, but systemic throughout the administrative structure.

There is hope yet for China: I recall how China and the Chinese Communist Party identifies, tests and selects the ultimate core of 300 men and women who govern China day to day.

A cadre begins his career at the village level selflessly working for the people. His immediate superiors report on his work performance. The central personnel department sends auditors incognito to the village, county and province to assess the cadre's character by mingling and speaking to the villager or ordinary man in the street. A CCP cadre cannot hide behind a facade and pretend to be what he is not.

It is a rigorous process of evaluating ability and character. This is of course an idealised model of human resource management. But even if half of the intention is realised, the men and women who rise to be mayors, party secretaries, ministers, and finally the Prime Minister and President of China will be extraordinary individuals who have earned the moral authority to govern.

I am confident that Prime Minister Wen Jiabao and President Hu Jintao will use their hard earned moral authority and power to rid China, root and branch, of the curse of corruption and nepotism. An open China will prove the sceptics and cynics wrong. For far too long, we Chinese have been resigned to the belief that corruption and nepotism are rooted in Chinese culture. To accept this grave prognosis is to repeat the tragic Chinese history of the rise and fall of dynasties and regimes.

The stability of China has to come from within. With political stability, China will indeed be unstoppable and a force for good in the world.

Epilogue: Mandarins in Context

Simon S.C. Tay

As editor, it has been my focus to allow Mr Ngiam to speak for himself in this book. Having offered an introduction, it is not my intention now to summarise what he has said. Rather, this brief epilogue seeks to suggest how Mr Ngiam's reflections may be seen in the broader framework of making public policy in Singapore.

What is the system of politics that effectively makes and implements policies in Singapore? What are the roles of the elite administration service officials in the civil service — the mandarins — to the political masters — the successive governments formed by the PAP, which has dominated politics since 1959? What are the roles of the civil servant in the context of the wider society like businesses and citizens and to political organs of the state? How should the administrative service change in the future as Singapore changes?

This epilogue offers a review of the relevant academic literature in Singapore to suggest how we might situate the writings and reflections offered by Mr Ngiam in the preceding parts of this book. First, I outline briefly what many consider to be the positive attributes and strengths in Singapore's public administration and civil service. This is an important foundation for understanding both the past success and future challenges for Singapore. Secondly, I consider the relationship of the mandarins and their masters in a broader political and constitutional context. Mr Ngiam's writings and reflections demonstrate the positive effects of having senior civil servants work closely to support their political masters in implementing policies, and yet remain professional and robust in policy debate. Thirdly, I touch on the relationship of the civil service to businesses in society. The writings exemplify — in both what they say and what they omit — the still evolving relationships with business and the broader society. Fourth and finally, I outline some of the present and evolving thinking on the future directions for the civil service. Mr Ngiam's writings will interest those who desire administration in Singapore to be at once stable and consistent, and yet also dynamic and even entrepreneurial, and open the way to think through the balances needed in going forward.

Attributes and Strengths of the Singapore Civil Service

In the telling of the Singapore story, a considerable part of the credit must be shared with the Singapore civil service and its elite administrative service officers. Many observers have acknowledged their role in helping make and implement the policies that fostered economic and social progress in Singapore, and in striving to be both efficient and free from corruption or other self-interest. Many developing countries set out ambitious plans that, almost inevitably, involved state-owned enterprises in jump-starting their economies. Some countries have also had charismatic and well-qualified leaders. But fewer states have managed to deliver on those hopes for development, empower and utilise state-owned companies for the greater good of the society and supply a core of able managers and administrators to follow up on the initiatives and ideas that leaders annunciate.

Commentators, academics and practitioners have described a number of positive attributes and strengths in the Singapore civil service that have allowed them to contribute to the Singapore story. One of these is that they have been fair and impartial in serving the public but not neutral about executing government policy. They have also been seen to have developed sound instincts of what are national concerns and interests, and a good understanding of national imperatives. They have shown commitment to the values of meritocracy and freedom from corruption and nepotism. Allied to this, they are noted for a mindset that judges effectiveness by results, and thus continuously strive for efficiency in implementation.[1]

From these attributes, key milestones and strategies in developing the civil service may be noted. From the early 1970s, the importance of efficiency and effectiveness was recognised with the setting up of the Management Services Department (MSD), now within the Prime Minister's Office. The late 1970s saw the pioneering efforts in computerisation for the public sector, with the setting up of the National Computer Board; an initiative in which government moved ahead of many private businesses. In the mid-1980s, the civil service notably introduced management tools to increase both efficiency

---

1   Lim Siong Guan, "Sustaining excellence in government: the Singapore experience", *Public Administration and Development* 17 (1977): 167–74. Jon S.T. Quah. "The Public Policy-Making Process in Singapore", *Asian Journal of Public Administration* 6 (Dec. 1984):108–26.

and accountability, such as performance budgeting, management accounting and activity-based costing.[2]

By the 1990s, the austerity of the early decades of the Singapore civil service gave way to a new policy that pegged salaries of civil servants to the private sector. This aimed to prevent an outflow of brains and talent from the public sector. At the same time, the first steps were taken to doing away with the "iron rice bowl" concept of life-time employment in the civil service, regardless of performance. The decade also witnessed more corporatisation and privatisation of government enterprise, and the establishment of more statutory boards. This increasingly meant that state-owned enterprises were run purely on a commercial basis, without political preferences and interference.[3]

In the mid-1990s, the initiative for PS 21 (Public Service for the 21st century) was started to nurture an attitude of service excellence in meeting the needs of the public and to foster an environment which induces continuous change for greater efficiency.

All in all, the civil service in Singapore has been justly acknowledged for its efficiency and ability, its strong foundations in rationality, financial controls, and technology and the underlying quality of its people. Efforts to make the civil service more responsive to citizens and to changing circumstances are also notable.

Mandarins and Masters: The Political and Constitutional Context

Notwithstanding its strengths, for many overseas commentators discussing the civil service and its relationship to political leaders, the starting point would be the principle of independence. This may be quite justifiable, given the British origins of Singapore's political and administrative system as embedded in the Constitution. The relevant provisions create a civil service that is given guarantees of independence, and subjects the hiring and firing of civil servants to an independent public service commission.[4] This ensures that they do not serve at the pleasure (or displeasure) of politicians. The original intention of such arrangements is that the civil service serves the state, and must enjoy some degree of separation in order to do his job with rationality, removed from political interference. Such arrangements assume that it is for the civil servant to provide continuity, regardless of which political party is currently government. In such a system, the assumption is that it is their political masters who may come and go, depending on the vagaries of the

---

2   UNDP. Ten Best Practices in the Singapore Civil Service. Article found in <http://magnet.undp.org/Docs/psreform/singapore_ten_best.htm> [13 Feb. 2006].

3   Ibid.

4   Constitution of the Republic of Singapore. Part IX, The Public Service.

ballot box. In contrast, the permanent secretaries who sit at the apex of the civil service in various ministries — as Mr Ngiam did for many decades — are indeed permanent.

This original design of a permanent and thus independent civil service rides on assumptions — drawn from modern Britain or indeed almost all liberal democracies — that governments change and political parties alternate in power. The political history of Singapore has challenged such political assumptions. As Mr Ngiam notes (more than once), the PAP swept into power in 1959. In the years since then, the PAP has been continually returned to power through general elections. In the 1970s, the PAP enjoyed a complete monopoly of all seats in Parliament. Even after a single opposition member won a seat in 1981, the political opposition parties have failed to offer any viable alternative government; with a "highpoint" of only four seats in Parliament and contesting less than half the seats in the general elections of 1993, 1997 and 2001.

This political dominance of the PAP, won at the ballot box, has altered the original design of relationships between the political leadership and the civil service. Indeed, from the early years it came into power, the PAP sought to align the civil service to its political objectives and campaign promises. This was a political necessity for a number of reasons.

First, some elites in colonial Singapore, especially among the English educated, had pinned their hopes for Singapore after independence not on the PAP but on "liberal" democrats such as the Progressive Party that won the Legislative Assembly general elections in 1948. When the PAP came into power in 1959, there were those who feared the strong socialist-communist strands in the PAP's statements and policies. Secondly, since the democrats within the PAP, led by Lee Kuan Yew, co-existed with the socialist-communist elements, there were differences and tensions between them. If the civil service were so minded, this would provide ground for them to cite uncertainty and delay projects and policies. A third and connected point was that, when the PAP came into power, there were perceptions that the civil service, installed before their entry into power and with Constitutional guarantees for tenure and independence, would resist their policies and stall implementation. If so, the PAP government feared it would fail to deliver on its campaign promises and lose power in the next elections.[5]

The PAP government leaders thus sought to discipline and bring the civil service into line. They cut the pay of civil servants. They also held camps to "educate" them on the new government thinking. Such measures were felt to be necessary to ensure that the civil servants would indeed implement, rather than delay or obstruct, the new policies and initiatives ushered in by the PAP government.

---

5   Dennis Bloodworth, *The Tiger and the Trojan Horse* (Singapore: Times Books International, 1986).

Mr Ngiam's reflections may be read in this broader historical context and show how the PAP succeeded in fostering a core of public servants who supported their policies strongly and indeed actively took the initiative to push ahead. Mr Ngiam entered the civil service in 1959, as he recounts, the same year the PAP entered power. Therefore, unlike others who entered the civil service before that year, Mr Ngiam served no other government other than that formed by the PAP. Mr Ngiam mentions the pay cut that the PAP administered to the civil servants (he notes that, unlike others, he did not serve prior to this, and thus did not feel the cut so badly in having to trim expenses). Mr Ngiam also briefly alludes to internal conflicts within the PAP, in which the largely English-educated democrats led by Mr Lee Kuan Yew had to deal with and separate themselves from a communist-socialist and largely Chinese-speaking quarter within their party.

More generally and most significantly, Mr Ngiam's reflections show how the mandarins and the political leadership came to work closely together to achieve a common objective of making Singapore succeed in the face of many challenges. Some civil servants, such as the late Mr Hon Sui Sen — whom Mr Ngiam served and admired — went further to cross the divide from civil servant to politician. Another civil servant who turned politician that Mr Ngiam names in this book was Mr Howe Yoon Chong, whom Mr Ngiam credits for taking a leading role in the HDB's early building programmes to supply much needed public housing. Following these and other examples from the founding years of Singapore, successive numbers of civil servants have continued to make the same cross-over from the civil service to the political office.[6]

The crossovers from civil service to politics have led some observers to suggest that the civil service in Singapore is no longer separate from the political leadership. From this, they argue that the civil service has become politicised and is subordinated and even subservient to the political leadership.

Mr Ngiam's recollections suggest that such arguments go too far. His reflections do show the close working relationship between the political leaders and the mandarins of the civil service. Indeed, Mr Ngiam recalls how ministers he served with would take the effort to personally correct his papers, to sharpen the thinking and arguments. But, as he also states, Mr Ngiam himself did not cross over into politics and indeed has not even joined the PAP as an ordinary member. His story leads us to focus not on those who cross from civil service to politics, but to note the many other senior civil servants who have not and have chosen to remain in the civil

---

6   For example, in the cabinet of 2005, three prominent cabinet ministers previously held senior positions in the civil service or government statutory boards: Lim Swee Say, the Minister (Prime Minister's Office) and a former Managing Director of the Economic Development Board; Khaw Boon Wan, the Minister for Health, and a former Permanent Secretary; and Tharman Shamugunaratnam, the Minister for Education, and a former Managing Director of the Monetary Authority of Singapore.

service. Even more importantly, as I have suggested in the introduction to this book, Mr Ngiam's recollections of several policy debates demonstrate the robust give and take between civil servants and their political leaders.

Thus Mr Ngiam's writings suggest neither a civil service so independent that it wilfully ignores the government (as the PAP were concerned might be the case when they came into power), nor one that is inseparable from it and subservient to political power. The relationship may instead be observed to be one that is closely intertwined. The government leaders have employed the civil service as the key institution in Singapore's developmental strategy. This has helped consolidate the PAP's position as the political party that is able to deliver on campaign promises and that has delivered the Singapore success story. In this process, the civil servants have become "politicised". But this term does not so much connote that they irrationally focus on narrow aspects of inter-party politics and are partial to the PAP as a party. Rather, the Singapore civil servant that has emerged is politicised in terms of needing to have some understanding of the broader and overall political consideration of a policy and to be politically sensitive and knowledgeable in serving the public.[7]

Yet even as the civil service in Singapore has been tutored by experience and time to time respond to the political leadership, their roles however remain different. As the current Prime Minister, Mr Lee Hsien Loong, suggests that it is not the civil servants' job to change the direction of the country or to judge what is politically sustainable or not, it is the Minister's responsibility.[8]

In terms of the decision-making process, the cabinet determines the general long-term direction of government policy. The civil servant's role is to implement, coordinate and promote specific policies.[9] Moreover, ministers in Singapore may be seen to be highly interventionist and be personally involved not only at the political stages of the policy process but also in the latter stages, and even to be involved in what others might think as more routine administrative tasks. This interventionist nature does not however obviate the need for a well qualified, and professional civil service, as they largely rely on the knowledge, experience and expertise of the bureaucracy, and the interventions remain exceptions, rather than the common practice.

Some studies have suggested that post-independence Singapore has been almost void of democratic competition between political parties because of

---

7 Ho Khai Leong. Chapter 7, "Bureaucracy and Policy-Making", in *Shared Responsibilities, Unshared Power: The Politics of Policy-Making in Singapore* (Singapore: Eastern Universities Press, 2003).

8 Speech by Prime Minister Lee Hsien Loong at the 2005 Administrative Service Dinner, Conrad Centennial Singapore, 24 March 2005. Source.

9 Ho Khai Leong. Chapter 1, "Analysing Singapore's Public Policy-Making", in *Shared Responsibilities, Unshared Power.*

the dominance of the PAP and that pragmatic policy-making and bureaucratic politics have filled this vacuum.[10] As such, without political competition, the political leaders and the mandarins have made the problem definition and agenda-setting in policy-making in Singapore an elite-driven process.

Wider Society: Bureaucrats, Business and Citizens

This leads to a second question in considering policy-making in Singapore: what are the roles of the civil servant in the context of the wider society like businesses and citizens, and to political organs of the state?

In the Singapore story, it is notable that the political leadership and civil servants did not only put in place policies to allow and foster the economy. They also participated very directly in the economic development of Singapore. For example, in fostering industry in Singapore, the government not only put pro-industry policies in place[11] but developed the industrial park in Jurong and then partnered some companies (including foreign companies) to begin production. In the provision of public housing and infrastructure, similarly, the government went beyond clearing land and providing broader development plans and went actively into the construction and funding of housing and infrastructure. In other sectors, similarly, when products, services and infrastructure were deemed important but found missing, the government grew government-linked companies (GLCs) that provided them. This is a result of the industrial and social policies in the early 1960s that called for bureaucratic intervention in state enterprises and statutory authorities (perhaps most notably the EDB and HDB). Thus, rather than being bureaucratic (with all the inertia and rule-bound behaviour that word implies), Singapore's governing elite has tended to accept a more varied set of values and mindsets that encompasses both bureaucratic and business perspectives. The making of public policy also involves not just the mandarins and politicians but also takes into account the concerns expressed by business actors.

Other countries have of course made similar efforts to utilise state-owned enterprises to jump-start and drive their economies. Few however have made a success of such an undertaking. In Singapore, much effort has gone into ensuring that the Singapore companies do not fall prey to inefficiencies, irrational political interference and (especially) corruption. Thus, balance between governmental and business perspectives interests in Singapore's development

---

10 Chan Heng Chee, "Politics in an Administrative State: Where has the Politics Gone?" in *Trends in Singapore*, ed. S.C. Meow (Singapore: Singapore University Press for the Institute of Southeast Asian Studies, 1975). Chan Heng Chee, *The Dynamics of One Party Dominance* (Singapore: Singapore University Press, 1976). Mauzy, Diana K. and R.S. Milne, *Singapore Politics Under the People's Action Party* (London & New York: Routledge, 2002).

11 For example, the granting of tax and other incentives for "pioneer" industries and the removal of tariff and other barriers for export-focused manufacture.

has been accommodated. Relations between private and public actors have increased over time but politicians and senior civil servants have never been completely isolated from business.

In this context, Mr Ngiam recounts some of these activities and the robust "can do" attitude to these undertakings by government agencies and government-linked companies. Indeed, his recollections spotlight the sense of not only "can do" but a "must do" attitude that was necessary as early Singapore struggled to meet so many challenges at the time. Mr Ngiam's reflections demonstrate how the civil servants spanned both public and private sectors, with the two sectors linked by shared interest, personal ties and overlapping career paths.

It is also notable that Mr Ngiam recounts, in a number of different sections, conversations with foreign business leaders and ideas that were gleaned from these engagements, and indeed partnerships that grew for Singapore. For, from the 1960s and onwards, most industrial policy initiatives in Singapore have largely relied on either government-linked enterprises or foreign investors. Even currently, foreign companies and government-linked companies are dominant in their contributions to the Singapore economy.

In contrast, local private sector businesses, while occupying a number of lucrative niches, have been largely sidelined in economic policy formulation and implementation. It is here that we may wish to note where Mr Ngiam specifically and positively refers to a number of private sector business leaders, like Mr Robert Kuok of the Kuok Group and Mr Ng Teng Fong of the Far East Organisation. Mr Ngiam also endorses the need for Singapore to foster our own entrepreneurs like Mr Sim Wong Hoo of Creative Technology and Ms Olivia Lum of Hyflux. These reflections by Mr Ngiam go towards recognising what has, relatively, been a historical gap in the relations of the civil service to the Singapore private sector, in contrast to the foreign investors and the Singapore government-linked companies. The government and civil service of the future, Mr Ngiam may be read to suggest, must encourage and support innovation and entrepreneurship from this Singaporean private sector businesses and (to use Mr Ngiam's phrase) "grow our own timber".

In comparison to his references to business leaders, Mr Ngiam makes few if any specific references to the prevailing opinions among the public or the views of ordinary citizens. Further, while he specifically mentions ministers he worked with, Mr Ngiam makes few specific references to Members of Parliament, whether individually in representing a constituency or collectively in the Parliament's law making function.[12] This may be interpreted as showing how the civil servants of that generation were relatively detached from direct relations with the public and their Parliamentary representatives.

---

12 An exception is where Mr Ngiam refers to an MP's effort to help government in ending the pig-farming industry, which was largely settled in his constituency, due to new government policies to curb water pollution that resulted from such farming.

They instead depended on the Ministers as their political leaders to serve as the main conduits to such constituencies and to judge the public good and what policies to put in place.

In contrast, the policy-making process is (arguably) today more open to such participants and the implementation of policies even more open and susceptible to popular feedback and participation. This results from the emphasis during the 1990s, given by then PM Goh Chok Tong, to increasing "consultation" for citizens.

Changes Ahead for the Singapore Civil Service

In reflecting on his past experiences, Mr Ngiam also deliberately discusses the present and future trends for Singapore. This ties to a third question of context: how should the mandarins of the administrative service change in the future, as Singapore changes?

Much depends on how we see the forces that shape policy-making and the policy-makers in Singapore. Some observers, including foreign academics.[13] suggest that policies in "Singapore Inc" are dictated by a small, inter-linked and somewhat insulated political and administrative elite. According to such a view, the pattern of policy-making in Singapore is very much result of the political dominance of the ruling party and the relative subservience of civil society. In other literature on the subject, the forces that shape Singapore's development have been and are still inextricably tied to the need to balance between domestic political choices and external trends in the world. From this second view, changes in Singapore have not been dictated by a local and largely PAP elite, but have more often and more profoundly motivated by external trends and forces, such as market competition, technology liberalisation and deregulation. Singapore, from this perspective, must make policies in a wider, global context.

The two views clearly have different implications for the policy-making process and the mandarins in Singapore. In what we may call the "Singapore Inc" view, which is clearly less than complimentary in its assessment of governance in Singapore, all that matters is domestic political power and the continued monopoly over that power by the PAP government. Policy-making is closely held and dictated by the senior figures and leaders within government. Civil servants learn to follow simple orders, efficiently and effectively, and not to question or debate. The people of Singapore matter as objects in the

---

13 Linda Low, "The Singapore Developmental State in the New Economy and Polity", *The Pacific Review* 14, no. 3 (2001): 411–41. Natasha Hamilton-Hart, "The Singapore State Revisited", *The Pacific Review* 13, no. 2 (2000): 195–216. Garry Rodan, *The Political Economy of Singapore's industrialization: National State and International Capital* (Basingstoke: Macmillan, 1989). Garry Rodan, *Singapore Changes Guard: Social, Political and Economic Implications in the 1990s* (New York: St. Martin's Press, 1993).

economic machinery, and not so much as citizens and participants in the fuller sense of development of the society.

In the latter view — which we could call, a "Global Singapore" view — the domestic domination of the PAP government is counter-balanced by external parameters. Their scope in policy-making is therefore not unrestrained. They must recognise the external forces and trends and seek to respond in ways that balance them with domestic concerns. The "global Singapore" would, in the present period, point to recent economic trends worldwide that give stress to issues such as good corporate governance; the trend towards privatisation in the provision of goods, services and even infrastructure that used to be considered government prerogatives and monopolies; and the need for companies to seek larger markets through global or regional expansion.

With this in mind, we can see many of Mr Ngiam's reflections and suggestions for Singapore's future in the context of "global Singapore". His thoughts about the need to find niche opportunities for Singapore and to expand our businesses through entrepreneurship and not just acquisition of existing companies are specific recommendations for strategy. Mr Ngiam's underlying premises that Singapore needs to remain competitive and that the civil service must avoid being on "auto-pilot" also resonate with the need to deal with a changing global context. In sum, Mr Ngiam's reflections could be readily associated with the "global Singapore" analysis, that emphasises that policy-making in Singapore — past, present and future — must contend and accommodate the broader concerns of increasing worldwide interdependence and competition.

Like Mr Ngiam, a number of academic commentators have argued that changes in nature and roles for the civil service are needed, beyond what have been done in past decades. One of the changes that most such commentators argue for is a mindset change in the civil service and the cultivation of an entrepreneur spirit to meet future external environments.

Although efficient relative to many other countries, it can be seen that there have been instances in which the civil service in Singapore has exhibited negative traits, such as bureaucratic red tape, and a lack of empathy towards citizens and businesses. While relatively unified too, there are instances in which the bureaucrats in Singapore tend still to react in their own, narrowly defined interests, rather than coordinating and working collectively as "one government" for the wider national interest.

Some scholars question whether Singapore's prevailing culture of "top down" leadership and its technocratic model will result in a diminishing ability to produce creative and innovative approaches in meeting future challenges. These future challenges especially include the advent of a knowledge economy in which Singapore faces increased competition not just among regional countries and developing economies but with the wider world and including developed economies. Another challenge is the ability to balance the need for government control of the economy and the cultivation of an entrepreneurial culture simultaneously. A third challenge that some commentators see ahead is for government-linked companies and statutory boards to be psychologically geared to operate in a disorderly, sticky and unpredictable environment.

The writings that Mr Ngiam has offered in this book touch on these and indeed many other challenges for Singapore and its policy-makers. He offers no easy, textbook answers. Rather, his experiences and perspectives demonstrate that a process of reflection is in motion, among the elite of Singapore on how to respond to these challenges that they increasingly recognise. This need for reflection lies not just with the younger and newer generation of policy-makers among the political leadership. From Mr Ngiam's example, we can see that this process of reflection can and should include those who have lived and served Singapore from its earliest decades of independence.

The processes of policy-making in Singapore, and the circle of those who actively participate in those processes may be widening, and may need further widening. But for the present, and indeed the foreseeable future, it remains a system in which relatively few participate. Such a system of policy-making will suffer if those who should be policy-makers descend to being parochial, "yes" men, or seek to influence decisions without sufficient regard to the wider national interest of Singapore in a global economy.

The relatively closed and limited processes in Singapore therefore (and quite conversely) require participants who are broad minded and who relish robust and rational debate. Those who aspire to such a policy-making process will find support in what Mr Ngiam has written and reflected upon. Those commentators who wish to understand and evaluate the policy-making processes in Singapore should do well to consider his experiences and perspectives.

INDEX

Editor's Acknowledgements

The editor would like to acknowledge the following people who have helped make the book possible:

- The National University of Singapore Press for publishing this book as part of the University's centennial celebrations.
- Susan Long of *The Straits Times*, Melanie Chew and Sonny Yap who gave their permission to use their interviews with Mr Ngiam.
- The Singapore Press Holdings, Editions Didier Millet and the Ministry of Foreign Affairs for their help and permission for the use of the photographs.
- Ms Joanne Lin, then a researcher with the SIIA, who helped read and footnote the text, and provided much of the background research for the epilogue. Mr Gavin Chua Hearn Yuit, a SIIA researcher, who helped with additional footnotes. Ms Sarah De Souza, my capable assistant at the SIIA and Mr Steven Ho of Mr Ngiam's office who helped to coordinate this project.
- And of course Mr Ngiam himself for providing the speeches and writings that make up the book.